Remains of Ritual

Northern Gods in a Southern Land

Remains of Ritual

Steven M. Friedson

The University of Chicago Press
Chicago & London

STEVEN M. FRIEDSON is Regents Professor of Music and Anthropology at the University of North Texas and the author of *Dancing Prophets: Musical Experience in Tumbuka Healing*, published by the University of Chicago Press.

The University of Chicago Press, Chicago 60637
The University of Chicago Press, Ltd., London
© 2009 by The University of Chicago
All rights reserved. Published 2009
Printed in the United States of America

27 26 25 24 23 22 21 20 19   3 4 5

ISBN-13: 978-0-226-26504-9 (cloth)
ISBN-13: 978-0-226-26505-6 (paper)
ISBN-10: 0-226-26504-8 (cloth)
ISBN-10: 0-226-26505-6 (paper)

Library of Congress Cataloging-in-Publication Data

Friedson, Steven M. (Steven Michael), 1948–
    Remains of ritual : northern gods in a southern land / Steven M. Friedson.
        p.   cm.—(Chicago studies in ethnomusicology)
    Includes bibliographical references (p.) and index.
    ISBN-13: 978-0-226-26504-9 (cloth : alk. paper)
    ISBN-13: 978-0-226-26505-6 (pbk. : alk. paper)
    ISBN-10: 0-226-26504-8 (cloth : alk. paper)
    ISBN-10: 0-226-26505-6 (pbk. : alk. paper) 1. Ewe (African people)—Music—
Religious aspects. 2. Music—Africa, West—Religious aspects. 3. Ewe (African
people)—Rites and ceremonies. 4. Dance—Africa, West—Religious aspects.
5. Spirit possession—Africa, West. I. Title.
ML350.F754 2009
781.7'9683374—dc22

                                                                      2008011084

♾ The paper used in this publication meets the minimum requirements of the American National Standard for Information Sciences—Permanence of Paper for Printed Library Materials, ANSI Z39.48-1992.

Angels (they say) don't know whether it is the living they are moving among, or the dead.

—RAINER MARIA RILKE, *Duino Elegies*

Contents

Additional materials can be found on www.remainsofritual.com.

Illustrations

Figures

Musical Examples

Acknowledgments

When you open the door wide, as in a sacrifice, or, in the case here, a book, you are never quite sure who might come in; it may not always be who was invited. That is why it is important to feed everyone who comes to the table—hungry souls can be problematic. For all those who have not been explicitly mentioned, and there are many, accept my apologies, know that you are acknowledged.

Specific thanks, however, go to Edward Tekpah, who for many years was my research assistant, more recently Christopher Akpeloo for help with translations, and Jemilatu Badiru and Peter "Papa" Kpodo for always being there. I know that working with an American professor sometimes can be a heavy necklace to wear. I want to thank Tɔgbui Gideon Foli Alorwoyie, who has been my back in Ghana on more than one occasion. A special thanks goes to Malena Kuss, friend and colleague, for her many helpful comments and suggestions. I also want to acknowledge the American Philosophical Society, which provided fellowship support at a crucial time, and the University of North Texas for sabbatical leaves and several research grants. Without their support this would still be a work in progress. A thank-you also goes to the Centro Incontri Umani Ascona for a subvention allowing for the publication of two color plates.

To my wife Elise, whose art inspired the title of this book, and who has been a collaborator in more ways than I can possibly put into words, and to my daughter Sophia, whose embrace of Africa has been a gift, a mere thank-you would not suffice. This book is dedicated to you and the *sofowo*—Kwamiga, Peter, Tᴐsavi, Nudedzitᴐ, Baniba, Alaga, and, especially, Kwasi Anibra—who opened the door of Lahare Kunde and invited me in. In the spirit of Ewe elders, a final acknowledgment: To my mother Mary, whose long life ended during the writing of this book, yours is of the cool sunset.

On Language

Eʋegbe (the Ewe language) is, as Ewes often would say, "deep" (*goglo*), full of analogy and allusion. There is a poetic bent to the language that lends itself to ambiguity. This is particularly true in the poetics of prayer, libation, and song, but is also evident in everyday discourse, where proverbial sayings are commonplace. This is why even native speakers of other Ghanaian languages will tell you that "Ewe is difficult."

Ewe is also a difficult language to pronounce, especially for English speakers, due to the presence of plosive clusters (*kp*, *gb*), nasalized vowels, onomatopes, tonemes, and consonants (*ɖ, f, ɣ, ʋ*) not found in most Indo-European languages. To facilitate reading, it is helpful to remember that every syllable ends in a vowel (*akpe* [thank you] is parsed *a·kpe*) unless it is in final position and finishes with an *m* or *n*. The consonant cluster *kp* is pronounced by placing the middle of the tongue against the roof of the mouth as if to say *k* and then saying *p*. For *gb* (as in *gbe* [voice, language]), the sides of the tongue are placed against the upper teeth as if to say hard *g* and saying *b*.

In its written form, codified by German missionaries in the nineteenth century, Ewe uses the Roman alphabet supplemented with international phonetic symbols:

ɖ   pronounced *d* but formed with the tip of the tongue against the ridge behind the upper teeth

ɛ   a half-opened vowel with the tongue on the hard palate like the English *e* in "bet"

ƒ   bilabial fricative somewhere between a stopped *p* or *f* but open

ɣ   produced with the back of the tongue raised toward the soft palate as for *ŋ* and *g*

ŋ   found in the final consonant cluster in English "sing"

ɔ   half-opened labial velar vowel as in English "ought"

ʋ   bilabial fricative somewhere between a stopped *v* and an open *w*

There is no *j* in the Ewe alphabet, which uses the consonant cluster *dz* to indicate this sound. In southern dialects *ts* is pronounced *ch*, and *x* represents the "German ch in 'doch, ach'" (Westermann [1928] 1973: v).

Spellings reflect standard practice: *Eʋe*, for example, is written as *Ewe*, the final syllable pronounced close to English "way"; *Aŋlɔ*, the major southern group and dialect, as *Anlo*. Plurals are formed by adding the suffix *–wo* to nouns. In literary Ewe, tones are not usually marked. The choices I have made in this book for rendering *Eʋegbe* follow these conventions.

Note on Transcriptions

Ewe songs are rarely, if ever, performed the same way. There are differences not only between separate musical events (variation from day to day), but also within the parameters of a contiguous performance (the rendering of a single song). This is more than the proverbial "never being able to step into the same river twice." As with other areas of Ewe culture, a structured ambiguity underlies the constantly shifting surfaces of musical praxis. Lyrics are not set in stone, but are templates for spontaneous variation, often across linguistic boundaries; instead of clearly delineated melodic contours, there are general pitch areas open to wide interpretation; and multiple rates of motion are always-already available for elaboration. Given this fluid musical field, transcriptions in this book are neither descriptive documents of past musical events nor prescriptive models for future action. Rather, they are visual modelings of particular grooves, deep acoustical spaces capable of continuous transformation. The use of staff notation to transcribe Ewe song should be taken as the metaphoric equivalent of translating Ewe into English.

Southern Lands

This book reaches back over a period of fifteen years—summers here, sabbaticals there—working with Ewe shrines. In many ways it seems overdue. Writing about the Ewe, however, is a notoriously difficult task, even though much has been written about them. More than one researcher has commented on a kind of Ewe chaos, a structured ambiguity that is resistant to synthetic analysis (Rosenthal 1998; Geurts 2002).[1] There seems to be no getting to the bottom of things, especially those things having to do with shrines, leaving a distinct impression that no matter how long you stay in Ewe country, you are never quite there. It is like the many clay Legbas, the god of the crossroads and thresholds, protecting the entrances to villages and homes. You see only the visible anthropomorphic figure, Legba's outward manifestation, not his power, the herbs, animal parts, and other things buried deep inside. Much in Ewe culture is similarly subterranean, not visible to the naked eye. Nothing is quite what it seems; everything feels submerged beneath at least two layers of clay.

A drive into Three-Town, an assemblage of small municipalities located on the Guinea Coast near the Togo border where I did most of my field-work, will confirm that fact.[2] If you happen to arrive at night, as you pass the Shell station just before the end of the Accra-Aflao road, you may catch a glimpse out of the corner of your eye of the night watchman sitting under the neon lights in his lazy chair, with his coat collar turned up against a slight night chill. An old man just trying to get through the night, most definitely, but earlier in the day he was carrying a duck in his mouth as he slithered along the ground in the guise of Da, the ancient snake *vodu*. It turns out that he is also a *midawo*, a priest of Xebieso, the wielder of thunderbolts.[3] Drive a little further and, on the right side of the road, you will see market women selling their wares by the light of kerosene lamps, the open-wicked flames giving everything a warm glow. The old white-haired woman sitting in front of a table of onions with her granddaughter on her lap, a rather gentle-looking soul, is also an *amegashi*, a diviner who deals with hot spirits, those who "died in the blood." The fishmonger sitting next to her, it turns out, belongs to the local medicine shrine, where, on a regular basis, she manifests a soldier god from the savanna, though when it happens she has no idea that it is in fact happening. And the man dressed in northern garb buying fish from her is not a Muslim from the *zongo* quarter of town, as one would assume from his clothes, but a Brekete *sofo* (priest). Continue down the road and you probably will overlook the unassuming kindergarten teacher standing in front of the "chemical store" (pharmacy) waiting for a taxi. From his looks and demeanor, who would figure that, on the weekends, he is a great shrine drummer, bare chested and drenched in sweat, chewing kola and taking shots of *akpeteshie* (local gin), calling the gods to dance themselves into existence.

Finally, at the end of the highway from Accra, you come to a crossroads. If you take a left, you will be headed for Aflao, some ten kilometers away, where there are plenty of drinking bars, illegal money changers, smugglers, and other somewhat nefarious characters typical of a border town. Take a right and you pass through Denu, then imperceptibly into Xedzranawo, and on to Adafienu (the three towns of Three-Town) toward the Keta Lagoon.[4] Although distinct towns, with different histories, different chiefs, different concerns, you can't really tell where one leaves off and the next begins. Most people either go left or right at the junction, but, if you decide to go straight, the pavement abruptly ends. Head down the dirt road and less than a kilometer away you will be standing on the eastern shores of the Black Atlantic, on the shifting sands of what was once called the Slave Coast. Whichever way you go, everywhere clay Legbas—small ones sitting at the side of the road, large ones protecting whole towns, hidden by the night—are reminders that much lies underneath.

Grandmothers and fishmongers, priests and diviners, gods and drummers populate a submerged life interlaced between heaven and earth, mortals and the divine. For the casual visitor—the new manager at the local Agricultural Development Bank, for example, who is working his way up the corporate ladder, or the Peace Corps worker working her way down—all this pretty much goes unnoticed (even for some Ewes). Most night watchmen, after all, are not thunder god priests (you do not choose that vocation, you are chosen); old ladies are usually just loving grandmothers, though occasionally, if their grandchildren are sick, they may consult a diviner; fishmongers are, for the most part, simply people from whom to buy that somewhat strange-named coastal delicacy "Keta schoolboys"; the majority of schoolteachers are Christians, having nothing to do with shrines; and it is a pretty safe bet that nine times out of ten the man in northern garb is not a worshipper of "idols," but will turn toward Mecca and pray when he hears the local muezzin call. As for Legba, well, he is the "divine trickster" (Herskovits 1938, vol. 2), and there is no telling what he may or may not be up to. If you don't know Legba's ways, it's better not to notice him at all, even if you see that he is there. Sometimes, however, this may be hard to do.

They say Legba has a penis so large he must carry it over his shoulder, a burden he carries with joy. His insatiable sexual appetite is always getting him into trouble; how he gets out of such predicaments, legendary. Legba loves to mislead, whether mortal or god. He is known for luring the unwary into intractable situations only he can resolve (that is, once the appropriate sacrifice has been made). Many are the woes of those unfortunate souls who have crossed his path when he was up to something. Even the gods have not escaped the machinations of his mischievous spirit. There is more than one story of how he fooled Afa, the god of divination, or deceived Xebieso, even played tricks on Mawu, the creator. No wonder the missionaries labeled him the devil incarnate.

A divine trickster, Legba, as with that other phallic god Hermes, is also the divine messenger, the linguist (*tsiami*) who speaks the language of the sky.[5] Because he patrols the borders and protects the threshold, all sacrifice, all libation, ultimately all meaning goes and comes through him, hence his infinite possibilities, his refusal to be pinned down. Translator, trickster, protector, linguist—all this and more comes under the sign of the crossroads where Legba rules, where there are always-already multiple paths, multiple meanings. And lest we think we have finally pinned Legba down as the phallic god par excellence, pregnant with meaning, it is helpful to remember that sometimes, though it is fairly rare, Legba manifests himself in female form complete with clay breasts. Nothing is quite what it seems.

The sand is quick along the Bight of Benin. There is no firm ground from which to take a stand, to get one's bearings, only crossroads at every turn. Whether the site where two roads actually cross, traced in the sand with powdered clay, inlaid with cowrie shells on an altar, danced or drummed in intricate cross-rhythms, the crossroads—walked, traced, seen, or heard—is a place of possibility where choices are made, paths followed or discarded, doors opened and closed. This is not a convergence of activity congealing into a series of options, but a thinning out of things, allowing room for something to happen. The crossroads—that resonant symbol of an Africa that is always on the move—offers by definition manifold ways, while simultaneously defining a center where paths cross and destinies intersect and intertwine. Perpetually in motion, the crossroads turns to that which is not there, and in this essential absence is danced to the core.

On the front cover of this book is a photograph of the remains of a ritual.[6] It is a picture of a crossroads drawn in the sand by Kpesusi, a Brekete priest, at the entrance to our compound. He made a circle and then cut it with a cross in white kaolin powder, then traced over it with water poured from the spout of a *buta*, the swirled-patterned plastic kettle used in shrines imported to the coast from the north. Nothing is as ritually powerful as the pouring of water, the only drink poured by man not made by man. It comes directly from Mawu's hand, unaltered by human process, and thus carries God's divine seal.

After he drew the cross, we sat down on our haunches and he poured a libation. As he let the spirits slowly flow over the rim of the glass, finding that exact place, the threshold, where the liquid overflowed, he called the old *sɔfowo*, those who have gone before—Kodzokuma, Mama Seidu, Zigah, Nudedzitɔ, Tɔsavi, Anibra—and I was reminded of how many of these priests I had the privilege of knowing, with how many I had danced.

Kpesusi called them to draw near and bind the gates: "Whatever evil is sent this way should find its owner." Gunpowder was set off at the four corners where the cross cut the circle, then in the center itself, closing the door against harm. This act of protection was followed by a blessing, when Kpesusi took the *buta* and reinscribed the circle and cross once again with water, then in a final act drew two lines from the gates through the circle leading into the compound, opening a pathway so that all that was good could still enter. This book, as with those traces of traces in the sand, remains of ritual, is an invitation to enter, to follow a path, above all, to heed the way.

Northern Gods

The following ethnography traces Ewe ritual life across the praxis of a northern medicine shrine that came to the Volta Region in the 1920s.[1] These strangers in a southern land were part of a larger movement of "occult economies" (Allman and Parker 2005: 14) that flowed from the savanna regions literally in the bags of ritual entrepreneurs (Werbner 1979: 668). As did their southern counterparts, these gods both came in material form as god-things to which sacrifices were given—the "fetish" in the bag—and also manifested themselves through spirit possession—the "wives" of the gods.[2] Although these northern gods were strangers (their otherness a source of their power), their ways, therefore, were not unfamiliar to Ewes. But it seems new gods were needed for new times, whether it was to address old concerns through borrowed means or to try to deal with disruptions of more recent origin. While virtually all the other northern shrines that came to Ewe country during this period eventually withered away, Brekete, the shrine with which this book deals, not only survived, but flourished, becoming one of the dominant ritual scapes along the Guinea Coast.[3]

The complex movement of these northern shrines has engaged the ethnographic and historical imagination of Africanists for generations, from virtually the beginnings of anthropology in Ghana (Rattray 1932; Fortes 1936; Field 1940; Ward 1956; Goody 1957a), with its concerns of effective governance and the changes wrought by new forms of solidarity, to more recent studies (Field 1960; Goody 1975; McCleod 1975; Werbner 1979; Parker 2004; Allman and Parker 2005), which have sought to understand the internal and external dynamics that created an opening for these foreign gods to operate, a space for these exotic others to inhabit.[4] Although this work collectively embodies a rich literature that significantly deepens and broadens our understanding of both local and global forces that shaped this north-south ritual axis, there is an important issue of aesthetic force, a proverbial elephant in the room, that largely has been ignored.

What has been lost among the various explanations, interpretations, and theories that focus on such things as occult economies and ritual entrepreneurs, the introduction and effects of new capitalist modes of production, the inner and outer workings of antiwitchcraft movements, searches for security in a rapidly changing world, ritual as a form of historical practice, counterhegemonic discourse, and so on, is the fact that when these gods came south they danced all the way down. This aspect of ritual praxis may be mentioned, but that is about as far as it goes.[5] We get no feel for the embodied presence of these dancing gods, the soundscape of a tuned world, the sheer intensity of being-with the gods in a musical way.[6]

Musical experience, the term used here to encompass the entirety of this way of being, something I have written about previously in my work on the dancing prophets of Malawi (1996), is not merely one more event among others that happens within the horizons of ritual life, but is the very terms of existence from which all else flows. People experience their gods and each other, first and foremost, in the immediacy of a musical way of being-in-the-world, sharing a specific time and space inscribed by cross-rhythmic effect, engendering a multidimensional movement that is always-already on its way. Drumming, clapping, singing, dancing— a list that already separates, thus does violence to the unitary nature of the phenomenon—create a soundscape beyond the acoustical, bringing into the world a way of being-there for the gods that is fundamentally a being-away.

Are you experienced?

—JIMI HENDRIX

Given the current emphasis on agency—gaining it, losing it, granting it, taking it, sharing it, dispensing it—what do we do with people who claim none, in fact are insistent that they are not there at all, are totally away, possessed by a god or spirit? How do we go along with ways of being-in-the-world so radically different from our own possibilities? If the people having such experiences can tell us nothing about it, and, given the fact that gods do not generally grant interviews to ethnographers, what kind of access can we have to such worlds? What does it mean to be embodied by a deity, to be-there and not-there at the same time? Is trance dancing inherently opaque, becoming a blank screen for our projections, power differentials cast before a silent landscape?

Spirit possession variously has been taken as the local equivalent of multiple personality disorder, Freudian sublimation, Jungian archetypes, the formation of right brain personalities, Lacanian manifestations of the Real, peripheral strategies of marginal peoples, the working out of colonial and postcolonial disorders, Marxist illusion, mimetic excess, and just plain good acting.[7] No one, after all, is "really" getting possessed by gods and spirits; they just think they are. To think otherwise is to leave ethnography behind and "go native," mistaking a worldview for a separate reality. What rarely happens is for spirit possession to be taken for what people who practice such traditions say it is.[8]

We can learn of the gods, their attributes, and lineages; pay attention to behavior, act, and word; track their movements across space and time; investigate the everyday life of devotees. We can even fill out such ethnographic detail with laboratory investigations into rhythmic effects on brain waves (Neher 1961, 1962); EEG readings in the field (Oohashi et al. 2002); analyses of autonomic responses to trophotropic rebound (Lex 1979); inquiries into the relationship of hypnosis to "monotonous drumming" (Maurer et al. 1997); or theorizing on how deep listening evokes deep responses in the lower regions of the brain (Becker 2004 by way of Damasio 1999). From these facts, we then can extrapolate complex chains of causality. But when these facts are linked to narrowly defined sequences of cause and effect, the resulting analyses tend toward a stasis that is antithetical to the multidimensionality of spirit possession. The unrelenting pulse to turn that which is possible into what is actual, hard facts ruled by the causal arrow of time, conceals more than it reveals. Suspicion always fills in the gaps with something concrete, leaving no room for silence to frame that which is already there.

If, however, we invoke a kind of *epoché* and explore the things themselves as they are given, go along with a way of being-in-the-world that is fundamentally a being-away, then perhaps we will stop listening to, thus dismissing, what people are telling us and, once again, begin to listen along with them. In doing so, we may begin to hear what the gods themselves have to say about the matter. In Africa—north, south, east, and west—this "saying" is most often a danced one.

I dance . . . therefore I am.
    —LÉOPOLD SÉDAR SENGHOR

Dance in Africa celebrates lives, commemorates death, consummates alliances, is part of the everyday lifeworld. We have nothing comparable in Western society, where danced bodies have been relegated to nightclubs, weddings, high school proms, and the occasional concert stage. In Africa, who you are often has much to do with how you dance. And nowhere is this more true than in dance's embrace of the other in its embodiment of a multiplicity of deities and spirits. This last dance—striking in its frequency (Bourguignon 1968)—is not merely the final item in a series, but marks the entire African continent. The Saharan divide—that somewhat suspect division of Africa—is not operative here. Trance dancing is an ancient practice that, to the consternation of both missionary and government officials, persists to this day. Divine horsemen still ride in the northern savanna as well as on the Guinea Coast (Besmer 1983; Erlmann 1982; Matory 1994), and drums of affliction continue to sound throughout Bantu-speaking Africa (V. Turner 1968; Janzen 1992; Friedson 1996).

No doubt trance dancing was never far from Senghor's mind when he predicated his ontological turn on dance's fundamental difference: its orientation toward the other. This was not merely a substitution of terms, but a reversal of effect. His philosophical take on négritude, part of that Left Bank efflorescence of the Black Atlantic (Mudimbe 1992; Jules-Rosette 1998), was the "weak beat" in a dialectical negativity (Jeanpierre 1969: 451; Sartre 1969).[9] If not for Africa, "who would teach rhythm to the dead world of machines and cannons?" (Senghor quoted in Vaillant 1990: 266). This parsing of vocations was part of Senghor's riff on a rhythmicized Africa that was always-already different.

If all this begins to sound somewhat familiar—African participatory reason confronting European analytical minds, the regionalized equivalent of black people clapping on "two" and "four"—it is not surprising. The tableau of Africans dancing into an exceedingly dark African night runs deep in the Western imagination. The rhythmic vitality that is the core of Senghor's négritude lent itself to a misappropriation aligned with oversexualized African bodies trapped in tropical climes (the overdeterministic view of weather), lost in a participation mystique (the overdeterministic view of mind). Yet, despite all the advances in microbiology, we never have found that ever-elusive rhythm gene.[10] Nevertheless, if you have been danced since you were in your mother's womb, rhythm can take on the dimensions of a cultural physiology (Moerman 1979), what Senghor understood as the psychophysiological contours of a "Black soul." The rhythm of African life made manifest in the beat of the drum was part of his poetry of retrieval, his project of recovering this negative stereotype of Africa in order to lay the foundations for an Africa worthy of its name.

Whether négritude is ultimately an inverted philosophy, Cartesianism in disguise, or antiracist racism (Senghor has been accused of all these; see Mudimbe's 1988 defense), it does not change its insight into African rhythmic praxis, regardless of how rhythm writ large was used in the imaginary of a pristine "Afrique-nature" (Jules-Rossette 1992: 22). This is not an essentializing of Africa, or rhythm, to reify its difference, as some have suggested (Agawu 2003), but rather an acknowledgment of the reality of a different way of being-in-the-world. Instead of suppressing the body as the antithesis of a higher spirit on the way to an ever more perfect knowledge, trance dancing privileges the body as the site of a gathering of mortals and the divine. Cartesian metaphysics seeks to overcome gods who may be deceiving; danced existences embrace them. What better place then to recover Senghor's ontology than in this dance that calls out to worlds that are both here and away?

A danced existence is, by its very nature, always on the move, a coming and a going, a continual leaving and approach. Arresting this movement in order to gain control over it, to categorize and analyze it into modes of behavior understood functionally, structurally, cognitively, so that it can be replicated and put to use in books, CDs, and videos, may make things more recognizable, thus more satisfying, but it turns what is there into a totality that overlooks that which is away. Claiming to understand more than it does, this stable ground gives way under the sedimented weight of dancing gods. A glance from the side, a fleeting glimpse of that which moves on the periphery, is much more in keeping with the phenomenon at hand, though it never will be as comforting as the cold discourse of certainty. This furtive vision, productive of understanding, is found in-between the being-there and being-away of trance dancing. To access such a world requires more than ethnography, more than ethnomusicology; it calls for an ontomusicology that engages music *as* ritual and ritual *as* music. Such an ontology moves us out of an interiority that projects a vision of certainty and into a world that calls the body to recognize itself in the contours of musical experience.

That much else happens—sacrifice and libation, divination and prayer, sometimes even possession—when music is largely absent will become evident in the following pages. But it will also become abundantly clear that musical experience is never far away: in the turn of the dance (chap. 1), the chanted call to prayer (chap. 2), the musical silence of sacrifice (chap. 3), the sounds and movements of wake keeping (chap. 4), the play of the drums (chap. 5), the poetics of divination (chap. 6). This is not a matter of building up ethnographic detail, chapter by chapter, into a context for understanding musical events. Rather, what follows continually unfolds from out of these peak musical experiences. The echoes of this structured ambiguity, enshrined, along with Legba, in the rhythm of the crossroads, resonate on every page, in every chapter, whether explicitly mentioned or not. They are the remains of ritual found interlaced throughout this book.

Brekete Pantheon

Major gods:

Kunde	Father and hunter
Ablewa / Tseriya	Mother
Sanya Kompo	God of the stone, linguist and secretary
Bangle / Ketetsi	Warrior and soldier
Sakra Bode	God of the land and Bangle's stool
Wango	God of the waters and roads

Minor gods (all work with Bangle):

Tsengé	God of the seven knives
Gediya	Policeman
Surugu	Lieutenant

Fig. 1.1 Northern gods dancing at a triennial cow sacrifice (Elise Ridenour)

The gods belong to what is.

—MARTIN HEIDEGGER, *Heraclitus Seminar*

Where Divine Horsemen Ride 1

Being-In-Between

It was right before the old woman became possessed. I was looking at the ground, fascinated by the play of light and shadow on the dance floor created by the sun coming through the woven palm-leaf roof covering the open pavilion. We had been up all night wake keeping, and I was feeling pretty tired. Now late afternoon, I found myself starting to doze but not quite going to sleep, in a kind of twilight existence, when a type of synesthesia set in, and the play of light and shadow started to take on a musical dimension. As this modality thinned, it simultaneously spread out and grew deeper. I was somehow between the light and the shadow, the sound of the drum and the rattle, between the call of the priest and the response of those who were gathered. Everything was on the move, including the ground, and I was suspended in between the shadows, the sounds, the smells, the heat, the wind. And this was precisely when the old woman leaped out of her chair, transposed into the sublime countenance of a dancing god.[1]

In Brekete shrines of West Africa ancient rhythms move bodies in spectacular ways. The power of repetition, inscribed in a soundscape of welcome and praise, calls northern gods to possess their devotees. These divine horsemen, so goes the trope, ride their mounts.[2] In the blink of an eye a person can become seized. Captured by their capacity to be taken, they are no longer aware of their bodily existence, for they are no longer themselves. It is not they who dance, but Kunde the hunter, or Ablewa his wife, Sanya the firstborn, or Bangle the soldier.[3] Embodiments of virtuosity, these gods are virtuosos of being-there. Dressed in swirling saturated colors, they dance themselves into existence. And as long as the gods are there, someone always must be leaving. What is a being-there for a deity is already a being-away for a devotee. And this is exactly what had happened to the old woman when she became possessed. No longer a widowed fishmonger with arthritic knees, she was Bangle the avenging and thus protecting deity, the soldier, the owner of *dzogbe* (the desert), where hot deaths reside.

Ketetsi (one of Bangle's many praise names) had been coming to Adzo for a long time and was as familiar with being in her body as she was with being-away. It was after several miscarriages, when she was in her midtwenties, that her husband first took her to seek the help of the gods. Shortly thereafter she became pregnant, and when she subsequently delivered a healthy baby boy, they were both, as it were, "born into the shrine." And soon after she joined the shrine, the god joined her. Adzo became a wife for a second time, a *trɔsi*, a spouse of the gods.[4]

Some forty years later, her first husband long since dead, Ketetsi was still working his way in her body. When he rides he puts her through paces she couldn't possibly imagine performing in her everyday life: spinning at a high rate of speed for fifteen or twenty revolutions and then landing on one foot precisely on the last stroke of the bell pattern to continue a dance that had been going on for hours; or sitting on the sharp end of a short spear, supporting a *brekete* drummer on each leg while gunpowder is being set off in her outstretched palms.[5] This and more happened that afternoon when Bangle came to ride.

Adzo, of course, knew nothing of the matter. Her knowledge of possession is restricted to arrivals and departures, of going into and out of trance, everything in between a total blank. Her ten-year-old granddaughter had experienced more of Bangle's presence than she had in the forty years he had been coming to her. But that is the nature, and irony, of possession: horses don't know they are being ridden. Only the day after would she feel the aches and pains of such physical exertion. After years of experience with "the day after," however, she is no longer confused over the exhausted state of her body when she wakes up the next morning; nowadays, she is accustomed to the aches, conversant with the pain. Being-away is just another kind of being-there, part of her life in the shrine.

Adzo is a fixture on the Brekete scene, a long-standing and well-known *trɔsi*. She, however, accumulated no particular spiritual capital as a result of this, was not considered to be enlightened in some special way, was not paid any special deference. No one confused fishmonger with divine horseman. True, it was generally assumed that she was of high moral character and followed the taboos religiously or Bangle would have left long ago, but other than that she was just one more member of the shrine. The fact that her old and partially crippled body could execute such impressive feats of balance and strength was confirmation for those who witnessed such events of Ketetsi's presence and her absence. How else to explain such goings-on?

Not everyone who joins Brekete, however, gets "married" to the gods. In a shrine such as the one Adzo attends, with some two hundred members, perhaps only twenty or so are *trɔsiwo*, three-quarters of them women. The gods choose only those who are worthy of their attention, those who follow the tenets of the shrine and keep the taboos. That is why there are more women who are *trɔsiwo* than men. The rules are many, and men, in particular, have a hard time following them. Women are not as morally lax as their male counterparts, who are more likely to sleep around, get in fights, deal with *juju*, drink too much, and pursue various other activities that are at variance with the laws of the shrine.[6] This particular assessment was not merely the negative judgment of women but was put forth by men themselves. This helps to explain why men are more involved with sacrifices than women—they are continually atoning for their sins and misdeeds—and offers a different take on women and trance than the theory of deprivation, with its attendant mechanisms of redress (Lewis 1971, 1999).

Though Adzo's status was not elevated as a result of being possessed, when she was away and Bangle was there her presence was a formidable one. Her entire physiognomy was transformed into the face of a dancing god. Not only was Bangle's dance one of divine virtuosity, but, when there, he was healer and protector, seer and judge. I have seen him grab a baby, take her into the shrine and smear her with protective medicines, then reemerge dancing with the baby on his back, all the while with the child sound asleep; heard him chastise a priest (*sofo*) for some infraction and demand a sizable sacrifice to rectify the matter and listened as no amount of pleading on the priest's part would change his mind; was present when a celebration was stopped in midstream and an entire congregation shaved their heads at his insistence (something I was, fortunately, able to avoid only because I was not a member). These and countless other acts characterized Bangle's ride and attested to his power.

This was not always so. When Bangle first came to Adzo, as with all *trosiwo*, the ride was a silent one. Until the mouth-opening ritual (*nuvuvu*) is performed, those possessed cannot talk, nor does anyone know which god has come. Dressed in simple white calico wraps, they are confined to a dancing that is yet to achieve the power and dexterity of a fully installed *trosi*. To open the mouth seven fowl are needed, along with two bottles of foreign drink, preferably schnapps, a calabash of kola nuts (roughly one hundred), and a calabash of kaolin. This can impose a formidable financial burden on new *trosiwo*, who often have difficulty procuring all that is required. If husbands and other relatives are not prepared to contribute, the ritual can be put off for months, sometimes years, which leaves the person in a kind of limbo, a potentially dangerous and vulnerable situation. But eventually people usually do help, sometimes even the gods, who may, as was the case with Adzo, increase a fishmonger's business to help cover expenses, and the ritual takes place in a timely manner.

The night before the mouth opening Adzo was taken to *dzogbe*, the desert where Bangle rules, a place near the shrine that is usually enclosed in palm branch fencing and accessible only to initiated members. In *dzogbe* she had to "clear her stomach" (*dome kokoe*), confessing all that she had done wrong in her life. If the person does not make full disclosure, serious consequences—sickness, even death—are sure to follow. Her head was then shaved (hair can accumulate negative forces), and she was bathed in the *amatsi* (herb water) of the gods. The next day prayers were made, and the kola, kaolin, drink, and some money were presented to the gods before the chicken divination began.

Death can give evidence of things unseen, and the way a chicken dies— more precisely, the position in which a chicken expires—reveals the will of the gods. If it dies on its back, it means assent; if on its stomach, refusal.[7] Ewes, as do many Africans, have a different take on what we would consider aleatory events. Instead of taking such chance happenings as the luck of the draw, Ewes see the work of the gods in these ritual situations precisely because human intentions are removed from the equation.[8] The divination got under way, and a fowl was brought into the shrine, its throat cut, and bled on Kunde, the father. The chicken was then tossed outside and, after it seemed as though it was going to die on its back, it flipped onto its stomach and expired—Kunde had said no. The same was done for Ablewa, the mother, and Sanya Kompo, the firstborn, who is linguist, secretary, and god of the stone, and each time the chicken took its last breath facing the earth.[9] But when it came to Bangle, the chicken jerked up once in a spasm and died straightaway on its back. Ketetsi had chosen another bride.

Just as all new trɔsiwo are marked, once the trɔ made himself known, three cuts about a half inch long were made at the corners of Adzo's mouth. The same medicines and herbs that are used to make the fetishes (see chap. 3), those objects that are the gods in their physical form, the things that sacrifice and libation, blood and drink, are directly given to, were rubbed into the wounds, creating a permanent tattoo. You can always spot a trɔsi as a result of these marks. The bodies of the gods are fused into the bodies of their spouses, not metaphorically, but literally. The trɔ, now installed, is given voice and released into the world of the living through the unique body of the one he or she has chosen. Once the mouth is opened, whenever the god rides a torrent of words pours forth in a multiplicity of languages—Ewe, Twi, Hausa, and others no one can quite identify—addressing a complex of issues of health and wealth, sanction and censure, that affect the members of the shrine. In the peripheral economy of a struggling Volta Region at the beginning of the twenty-first century—as it was at the turn of the twentieth century, when colonialism was firmly taking hold in the far eastern part of what was then called the Gold Coast—a search for some kind of security, to echo Margaret Field (1960), was, and is, often a difficult and elusive task.

The coastal plains of the Volta Region, with its infertile soil and low rainfall, its lack of natural resources, and a fishing industry that at best barely supports the many fishermen that dot the coast, are one of the poorest areas of Ghana. No goldfields here, no fertile fields for cocoa production—the main export earners for Ghana. What we cannot take from this depressed economic condition is a direct causal link to shrine activity. In fact, the explosion of cocoa production as a cash crop in the Akan forest region is often cited for the many witchcraft accusations, which precipitated bringing northern gods south. There are myriad contexts that frame who came where and why. Ewes don't turn to Brekete just because they are mired in seemingly intractable economic difficulties, which indeed may strain social relations, exacerbate health-care problems, and so on, just as the uneven distribution of wealth from cocoa is not the sole answer to the many antiwitchcraft movements that were powered by northern fetishes. Much more *and* much less is at work here.

Kola-Nut Gods

Brekete, officially known as Lahare Kunde, was, as was previously stated, but one of a wave of "medicine" shrines (*atikevodu*; literally, "tree-root vodu") brought to southern Ghana in the early to mid-twentieth century.[10] They offered cures for all kinds of afflictions and protection against sorcerous attacks, which for the Ewes is generically referred to as *juju*. For generations, people along the Guinea Coast had turned to more indigenous medico-religious practices to address the vicissitudes of daily life. What, then, was going on in southern Ghana that moved people to actively seek foreign gods, especially northern ones? Why this influx of northern shrines at this particular time?

Part of the answer had to do with a general belief that the north had resisted European domination more effectively than the coast, and therefore their gods must be stronger. That this had little basis in fact did not deter southern peoples from positing a northern resistance that was effective, thus giving hope for a reversal of fortunes.[11] Although this was not the only reason for their adoption—they already fitted into a long-held conviction that northern strangers had access to occult powers not available in the south—northern gods did find fertile ground in the disruptions of colonialism.[12]

When Kunde moved south, he and his family rode into a long and complicated history of north-south contact in trade and conquest, religion and ideas. They found themselves part of an ambiguous discourse that was both receptive to such northern strangers and also extremely suspicious of them.[13] There is a strongly held ethos among Ewes concerning "strangers" (*amedzrowo*) that is summed up in the frequently heard statement that "you should treat strangers with respect and hospitality, for you never know when you may also find yourself one," a situation Ewes found themselves in many times during their long migration from points further east to their present home.[14] This ethos of the "stranger," however, is tempered with a certain wariness when the strangers in question are Muslims. Most Ewes, then and now, imagine the "north" as an Islamized region of "otherness"; its people, regardless of where they come from or what ethnic group they belong to, are all considered to be Hausa, Islamic traders not to be trusted in business or, for that matter, in religion.[15] As sententious wisdom would have it, "If they can get away with cheating you, they will, and if they profess to be pious Muslims, you know that after prayers they are not averse to having a beer or two, or a couple of tots of gin in private." This negative attitude of Ewes toward Muslims is vividly displayed in the painting on the front wall of a Brekete shrine in the border town of Aflao. A python is depicted with the turbaned head of a bearded northerner, with his tail wrapped around a tree, looking piously toward heaven, but with crossed eyes. The inscription below the painting reads, "God hates hypocrisy." That the shrine displays such attitudes prominently while simultaneously aligning itself with certain Islamic practices is a kind of cognitive dissonance that is carefully managed by members of the shrine. At best, Islamic practice in Brekete is but a thin overlay.[16] There is no deep syncretism here, such as the kind that can be found among the Tumbukas of northern Malawi, where Christianity has been fused with a traditional drum of affliction (Friedson 1996). All Tumbukas profess to be Christian; virtually no Brekete member would claim to be a practicing Muslim, someone who follows the five pillars of the faith. Islam in Brekete always has been a matter of geographic fact rather than religious belief.

Needless to say, this diverse group of people—Mossi, Fulani, Zabrema, Songhay, Mamprusi, Dogon, Gonja, Dagbamba, "real" Hausa, and others that make up these generic "northerners"—resent this stereotyping, and, of course, not all southerners subscribe to such labeling. Although Islam is an established presence in Ewe lands—most towns of any size have a mosque and a *zongo* (Islamic or stranger quarter)—Islam, unlike Christianity, has made few inroads into Ewe society and even fewer converts. It was, and remains, the northern "other," and it is within this context that these northern gods were adopted.

All of this is further complicated by the fact that, according to shrine history, Kodzokuma, the man who brought the gods south, received them from the hands of the Dagarti of what is now officially called the Upper West Region.[17] Ironically, the Dagarti are one of the northern peoples who instead of coming under the sway of Islam were heavily missionized by Catholic white fathers (the Society of the Missionaries of Africa). They were an island of Christianity amid a sea of Islam. This seeming incongruity, however, was easily explained by shrine members who either didn't know the Dagarti were not predominantly Muslims, and whose religion was therefore not an issue, or, if they did, reminded me that not all Dagarti were Christians, such as the ones who were taking care of Kunde and his wife Ablewa.[18] When it serves their purposes, at least some Ewes have no trouble executing more fine-grained discriminations regarding northern peoples.

When Kodzokuma went north, he didn't go looking for the gods, according to his son Kwasi Anibra, who, at the time of my research, was head priest of all of Brekete; they instead found him. After all, as he recounts it, his father back then was only a boy of thirteen:

Between 1916 and 1918 three chiefs were enstooled in Kpando and three chiefs died. There was *masɔmasɔ* [confusion] in the town, and *juju* had killed all three. The elders finally turned to the maternal side of the royal family to choose a new chief, but the queen mother would not let her son be put on the stool unless they brought a fetish from the north that could protect him.[19] A delegation was formed of six elders and my father, Kodzokuma, who was the water boy. They set off on foot for a town called Dukuma where Kunde was worshipped. After several weeks of travel, they finally arrived in Dagarti country and the owner of the fetish was informed of their mission. He said he would give them the fetish if Kunde agreed. He instructed them to gather seven chickens for a divination to find out Kunde's wishes. But each fowl that was sacrificed died on its stomach, a sign that Kunde refused to go with any of these men. Having failed in their mission, they gathered their things and were beginning to leave when an old woman in the fetish house said: "You haven't tried the young boy who is carrying the water jug. Is he not too a human being?" So they threw a chicken and it landed on its back, and they threw another chicken and it died on its back, and another. Each one confirmed that Kunde wanted to go with my father. He was carried on the delegation's shoulders, and they returned to Kpando. Kodzokuma was thirteen years old at the time. But the other members of the delegation were jealous and tried to undermine him. He moved away from Kpando and became a fitter (auto mechanic) in Kumasi.[20] In his twenties he eventually returned to his home and established a shrine, but the elders of the community were jealous and told the Europeans it was a place for *juju*. The governor came and asked my father: "Does the shrine punish evildoers"? My father said, "Yes," and the governor told him to go about his work.

From Kpando, a town in the northern Volta Region that had been a center for German economic and missionary activity at the turn of the century when this area was part of the Trans-Volta region of Togoland, the shrine spread first to the coastal border town of Aflao, then shortly thereafter to Lome, the capital of Togo, and to Accra, the capital of what was then the Gold Coast. Thus there was a second migration of the shrine from the north to the south, but this time it was taking place among different groups of Ewes with different traditions.[21] By the early 1960s Brekete was well established in Ghana and Togo, wherever there were large groups of Ewes. The *trɔwo*, the spirit-gods that Kodzokuma had brought back from the Dagarti, were proving more successful than he ever could have imagined. Kpando became a kind of Mecca, and Kodzokuma became the pope for an ever-increasing number of shrines.

What Kodzokuma received from the Dagarti was not esoteric knowledge of gods and their rites, but the gods in their material form, what Ewes still refer to (as we just read in his son's account) as "fetishes."[22] For the peoples of the Guinea Coast, the word is not a loaded term burdened with sexual overtones and Marxist theory (see chap. 3), but rather points to those powerful "things" found in shrines. This is not to say that some Ewes, particularly Christians, don't see fetishes as evil, the work of the devil, which ironically confirms their reality (Meyer 1999), but the term itself is not pejorative. Whether taken as something good or bad, fetish merely speaks of those things that receive sacrifice and libation. All the northern shrines that came to the coast brought with them these god-things, which were collectively known as *gorovoduwo*, a name that points both to their northern origin and their southern embrace. The first part of the name, *goro*, is the Hausa word for kola nut, the medicine cum sacrament of these shrines, and a commodity with a long history of trade between the Sahel and the forest zones of central Ghana, where the most sought-after variety (*Cola nitida*) is grown (Hiskett 1984; Abaka 2005). Islam came to Ghana, in part, following the trails of these kola-nut traders. In a religion with strong sanctions against mood-altering substances, kola became the recreational drug of choice—albeit a rather soft one—for many Muslims in West Africa. These days in Ghana, pretty much the only people who chew kola on a regular basis are Muslims and members of *gorovodu* shrines. The former use it as a stimulant, the latter as part of medico-religious practices. Whenever prayers are made—to Kunde or Ablewa; Sanya or Bangle; Sakra Bode, the god of the land, or Wango, the god of the seas and roads—kola is an obligatory offering because that is what the gods were offered in the north. And, as in the north, after contact with the fetishes the kola—distributed to members in its transformed state as the food of the gods—both heals and protects. It is the kola sacrament perhaps more than anything else that, in Ewe eyes, separates these gods from the second part of the name, *vodu*, the word for spirit-god in many Kwa / Gbe languages of the Guinea Coast.[23] *Voduwo*, as with Kunde and his family, are both fetishes and dancing gods who possess their devotees.[24]

What this all suggests is a single widespread West African religion with

Fig. 1.2 Bangle / Ketetsi as *gorovodu* fetish (Steven Friedson)

different denominations in the north and south that probably have influenced each other for centuries. Greenberg (1941), in fact, makes one-to-one equivalences between *iskoki / bori* spirits and such coastal gods as Xebieso, the thunder god of the Ewe and Fon, and Shango, a similar thunder god of the Yoruba; Aido Hwedo, the rainbow snake god of Dahomey, and Legba, the messenger and *vodu* of the crossroads. But the history of these connections, contacts, influences, exchanges, and interactions is yet to be written.

To trace but one such possibility, the horse in West African history has been well documented (Law 1980; Webb 1993), but there is virtually no work on the relationship between this history and the widespread trope of divine horsemen. Given the fact that horses were introduced to the Guinea Coast relatively late (probably no earlier than the nineteenth century) and were extremely hard to maintain as a result of this area's being a vector for trypanosomiasis, spread by the tsetse fly (Law 1980: 77), there seems to be at least circumstantial evidence that the trope migrated from the north to the south long before kola-nut gods arrived.

Through the Middle Passage, divine horsemen traveled to Latin America and the Caribbean (Matory 2005; Bastide 1978; Deren 1953; Métraux 1972; Walker 1972; Houk 1995) and, in a second and more recent dispersion, to such cities as Miami and New York (Brown 1991; Vega 1995; Lefever 2000). We are confronted here not with the history of the movement of localized cults, but with the workings of what amounts to a world religion. In 1983 the World Council of Churches acknowledged this fact by officially recognizing Vodu (Fleurant 2007: 237). Today, divine horsemen ride throughout, to appropriate Thompson's (1983) suggestive phrase, the Black Atlantic (see also Gilroy 1993; and Matory 2005). Vodu is not some historical curiosity, but a living reality.

Drum Brekete

By the time I arrived on the eastern shores of the Black Atlantic, Brekete was one of the fastest growing shrines in all of West Africa, found as far east as Nigeria (recently a shrine was even established in Gabon) and extending in the west to Côte d'Ivoire and beyond. It seems to be only a matter of time, if it has not happened already, that the Brekete gods will follow the lead of other divine horsemen and start to ride on other western shores. Of all the *gorovoduwo* that came to the Guinea Coast, Brekete was the only one that had any staying power. Tigare, as most witchcraft eradication movements did, burned itself out relatively quickly, and, though Alafia is still around, it only has a small following.[25] Why those failed and Brekete flourished is not entirely clear. No doubt it was partly due to the combination of a charismatic founder who seems to have had superior organizational skills, his ritual genius in combining what had been different fetishes with separate shrines into one single pantheon, the belief that it addressed a wider range of problems than just witchcraft (see n. 22), and, perhaps the most important reason, something that we cannot just dismiss out of hand, that this group of gods simply proved to be more effective than their northern counterparts, and they did turn out, as people had thought, to be more powerful than their southern cousins. They were more successful in solving the problems of those who sought their help: they promoted fertility, cured intractable illnesses that proved resistant to other remedies, protected against the evil intentions of others, restored balance in personal relationships that had turned poisonous, and ensured success in business as well as other aspects of life in both urban and rural environments when people invoked the intervention of powers greater than that of mortals.

But the shrine also flourished in no small measure because of its art, the spectacle brought forth at a Brekete shrine during times of celebration, the center of which is, as it is with much ritual and celebration in Africa, a potent and powerful musical experience. Significantly, while the gods, Islam, and kola nut came south, northern music, for the most part, did not. The music of Brekete for all practical purposes is the music of the Ewes of the Guinea Coast. Ewes may have been looking for new gods, but they were not looking for a new musical world; the gods were assimilated into Ewe religious life but were totally adapted to southern ways of making music. Brekete was, in a sense, domesticated, made familiar, to a large degree through musical means.

Pretty much all that remains of northern musical practice, besides snatches of songs and lyrics here and there, is the double-headed drum that followed the gods and some of the praises played on them. This organological evidence of geographic origin, however, turns out to be no small matter. Transformed from a shallow wooden drum in the north into one made from used metal chemical or oil barrels in the south, which are about twice the length, it has a low booming sound with a buzzed edge due to the string snares affixed to each head, a feature typical of northern drums.[26] When they are played correctly, the resonance, though low pitched, is focused and penetrating. Standard practice is for two of these drums to play at the same time, individually elaborating on stereotypical patterns, creating a synergistic effect that produces a truly impressive sound.

Northern drums playing within the context of a southern style is consistently cited by Ewes as one of the main reasons for the success of the shrine; it caught the aural imagination of coastal populations. That a phenomenon as aesthetically charged as musical sound would have a direct influence on the acceptance and adoption of ritual change is something most anthropologists not only haven't heard, but have never even considered. In anthropological thought about ritual, if music is mentioned at all, usually it is relegated to the status of an epiphenomenon, something accompanying other more important ritual happenings. The soundscape of two *brekete* drums, however, may have something to say to us about the ontological contours of a particular way of being-in-the-world that all the nuanced analyses of peripheral strategies, subaltern tactics, gendered hegemonies, political economies, social histories, structural relationships, thick descriptions, and so on, can never reveal. In essence, drumming may be a form of Ewe philosophy, one not done with words but through musical sound (see chap. 5).[27] Whether this is so might be open to debate, but its importance to the shrine is undeniable. Brekete, after all, took its name from the drum that accompanied these northern deities when they were brought south and the one still used to call the gods to descend and dance, as it had that afternoon when Bangle came to ride.

Fig. 1.3 *Brekete* drummers kneeling out of respect for priests who are dancing (Steven Friedson)

Being-There

When Adzo became possessed, it was the third, and next-to-last, day of a *fetatrɔtrɔ* (literally, "the year head turning"), a triennial cow sacrifice. No one had gotten much sleep, for at a *fetatrɔtrɔ* every night is a wake keeping and every day a jubilation. What little rest we had managed consisted of short naps here and there. REM sleep was beginning to work itself out whether we knew it or not, and by that penultimate day we were all in an altered state, some obviously more than others. The almost constant music making, and three days of chewing kola nut and drinking *akpeteshie*, the potent locally distilled gin, more than contributed to the mood. A cow sacrifice, of course, is serious business: gods must be fed, libations poured, ancestors remembered, debts repaid, and pledges redeemed. Gods in West Africa, however, also simply love to celebrate with their children. Whatever else this sacrifice was about, whatever stories people were telling themselves about themselves, a *fetatrɔtrɔ* was always a good party, and this was no exception.

It was taking place at Sofo Peter's shrine, located in his natal village a few kilometers from the Togo border in the eastern part of the Ketu District just a hundred meters or so from the high-tension electricity pylons

that go directly from the Akosombo Dam to Lome and beyond.[28] Surrounding the main shrine building were the houses for himself and his
wives, his brothers' families, and other patrilineally related kin.[29] Lente
(population roughly 250), the name of the village, always seemed to have
a cool breeze blowing through it, a peaceful air, and while Peter's shrine
had gone through some rough times in the recent past, it currently was
prospering, with over two hundred members.

Although it had seemed like days ago, it was only earlier that morning
that the fetishes had been brought outside and "washed" in the blood of
the cow. Inside the shrine-house, each god has his own *kpome* (literally, "in
the oven," but here meaning the home of the god), a half-walled cubicle
where sacrifices and libations usually are offered. For a cow sacrifice, however, the fetishes are gathered together, put into a large metal basin, and
placed in the courtyard in the middle of the dance floor in front of the
shrine-house. It is one of the only times when the gods are taken from
their altars and displayed publicly, and one of the only times they are in
physical contact with each other, which is no small matter (fig. 1.4).

As the gods were brought out that morning, several of the *bosomfowo*,
who are especially initiated sacrificial priests, led a large bull into the courtyard.[30] The bull, not surprisingly, was not very cooperative, and it was
only after several tries they finally got him on his side and proceeded to lift
him over the basin, which had been placed in the center of a cross drawn
inside a circle with kaolin powder, an invocation of the power of the crossroads. One man put his fingers inside the bull's nose and pulled back the
head so that the neck was exposed as one of the senior *bosomfowo* emerged
from inside the shrine with the special cow-sacrificing knife (*nyitsohɛ*) in
his hand. He walked over to the cow and with several quick slashes nearly
decapitated it. Blood gushed out of the jugular vein, pouring out all over
the gods. When the blood quit flowing into the basin, the cow was tossed
to the side and the *trɔwo* were taken inside to be "polished." As always,
there was an almost eerie silence when the gods were fed. There was no
music, no dancing, and most people kept quiet; it is not polite to talk when
the gods are eating.

After the bull died and was removed, however, the special hunting songs
of the *bosomfowo* were raised as the sacrificial priests processed out of the
shrine led by a drummer playing on the *apentema*, a small footed hand drum
of Akan origin now associated with Ade, the indigenous god of hunting,
and also part of the *brekete* drum ensemble. Associations with hunters and
hunting are many in Brekete, especially around Kunde, the father of the
pantheon. Not only is he considered to be an *adela*, a hunter, and often

Fig. 1.4 *Gorovoduwo* fetishes gathered together in pans to receive the sacrifice (Elise Ridenour)

depicted as such in paintings that decorate the outsides of shrines, but he is also referred to as a lion, the ultimate predator. One can often hear the drums calling out *dzata gbɔna*, "the lion is coming," a warning to his prey, in other words, those who have offended him in some way. His children, the members of Brekete, are referred to as the *adehawo* (literally, "the hunting group"), and when he rides, his Kundesiwo (wives of Kunde) often carry a hunting bow and quiver of arrows or a wooden gun. Although Kunde is specifically aligned with Ade, they are not isomorphic. Many *sofowo* have an Ade shrine at their compound, separate from Kunde—easily identifiable by the many animal skulls around the entrance—that is handed down from father to son. In contrast to Brekete ritual and ceremonial, which is open to a congregation of adherents, Ade ritual is usually a private family affair. Much of the ritual surrounding this god has to do with appeasing the souls of the animals that have been killed by ancestral hunters.[31] Kunde, on the other hand, is a hunter not in the sense of a skillful stalker and killer of animals but in the moral sense of a hunter of wrongdoers, both those who try to cause harm to the *adehawo* and those who are members and break the laws of the shrine.[32]

When the *bosomfowo* came out of the shrine after having polished the gods and sacrificing the other animals required when a cow is offered (see chap. 3), each was wearing his bloodstained *adewu* (hunter's shirt). These ritually charged tunics with their sewn-on talismans (*tsila*) and other medicines are always worn for sacrifices, offering protection (resonant with Ade practice) to the sacrificer from numerous dangers associated with the ritual killing of animals. They are never cleaned, and years of caked-on blood have turned the fronts black. As the *bosomfowo* circled the dance floor in their *adewuwo*, they periodically stopped to sing the ritually charged songs of *ase* (see ex. 1.1).

Ase I ye	[Vocables]
Ekraa ɖaɖea mewua	Holding a cutlass, we saw it
(Wokura dadeɛ o, Yehunu oo)	
Enua basa mewua	The arm is strong
(Basa mu yɛdwru o)	
Egble o, enyo o, ahoo!	Whether bad or good, ahoo!

Ex. 1.1. Ase

Lyrics in parenthesis are the Twi equivalents of the Eweized version of that language.

While the song is in Twi, the last line is Ewe and sums up an approach to the vicissitudes of life; it is an acceptance of what is—not a defeatist attitude, but a pragmatist's understanding expressed in musical terms.

Ase songs are sung in free rhythm, punctuated now and then by the drum.[33] Everyone kneels down when singing, and plenty of gunpowder is set off. The songs and gunpowder are meant to increase and raise the level of excitement, to inject energy into the proceedings. The word *ase* itself, probably borrowed from the Yoruba language, points to spiritual energy, power, and life force. This style of music seems counterintuitive to the usual attribution of highly charged polyrhythmic percussion ensembles as a main ingredient of musical energy and excitement, but *ase* songs are intensely felt and build ritual tension.

After the *ase* songs were finished, the *bosomfowo*, as metaphoric "hunters" who deal in the sacrificial immediacy of life and death, once again took up the songs of their vocation and one by one danced the hunt. This individualistic display of the hunters—stalking the prey, capturing and slitting its throat, leaping into the air from sheer exuberance—can be, in its own way, as visually spectacular as the ride of divine horsemen. If one hadn't known better, if one had been just looking at their behavior, it would have seemed as if they were totally possessed. But possessed they were not; in fact, it was just the opposite. Instead of being away they were fully there, overcome by the intensity of sacrifice and the power of the music. It was an inspired dance, not a possessed one (see Rouget 1985).

As the hunters continued their dance, eventually new songs were brought forth and the *brekete* drums reentered the soundscape and once

Fig. 1.5 *Bosomfowo* in sacrificial shirts singing *ase* songs (Elise Ridenour)

again resumed their prominence. As the level of excitement continued to increase, the *lātsohawo* (literally, "animal-cutting-songs") were introduced and the whole atmosphere reached an intensity that verged on chaos. These songs (each god has his or her own) are sung only after sacrifices and are different from other *brekete* songs in melody and text, though rhythmic practice remains the same (see chap. 5). It is during their performance, however, that drummers can apply their vocation; this is a time for them to dig into their repertoire of "licks" and revel in their competence to continually and spontaneously transform them. These are considered the most potent *brekete* songs, and, when they are sung, many *trɔwo* come to ride their horses. By the time Sanya's song was sung (ex 1.2), followed immediately by Bangle's (ex 1.3), the most compact songs of the set of *lātsohawo*, both continually repeating only a few words, the dance floor was filled with *trɔsiwo*, many of whom were wielding knives and spears, performing feats of bravado only northern gods would dare.

Sanya ɖoɖo   Sanya's *ɖoɖo* (hourglass-shaped tension drum)
Ɖoɖo nye ɖe?   Where is my *ɖoɖo*?

Ex. 1.2. Sanya's *lātsoha* (song for animal sacrifice)
Call-and-response form is most commonly mapped across the distinction between solo and chorus—the soloist calls and the chorus responds. For these two *lātsoha* songs, however, the reverse is true—the chorus calls out and it is the soloist who responds. (See www. remainsofritual.com for transcriptions of the full set of *lātsoha* songs.)

And this was when Adzo the fishmonger became possessed for the first time that day. After the possession was settled in her head with the help and under the ever-watchful eyes of the *senterwawo*, who are especially appointed women "sentries" who attend to the needs of the *trɔsiwo* when possessed, Adzo stormed into the shrine, picked up the trident that is Bangle's spiritual weapon, and joined the other gods.[34] But it was only for a short stay—gods come and go as they please—and within the hour he

Atsidzé, atsidzé Ɖiamlo
Bangle Ɖiamlo[35]

Ex. 1.3. Bangle's *lātsoha* (song for animal sacrifice)
Most priests and members do not know the meaning of this song, nor could
they identify the language.

took his leave. As usual it took a while for Adzo to completely come back
to the everyday world, but soon she was sitting with the other *adehawo*
singing and playing the *akpé* clapping sticks.

The celebration continued throughout the day, and by late afternoon
most of us were running on empty, moved on by the sheer energy of the
music—and the continuing rounds of kola and *akpeteshie*. I was drifting in
and out and had totally given up any pretext of being the resident ethnomusicologist. I no longer cared what songs were being sung or who was
playing the *brekete* drums; whether the rhythms I was hearing were syncopated, polymetrical, or just plain unfathomable; who was or was not possessed, inspired, participating, or bored; and countless other things I was
supposed to be concerned with in the field as a researcher. Instead I just sat
there somewhat in an alcohol-induced and sleep-deprived fog as twenty or
so *trɔsiwo* continued to appropriate the dance floor, taking up the entire

space in their expansive and highly articulated movements. Visually it was stunning: the gods' northern-style dress, with its striped cloth in primary colors highlighted by the stippled effect of the filtered light. Acoustically it was overwhelming: songs of deep Ewe filling the air as they began playing Bangle's music.

Befitting a soldier, his music is that of *agbadza* (usually translated as "gunbelt"), the classic war drum of the Ewe. In the olden days, when it was known as *atrikpui*, it was performed only on the outskirts of the village by returning warriors, or at the funerals of those who died a hot death (Fiagbedzi 1977: 57–58; Jones 1959: 162–63; Alorwoyie 2003). Now it is mostly heard at wake keepings and burials, both for those who died coolly in bed at an old age (*afemeku*, or "house death") and those who "died in the blood" (*vumeku*) as a result of some kind of accident or other misfortune. This music touches people deeply, seeming to embody core features of an Ewe sensibility. At a wake keeping, I have seen more than one old man inspired by memories past—and a bit of *akpeteshie*—dance to this drum with a force and grace that gave those who were gathered pause.

And this is when Adzo became possessed for the second time. She joined three or four other *trɔsiwo* who were already manifesting Bangle, which seemed totally normal to everyone else, but always struck me as a bit strange, especially when the various Bangles would engage each other in animated conversation. Eventually, however, I began to realize that Bangle in Adzo is something slightly different from Bangle in someone else, which is different from Bangle as fetish. The gods are not a single transcendent entity analogous to a Western projection of personhood with a bounded identity and delimited personality, but always a multiplicity of effect. These were not gods frozen in an eternal bond of always the same, but a dynamic presence of difference. Bangle is always a particular Bangle.

As I sat there watching the multiple Bangles dance, every once in a while one of them would stop in front of me to offer greetings and give his blessing with the typical handshake of the gods, a hard slap of the hand. In West Africa you can shake hands with your gods, engage in face-to-face interaction, experience them in immediacy. They are not "other worldly" but decidedly "this worldly" (Horton 1971: 86). If I had been daydreaming or nodding off to sleep, which by this time was a frequent if not almost a continuous occurrence, the hard slap would immediately pull me back into my body and an awareness of my immediate surroundings. And just as suddenly I would start to drift off again. The time between the shifts became slower yet somehow closer together. I started getting confused about which mode I was in. Being-away started feeling like being-there, and in this liminality the texture of light and shadow, sound and movement, began to separate and coalesce at the same time.

Being-Away

Of course, we all have experienced being-there while being-away to some degree: daydreaming while driving a car, attending a lecture, listening to music, or in countless other ways. During those moments, we somehow manage to withdraw our awareness of bodily emplacement even while we continue to do complex tasks, such as drive a car or even play in a symphony orchestra, as happens sometimes with professional musicians playing Beethoven's Fifth Symphony for the hundredth time. It is not something we willingly do, even though sometimes we might think so. We may consciously want to think about being somewhere else when, for example, listening to a boring lecture, but thinking it and doing it are two different things. Of course, you can be thinking of something else and still be there at least half-listening to a lecture. But when you are truly daydreaming you are "away," the very definition of the phenomenon. Daydreaming comes over us of its own free will at the moment of its happening. And just as suddenly, without warning, we are once more back in our bodies: someone asks us a question, a car pulls out in front of us, the speaker stumbles over her words, a string breaks. The dis-placement itself is displaced as it withdraws.

This is to say nothing of sleep, a much more radical attunement of being-away. When we are sleeping, our bodies are not so much displaced as bounded in immobility. And, just as we cannot willingly daydream, we cannot willingly go to sleep. This is evident when we nod in and out while dozing, but it is also true when we go to bed. As Merleau-Ponty (1962: 189–90) reminds us, interestingly relating sleep to possession, before we actually go to sleep we assume the position of someone already asleep:

> I lie down in bed, on my left side, with my knees drawn up; I close my eyes and breathe slowly, putting my plans out of my mind. But the power of my will or consciousness stops there. As the faithful in the Dionysian mysteries, invoke the god by miming scenes from his life, I call up the visitation of sleep by imitating the breathing and posture of the sleeper. The god is actually there when the faithful can no longer distinguish themselves from the part they are playing, when their body and their consciousness cease to bring in, as an obstacle, their particular opacity, and when they are totally fused in the myth. There is a mo-

ment when sleep "comes," settling on this imitation of itself which I have been offering to it, and I succeed in becoming what I was trying to be; an unseeing and almost unthinking mass, riveted to a point in space and in the world henceforth only through the anonymous alertness of the senses.

We may call sleep to visit us, but, as with Dionysian frenzy and the dance of northern gods, the moment of its arrival is not under conscious control. I am not suggesting that possession trance is somehow an extreme form of daydreaming or some kind of sleepwalking, but that there is a resonance bringing us somewhat closer to an understanding of how someone entranced can be there and away at the same time.

No matter what the similarity may be, however, a gulf remains between the two that never can be bridged. For a trɔsi, to dance is to dream of nothing. In our dreams, whether they be of day or night, we are always involved, in some way, with the dreamplay that unfolds; we hold on to who we are. While they are happening, we are definitely there, even if we have absolutely no memory of the dream when we awake. But dreaming of nothing is a whole other matter. Waking and sleeping are neither equivalent to consciousness and unconsciousness nor coterminous with being-there and being-away, but the latter are present in both.[36] Likewise, just because the trance of a trɔsi entails a complete sacrifice of persona and a total concealing of identity in order to allow the unconcealing of a trɔ, it does not necessarily mean that there is no experience at all. Possession trance may not be remembered because the happening is not so much linguistically encoded, and thus not amenable to a retelling, as for much of the time an embodied musical experience not tagged by syntagmatic chains. This kind of experience moves back on itself in a continual round of polythetic retrieval (Schutz 1951). It is an example of why a logocentric bias blinds us to a hearing of what happens in spirit possession. Recollection, recounting, retelling, or just telling, if nothing else, is something that takes time—precisely why Adzo can tell me in vivid detail of Bangle coming in her dreams as an Arabic man dressed as a mallam, a learned Muslim scholar, but can say nothing of being-away when Ketetsi comes to ride. Possession for Adzo is something that takes no time at all.

This lack of a "present" characterizes possession trance in two significant ways: it aligns it to animality, hence the horse metaphor, and simultaneously projects it within a temporal horizon, an ontological dimension overlooked in most studies of trance. First I turn to horses, a trope that seems to have provided diverse peoples a way to talk about the experiences of trance. In its classical inner Asian form a shaman's frame drum is his horse, and the beater his whip (Eliade 1964). As he plays the drum, he rides to the upper and lower worlds in search of lost souls, to act as a psychopomp for the departed who are on their final journey, to do battle with spirits, gods, and other shamans, and sometimes for no other reason than to gain a deeper understanding of this complex geography. The shaman is in control of his trance when he is away; in other words he is totally there, intensely aware of everything that is going on: the look of an insect in the underworld, the smell of a person when sensed from above, the feel of the air when riding, the sound of the drum with its subtle timbral changes. Instead of being the horse of a god—that a god would ride a man must be a strange thought to a shaman—the shaman is the one doing the riding. As Rouget (1985) has pointed out, this is almost exactly the opposite of West African spirit possession: the shaman appropriates the energy of his "musical" horse (his drum) to take him on his journeys; when Adzo is possessed, she is the one whose energy is appropriated by the god to ride in the world of humans.

If horses, both metaphoric and literal, were truly aware of being ridden, the question of who exactly was riding whom would inevitably arise; the fact that it doesn't is why a horse can be ridden to death and Adzo can be put through such physically demanding paces.[37] It is precisely this captivating quality of animality that makes the metaphor of divine horsemen so compelling. Horses and trɔsiwo are captivated in an "environment," totally transposed into the happenings of their behavior. Unlike human comportment, which is world-forming, they both ride in fields not of their own making. When Adzo is possessed, she is temporarily released from her own rings of contextuality and thrown into a being-there that is a being-away. But this is also precisely what separates one who is possessed from real horses, for animals can never be-away because they can never be-there in the world.[38] It situates someone like Adzo in a certain kind of animality while simultaneously moving her toward a certain kind of divinity. It is this double move that characterizes spirit possession in West Africa. When Bangle rides, he is not poor in world, as with a horse, nor is he world-forming as with a fishmonger; he is by his very nature, world-possessing. By possessing a world Bangle is moved toward the being-in-the-world of humans just as Adzo is moved toward the captivating world of animals; both are a step down in the ontological hierarchy of the Ewe cosmos.

This brings us to the second moment of the metaphor: the significance of temporality. What trɔsiwo and gods have in common is not so much the relationship between real horses and their human riders as a strange time-out-of-time temporality that binds possession to animality, gods to horses. Ask a *trɔsi* after she has come back how much time has elapsed, and she will invariably tell you that no time has passed: one minute she was sitting there singing, and the next she found herself drenched in the herb water (*amatsi*) of the god. Where Adzo and other *trɔsiwo* go when they are away no one knows, nor are we likely to ever find out: this temporal disruption of the body precludes such tellings.

Instead, it is northern gods, those timeless beings, who, when they are there, take up temporality, the projects and possibilities, cares and concerns of being-in-the-world. They do so, however, in a different mode than that of mortals. Bangle's being-there is not in time, nor does he have time; he cannot lose it or save it, because he does not exist within the "ekstatic" temporal horizon of human comportment and therefore cannot fold back the possibilities open to him into having been.[39] Gods cannot grow older surrounded by a field of finitude because only humans can die. (Animals may expire, but they are not thrown, or are caught, in an understanding of this mortal coil.) As Gadamer once put it for a different set of immortals, that is why "none of the gods philosophize" (1976: 121). This does not mean that *gorovoduwo* cannot cease to exist, that they necessarily live forever. If not taken care of, paid attention to through sacrifice and libation, they eventually may be forgotten and, as with old soldiers, just fade away, as seems to have been the case with many other kola-nut gods that were brought south.

But this day at Sɔfo Peter's shrine the gods were well fed and well feted. Bangle was in his prime even though he was in the arthritic body of a sixty-eight-year-old woman who had worked hard her entire life. Once again he had transcended her physical limitations and danced himself into existence by going along with her, not so much inside her, as it is usually depicted, but by being by her side, as it were, thus *trance*-posing human experience into the time-out-of-time temporality that is the *trance*-action of being-in-between.

And that is where I found myself late in the afternoon when Adzo became possessed and Ketetsi stood up to dance, suspended in-between the symphony of drumming, dancing, and singing that takes place at a Brekete shrine. Everything was in slow motion: the cross-rhythmic density of drums, bells, clapping sticks, and rattles separating themselves out into distinct "timbric" bands (Léon 2007); the play of light and shadow, color and costume, call and response in a continual flux, coalescing under the weight of fluid synesthetic boundaries. It was the rhythm of the crossroads inscribed in the flesh of the world.[40]

Adzo became for me a strange kind of doppelgänger, both there and not-there at the same time. She was the site of an interval in-between the customary terms of existence, a reversal in the density of being that loosened the intentional threads that bind us all to particular places and times. In the moment of that reversal, time was stilled and my leaving seemed no different from my arriving. I was somewhere I had never been, though it all seemed so familiar I could have sworn I had been there before, that there had been other sunlit afternoons like this that I somehow must have forgotten.

Being-There-and-Away

The late afternoon sun eventually turned into that distinctive equatorial twilight that makes everything seem bathed in shadows. The celebration was breaking up, and the brilliant colors of the afternoon were giving way to a more monochromatic hue. The gods decided that it was time to leave, and each *trɔsi* was washed in the special water of the deity who possessed her or him, bringing the *trɔsi* out of trance and back into the world of everyday cares and concerns. Most people started heading home, and the *brekete* drums were taken inside the shrine house and put away till the next ride, which would take place the next morning, when *salah* prayers would be said and the "breaking of the head" (*lātagbagba*) would take place. The only people remaining in the courtyard were some women and young girls, mostly the wives, sisters, and daughters of the head priest, who were cleaning up the courtyard and surrounding area.

Off to the side of the shrine house, however, all by herself, was Adzo, who was still twirling around, dancing to music that no one else could hear. Bangle was not yet ready to let go, intent on taking one last turn with his horse. No one tried to stop her, or seemed to pay much attention to what she was doing. After all, it was the god who was dancing, and gods do what they want. I, on the other hand, sat there fascinated by this silent dance, realizing in the moment of its happening that music for Adzo, Bangle, and myself was not, as I always had assumed, something dependent on the compression and expansion of air molecules. This was a musical experience born of its own ekstatic time, an original leap out-of-itself.

I think somehow Ketetsi knew that I too was listening, for he suddenly stopped dancing and came over to me. Welcoming me in Hausa, he knelt down and grabbed both of my hands, his right hand holding my right hand, his left, my left, thus causing them to cross. Different from the hard slap of earlier greetings, this was the traditional way Bangle's priests shake your hands after offering prayers to the fetish. It is Ketetsi's particular way of blessing. Then he did something that was not traditional; he rested his head on our crossed hands. Adzo's breathing was so intense that her entire body was shaking in a kind of fine muscle tonicity. It felt like she was giving off electrical shocks. I had learned from watching others that it is impolite to look directly at the god, so through all of this I was averting my gaze, only seeing Bangle off to the side in my peripheral vision. Then, without warning, he jumped up and took his leave, dancing his way into the shrine house. It was the last time I would see him that day, because twenty minutes later Adzo, the fishmonger, emerged dressed in her everyday clothes, walking slowly because of her arthritic knees.

Where Divine Horsemen Ride

The spirit is made flesh in West Africa in very particular ways. Divine horsemen ride their mounts in an extravagant immersion into the sensorium of human experience. It seems that West African gods have an intense desire to feel the sweat and smell of finitude, to sense light set upon the eyes, the pull of gravity holding one close to the earth, but, especially, to experience a rhythm upon the body, music that fills the ears. Gods dance themselves into existence, living the death of another while those whom they ride die the life of the other. This dark formula is what allows gods to be gods, and humans sometimes to be horses.[41] For the Vodu shrines of West Africa, Léopold Senghor's (1974) ontological turn—"I dance . . . therefore I am"—is not a statement of a devotee, but a declaration of the gods. In the in-between of a danced existence, divine horsemen ride in musical fields.

Fig. 1.6 Kunde (Elise Ridenour)

Prayer! Prayer!
Prayer is better than sleep
—Muezzin's call to the first morning prayer (Fajr)

Salah! Salah! 2

The final day of a *fetatrɔtrɔ*, when *salah* prayers are performed, starts at the break of dawn with the "breaking of the head" (*lātagbagba*).[1] "If you don't break the head," say the *sɔfowo* (priests), "then you haven't done anything," and all the sacrifices and prayers for the previous three days are for naught. The head is the cow's, and "breaking it" is a rather simple procedure: it is cooked, and the eyes, nose, ears, tongue, and mouth (lips) are removed and divided among the gods. Watching this being done at six o'clock in the morning after several days of fairly heavy drinking, however, actually was not that simple. I had seen enough cutting up of animals by then—cow, ram, goat, dog, cat, and various fowl—that it was no big deal, except for the dog and cat, but more about that later. Even watching the cow's eyes being removed with the occasional squirt of eye juice wasn't too bad; if anything, it was more comical than disturbing. But I was sitting inside the shrine with the *bosomfowo* (sacrificing priests) on a stool directly over the basin that held the head, and if you have ever smelled a boiled cow's head that has been sitting in the heat for over twenty hours sans refrigeration, then you know what was making me queasy.

While we were sitting around the basin and the *bosomfowo* were carving out eyes and cutting off ears, there was a continual coming and going inside the shrine. Members were arriving and entering to kneel down and pay respects to each of the *gorovoduwo* (fetishes);[2] *sofowo* from the many different shrines who had come to celebrate *fetatrɔtrɔ* were attending to the fetishes, offering prayers, kola, and drink; and, most prominently, *trɔsiwo* were becoming possessed. Because all their outfits and accoutrements were stored in bundles on the floor, they would burst inside to get dressed and have their faces and bodies marked in special designs with kaolin powder. Properly attired and decorated, without warning they would rush outside to shake hands with the *adehawo* (shrine members), give advice, talk to each other, break into dance, and, just as suddenly, decide to come back in and sit on their stools, put sticks of kaolin up their nose, take kola from their *kpomewo* (enclosed altars) and offer it to people, and do whatever else might strike their fancy. The gods may be serious, but they are also playful. They moved in and out of the shrine as if they owned the place, which they did. And while doing all of this, they were constantly singing, sometimes their voices breaking out into beautiful harmonies. It was as if their hold on this world depended on song, relied on dance. It was not that they were singing and dancing all of the time, but that they were never far from it. One moment they would be talking to you, shaking your hand, and, in the next, singing a song in Hausa, spinning and dancing in a feat of balance and bliss. *Trɔsiwo* are always on the move, even when they are standing, frozen in the classic bent posture of the onset of possession (figs. 2.1, 2.2).

Through all of this the *bosomfowo* paid virtually no attention to what was going on unless a *trɔsi* happened to come over to greet or offer one of them kola or a drink of gin. Their focus was on preparing the cow's head, all the while carrying on a lively conversation among themselves, joking and giving each other instructions on how and what to cut out next. When they had finished, the required parts were put in a bowl, and the owner of the shrine, Sɔfo Peter, who was sponsoring the *fetatrɔtrɔ*, entered to give the gods the cow head. Ablewa (the mother) and her firstborn, Sanya (the linguist and secretary), as always, were given one eye. If two cows are killed, which sometimes happens for a particularly big *fetatrɔtrɔ*, or when

Figs. 2.1 and 2.2
Onset of possession
(Elise Ridenour)

a new *sɔfo* is "outdoored," then Bangle, the soldier, and Wango, the god of the water and roads, also receive an eye. Regardless, they all get a piece of the tongue, lips, and ears. The only one who doesn't get food that day is Kunde, the father and hunter, for *lātagbagba* takes place on Monday, one of his days of rest. It is also one of Ablewa's, but the cow is mainly for her, and the white calico that covered her on this day was temporarily folded back so that she could receive her portion of the head along with balls of *dzekple* (maize flour that is boiled with salt), which had been cooked earlier. Although this is usually the province of women, men did all the cooking that morning. As the cow's eye was put on top of the fetish, the *sɔfo* spoke to Ablewa, telling her that she should take this eye in order to see all that was good and bad. Then he gave her a piece of the ear so that she could hear that which was good and that which was bad, part of the lips and tongue so that she could tell what she had seen and heard, and, finally, part of the nose so, of course, she could breathe. The homologic impulse in Ewe religion is strong and deep. The same was also done for Sanya, Bangle, and Wango, but, as already mentioned, without an eye for the last two.

The remaining meat from the head was cut into small pieces, mixed with *dzekple*, and distributed to the priests and *adehawo* as a type of communal meal. Significantly, this is not only a sharing of food among members, but also a partaking in a feast with the gods. And when the gods eat, as when the cow is sacrificed, there should be silence. Once again, no songs were sung, nor was there any kind of musical activity while the fetishes were eating. Even the *trɔsiwo* stopped singing. When one of the younger *brekete* drummers, anticipating the music that was to come, picked up one of the drums outside and struck it several times to see if it was properly tuned, he was instantly and roundly yelled at by the *sɔfowo* for committing this infraction and disturbing the gods during their meal. What followed this relative silence of *lātagbagba* and, in many ways in direct contrast to it, was the performance of *salah* (the Arabic word for prayer), the most overt expression of Islam in all of Brekete.

Sleep Is Better than Prayer

With an ease that goes unmarked, the *adehawo* move from sharing a silent meal with the fetishes to the sounds of *salah*, which these days includes such orthodox elements of Islamic prayer as the *adhan* (the call to prayer), the *shahada* (the profession of the faith), the *basmalah* (a recitation spoken before each chapter of the Qur'an) and parts of the al-Fatihah (the opening *surat* [chapter] of seven verses).[3] No member of the shrine, however, wakes up before dawn to the call of the muezzin: "Prayer! Prayer! Prayer is better than sleep." Nor do they perform ablutions or face Mecca. As with most things Islamic in Kunde's house, *salah* has been appropriated to a traditional Ewe sensibility that also features praise singing to the *trɔwo*, dancing and drumming, and *trɔsiwo* going into trance, all very un-Islamic things. Although some elements—trance dancing, in particular—are found in certain Islamic brotherhoods with their Sufi practice of the *dikhr*, it is nothing remotely like the ride of divine horsemen. A large public *salah*, such as the one at the end of Ramadan sponsored by the local Islamic community, is something entirely different from what occurred on that final morning of the *fetatrɔtrɔ*. The former is one of the five pillars of the faith as old as Islam itself; the latter a rather recent innovation in praise of different northern gods.

Salah, as practiced in Brekete, began in the early 1950s when the now practically ancient *kpomega* (an administrative head) of Sofo Tɔsavi's shrine in Accra had a dream (fig. 2.3). When I first met her in the early 1990s she already must have been in her late eighties. As she told it to me, in the dream the linguist, secretary, and god of the stone, Sanya Kompo, came to her accompanied by two *mallams* dressed in northern robes. They had come to show her *salah*, to teach her the prayers, the songs, and the circular dance; to explain the importance of *sadaqa* (alms), why giving is better than receiving; and to teach her how to perform a *rakat* (prostration) and give it a rhythm. But when she awoke, she forgot the dream, as if it had never happened. The next Sunday in the midst of the weekly Brekete celebration, Sanya came to her once again, but this time in the form of a *trɔsi*, and, in passing, asked: "Why have you forgotten *salah*"? At that moment the dream came back to her in full force. Everyone was dressed in white, dancing in a circle, singing out to Sanya:

Sanya Kompo, Sanya Kompo
La ilaha illallah   There is no god but Allah.

In her dream this was no ordinary profession of the faith; it came in call-and-response form, and every call was an invocation of a northern god and every response the last part of the first verse of the *shahada*, an attestation of Allah sung in three-part harmony.[4] With this song the elegance of *salah*, thus the parallel nature of Islam in Brekete, was revealed. And thus a new kind of prayer was born from the dream of an old woman. Sometimes, it turns out, sleep *is* better than prayer.

Fig. 2.3 Dreamer of
salah (Steven Friedson)

What began as a weekly affair on Friday mornings at Tɔsavi's shrine in
Accra soon spread and, in short order, became standard practice for all of
Lahare Kunde. In its early days, *salah* was strictly a local affair that varied
from shrine to shrine with little in the way of actual Islamic prayer. But
with the introduction of large *salahs* in the past several years, taking place
once a month and involving all the shrines in an area, or, as is the case
here, after the breaking of the head at a *fetatrɔtrɔ*, which is another recent
innovation, a more fixed Islamic liturgy has been introduced.

This move to a large and more formalized Islamic practice—over two
hundred women were gathered for the *salah* at the *fetatrɔtrɔ* that day—
coincided with a marked increase in evangelical Christianity in the coastal
areas of the Volta Region. Long resistant to missionizing activity, the southern Ewes were, and still are, well known for their strong adherence to traditional religious forms. The German Pietists in Ghana had much more

success among the northern Ewes around Kpando and Peki than they did with their southern brethren on the shores of what was then called the upper Slave Coast. Only since the 1990s has an indigenous charismatic Christian movement finally taken hold along the coast to any significant degree, with more and more Ewes becoming baptized and increasingly agitating against traditional religious practices as the work of the devil, taking up a favorite theme of the Pietists centuries before them (Meyer 1999).[5] It seems that the introduction of *salahga* (*ga* is the Ewe suffix indicating something that is large or big), with its expansion and forefronting of Islamic prayer, has been partially a response to this increased pressure from Christian fundamentalists. Brekete presents itself to itself and to the large crowd of spectators it invariably attracts as being tied to a different northern religious tradition from that of Christianity.[6]

During this same period, Islam has made virtually no overt attempts at proselytizing. In their *zongo* quarters, Muslims are considered by others and see themselves in many, though not all, ways as permanent strangers and always have been careful to keep their religion to themselves. As the author of the report on the 1891 Gold Coast census made clear, "The Mahommedans, who are found mostly along the trade routes and in the trading centres, do very little proselytizing among the native populations" (quoted in Abaka 2005: 92). The same holds true today. There has been no active attack on traditional shrines, for example, such as the attacks more recent Christian converts have made. Muslims merely dismiss such religious practices as the wayward worshipping of idols (*tagut*) that Allah would duly note and take care of on Judgment Day. There has been no interest in "transforming the *Dar al-Kufr* in which they lived into a *Dar al-Islam*" (Robinson 2004: 56). Furthermore, the *trɔwo* (spirit-gods) are not considered *jinn*, that third species of beings Allah created along with humans and angels, as they are in some northern possession cults such as Bori (Besmer 1983).[7] Islam has remained relatively static in regard to actively recruiting new adherents from the local Ewe population, though this is not to say that there haven't been conversions to Islam in the area.[8]

Although the *adehawo* are not converted but wayward Muslims, they are, nevertheless, "Islamic," for their gods are northern and the "north" always has been part of the power of an Islamized other. When "commerce and Christianity" first came to the Guinea Coast, they were received as a southern phenomenon, coming from the waters beyond a coast that faces directly south. These days, however, everyone is aware that Christian missions had their origin in a cold "European north." Nevertheless, as it did during its adoption in the 1920s, when it was tied to the perception of an effective northern resistance to southern colonial powers, Brekete seems to have reemphasized and highlighted its Islamic northern roots in these large public *salahs* as a force to counter the pressures of a southern and now homegrown evangelism.

An effective recruitment tool of evangelical Christianity in this part of Africa has been its appeal to economic gain—"make yourself right with the Lord and ye shall be rewarded here on earth and in heaven." Likewise in Brekete, a "polish the gods and they will polish you" sentiment is at work, though heavenly rewards are not, nor have they ever been, of particular concern to traditional-minded Ewes. *Salahgas*, as with *fetatrɔtrɔwo*, are visible and tangible proof of this dictum. Only a successful shrine could afford the expense of putting on a three-day *fetatrɔtrɔ*, followed by a *salahga*. The very size of the gathering attests to the power and success of Lahare Kunde.

For someone whose life is not going well and who happens to come across one of these celebrations, seeing and hearing a crowd rejoicing in a different kind of Islam, someone for whom Christianity is too far afield from traditional religion and the *voduwo* too far removed from the increasing problems of a complex sociopolitical landscape, Brekete might suggest a viable alternative. The coast of the Volta Region has been and continues to be one of the poorest areas of Ghana. Despite the ever-present government rhetoric of development, things seem to be getting worse instead of better. An unstable political situation next door in Togo, exacerbated by the death in 2005 of President Eyadema, sharp increases in the cost of living accompanied by stagnant wage structures, AIDS, and armed robbers have all contributed to an increased sense of unease and instability in a region that already was suffering. Brekete offers a way through this morass, a third stream in between the "transcendent" religions of the north and the morally ambiguous traditional religions of the coast, with their own long history of contact and influence with a north closer to home. While holding on to the core practice of spirit possession in Vodu, a powerful experience of seeing and touching the gods directly, Kunde's moral dictates are clear and, by the immediacy of their rewards and punishments, offer a sense of stability in troubled times.

Salah in Two

As the communal meal of the cow's head was nearing its end, mats were spread out under the shed and the women, all dressed in white calico with white scarves covering their heads, sat down in rows with their legs outstretched (fig. 2.4). The only men who were actively participating were three who sat in the front: two were there to play the *atoké* (boat-shaped iron bell) that accompanies the singing, the third was Bisi Kwasi, son of one of the older *sɔfowo* who, while living in Accra, learned the Islamic way of praying and was one of the people who introduced it into *salah*.[9] Although he led the prayers, it was the women who were the focus of this, to borrow Erving Goffman's (1961) terminology, focused gathering. *Salah* was, and always is, overwhelmingly an affair of the women. This is not a proscription from the shrine but a reality of practice—a majority of men simply have no interest in attending weekly *salahs* or participating in the larger monthly prayer gatherings. One might think that the introduction of more classical features of Islam, with its theological and sociological focus on maleness, would be a way for the male minority membership to assert itself within the structure of the shrine, but the opposite seems to have taken place. It is the women who have appropriated *salah* and its Islamic cloak as an expression of solidarity, a sisterhood of the *adehawo*. This also contrasts strikingly with the possession strategies of women in the north, where Islam is the religion of the majority.

Fig. 2.4 Women at *salah* prayers (Elise Ridenour)

Salah at a *fetatrɔtrɔ* is a gendered negative image of public prayers in the Muslim communities of the many *zongos* found along the Guinea Coast. This difference was forcefully brought home to me when, a month after the *salahga* at Sɔfo Peter's *fetatrɔtrɔ*, I was invited to a large *salah* for Eid-ul-Fitr, the festival of fast breaking celebrated on the first day of the tenth Islamic month, following Ramadan. Sponsored by the *zongo* community of Three-Town, around two hundred people came early on a Saturday morning to the beachside at Xedzranawo to pray. Seated in front on prayer mats facing east were the men, in fairly organized rows. They were all wearing their finest and most colorful dress, mostly in the northern *agbada* style (called "three piece," consisting of pants, shirt, and large smock) or *jalab* (long gowns that come to the knee), both worn with elaborately embroidered caps. This northern-style clothing is also the way most *sɔfowo* dress at important functions, including the caps, further aligning them with a northern African Islam, but in addition to the embroidered kind, the red fez, that famous marker of the other, was alive and well in Brekete (Kramer 1993).[10] Behind the men, separated by a space, were the women and children, also in their "Sunday best," to borrow from that other northern religion. They occupied a much more loosely defined area, with people coming and going, visiting and renewing acquaintances. In front of them all was the white-bearded chief imam, dressed in robes of green, holding a staff. Silhouetted against the rising sun spreading across the southern face of the Gulf of Guinea, it was a striking tableau. I was immediately struck by the almost exact opposite picture presented at the *fetatrɔtrɔ*, where the mats were filled with women and young girls in white, and a few men, including me, sitting on benches along the sides and back.

At the congregational *salah* for Eid-ul-Fitr the men led the prayers and were the main participants, with women occupying the periphery both figuratively and literally. Much has been made of the status of women in African Islam, especially regarding possession cults (Lewis 1986, 1999; Bourguignon 2004)—the gender war thesis of peripheral cults for marginal people. But as Boddy (1994: 410) and others (Donovan 2000) have pointed out, this deprivation theory often obscures more than it reveals. For Brekete its salience is limited at best, since possession is seen as positive, with those possessing, though foreign, upholding the moral order (see chap. 1, n. 32). What strategies of redress are being worked out here? Are women merely projecting deep-seated and unconscious cries for transitory agency that, while they are possessed, completely escapes them? Boddy's (1989) reworking of subaltern lines of discourse—possession as a woman's domain in contradistinction to men and the wider external world; a metacommentary on moral life realized in an ethical geography of town and countryside—actually isn't much help here either. Brekete is equally robust in both urban and rural settings. In addition, Islam in Brekete and Brekete in Islam present a unique configuration that differs from such possession cults as Bori in the Sahel or Zar in the Sudan, where Islam occupies the space of a main morality cult, to adopt Lewis's center-periphery terminology. Islam among the Ewes is far from central or, for that matter, at least according to local perception, particularly moral. The confluence of northern peoples and northern gods in southern lands not only presents a different profile, but also unfolds different dynamics. Among Ewes, Islam itself is peripheral, with Brekete and its emphasis on possession trance occupying the status of a main morality cult.

One of the most striking differences between the *salah* that morning at the beach and the one at the *fetatrɔtrɔ* was the lack of music in the former and its central and indispensable role in the latter. Music in Islam, a vast subject that I can only touch upon here, is a contested site both within and outside the faith. In Sufism, the correct kind of music can bring you closer to Allah, even into an ecstatic trance of communion, but not possession (Becker 2004: 78–79; Rouget 1985: 255–314). In more orthodox interpretations, music is too sensuous a medium to be used as a vehicle for bringing one closer, invariably leading into a state of aesthetic contemplation that in fact leads one away from God. Regardless, all agree that the recitation of the Qur'an is most definitely not music (Nelson 1985: 188–91), which is not to say that it is not intensely musical, a reality I experienced years later.

Shortly after completing our house in Adafienu (see chap. 6), I invited all of the *mallams* in Three-Town, including the head imam, to do a recitation of the complete Qur'an at our compound. For one who sponsors such an event, it is supposed to bring a blessing to the entire household. On the appointed day around eight o'clock in the morning the *mallams* started arriving. We had cleared the reception area of all the furniture and had put down mats on the floor. By nine o'clock most were there, and an hour later the some twenty people who had gathered began the recitation. For occasions such as this a special Qur'an which has each *surat* (chapter) separately bound is used. Everyone took one of the bound chapters, and all began reciting at the same time. As soon as one *surat* was finished, another one was picked up until all 114 chapters had been chanted, something that took about an hour to perform. As I sat there listening to this amazing amalgamation of voices, it was as if a veil of sound was being lowered and raised simultaneously. And although I understood nothing beyond the fact that it was Arabic, it seemed to my ears deeply musical. While music may be a contested site in Islam, there is no doubt about Qur'anic recitation. It is an approximation of the way the archangel Jamil (Gabriel) revealed the word of God to Muhammad, and no human music can approach that.

Later that night, after we restored couch and chairs to the reception area, I had a couple of beers to ease the heat of a rather hot night with more than a few mosquitoes. I went into the bedroom to put on some repellent and, accidentally, had the nozzle on the bottle turned the wrong way, which proceeded to spray 95 percent deet directly into my eyes, resulting in a chemical burn. After rushing me to the hospital to have my eyes flushed out with saline solution, the Islamic friend who had taken me there told me, as he was driving me home, that having the entire Qur'an recited at your house is a great blessing, attracting many angels. Drinking alcohol in their presence was not a good idea and the reason why I ended up at the hospital—a lesson well learned that, luckily, resulted in no permanent damage.

Music as Prayer

For those who partake in *salah* at a *fetatrɔtrɔ*, however, there is plenty of alcohol and music *is* the prayer. Even the *adhan* (the call to prayer) is heard as music, the opening verse to an extended song. In *zongo*, the local muezzin calls out to the faithful to turn toward Mecca and pray. But when Bisi Kwasi stood up with a white scarf covering his head, holding a set of *tsebu* (worry beads) and called in full melismatic style the *adehawo* to *salah*, it was a different matter altogether (see ex. 2.1).

Allah-u Akbar (4×)	Allah is the greatest
Ashhadu anla ilaha illallah (2×)	I bear witness that there is no deity but Allah
Ashhadu anna Muhammadar rasulullah (2×)	I bear witness that Muhammad is the Messenger of Allah
Hayya alas salah (2×)	Come to prayer
Hayya alal falah (2×)	Come to your Good
Allah-u Akbar (2×)	Allah is the greatest
La ilaha illallah	There is no deity but Allah

(Transliteration and translation quoted from *Salah: The Muslim Prayer*, one of the many small booklets sold on the streets in front of mosques)

Ex. 2.1. Call to prayer (*adhan*)

Although both the muezzin and Kwasi chant roughly the same words in a similar way, their actions have very different meanings. For Muslims the *adhan* is a call to serve Allah; for the *adehawo* it is a time to celebrate the *trɔwo*.[11]

The *adhan* was not always done in this way at the shrines. When I first started attending Friday *salahs* in the early 1990s, the call to prayer consisted of only the recitation of Allah-u Akbar, the *takbir*. It was Bisi Kwasi who, after learning this standard version in Accra at a local mosque, and from a small booklet that he had bought that gives instructions on the correct performance of prayers, introduced this orthodox version of the *adhan* to the Aflao Association of Lahare Kunde, which comprised thirty-four shrines, and where I did most of my fieldwork. These small *salah* manuals, virtually all printed in Lagos, Nigeria, are for sale along with Qur'ans, worry beads, and other Islamic religious paraphernalia near most of the mosques in Accra.

As the women settled in, with late arrivals trying to find space to sit on the already crowded mats, Kwasi followed the *adhan* with the *basmalah*, the invocation that precedes each chapter of the Qur'an, and then recited a truncated and somewhat altered version of the al-Fatihah, the opening *surat*, which most Islamic scholars cite as the "perfect prayer" and contains the essence of the entire Qur'an.

Basmalah:

Bismi la hir rahman ir rahim
In the name of Allah, the Beneficent, the Merciful

Al-Fatihah:

[Alhamdo lil lahi rab bil a'lamin
Ar rahman ir rahim]
Maliki yau mid din
Iyya ka na bu do wa iyya ka nas taeen
Ih di nas si ra tal mus ta qeema
Sira tal la zina amta alaihim
[Ghairil magh du bi allaihim, wa lad dall lin]

[Praise be to Allah, Lord of the worlds
The Beneficent, the Merciful]
Master of the Day of Judgment
Thee alone we worship and to Thee alone we turn for help.
Guide us in the straight path
the path of those whom You favoured
[and who did not deserve Thy anger, or went astray.]

(Cited from the *salah* booklet purchased by Kwasi Bisi)

He omitted the first two verses, as he always does, and started with "Maliki yau mid din" (Master of the Day of Judgment), also skipping the last verse but instead inserting a version of the profession of the faith at the end. Kwasi's understanding of what he was saying was also far from complete—he neither spoke nor read Arabic, using the transliteration provided in the booklet—but he understood far more than the rest of the *adehawo*, virtually none of whom "heard" Arabic. Probably, this is also the case for many Muslims who attend congregational prayers at the mosque on Fridays in Three-Town. The recitation of the *basmalah* and al-Fatihah was followed by three *rakats* (prostrations) performed by the entire congregation, something that he had taught to the rest of the members, having himself learned the proper way to do it from the instructional manual he purchased. All of this, too, was a relatively recent innovation, once again aligning Brekete with an Islamic soundscape and physicality devoid of any accompanying religious devotion or conversion. No *adehawo* performs ablutions and prays five times a day, or goes to mosque on Friday afternoons.

Fig. 2.5 Wives of Bangle and Wango at a *salah* (Steven Friedson)

After the recitation of the al-Fatihah, Kwasi said blessings in Hausa, a linguistic marker pointing to the northern origin of the *trɔwo*:

Allah badesaa	May God give us good luck
Allah tenyemu	May God help us to be strong
Allah bada hamkudi	May God forgive our sins
Allah dziken marayu	May God take care of orphans
Allah dziken merigayei ku	May God take care of death
Allah bamu kasuwa	May God give us good market
Allah bamu kudi	May God give us money

Each blessing was repeated twice, the women responding with "Amin" after each one, even though, once again, they had no idea, for the most part, of what was being said. These blessings, which are part of standard Islamic practice in West Africa (they are said not only in Hausa but in whatever local language is deemed appropriate), are reminiscent of exactly the kinds of things asked for in typical prayers to the *trɔwo*, except for the appeal to care for orphans and the request for forgiveness of sins. Given the extended family structure of Ewe social life, orphans are virtually nonexistent, and sins within the structure of the shrine usually are taken care of through sacrifice—the bigger the sin, the more expensive the sacrifice—and that doesn't involve forgiveness but bargaining with the gods (see chap. 3). To end this section of the *salah* a short prayer was said in Ewe. Sometimes, however, the blessings in Hausa and the prayer in Ewe are situated later in the service. Nothing is exactly prescribed in *salah*, including the order of events. There is a certain freedom at work here that allows for substitutions, additions, and deletions, depending on circumstances and, in no small measure, on how Kwasi decides to do the service that day.

With these preliminaries over, Kwasi "knocked" on Allah's door— "Salam Alekum"—and the members responded, "Alekum Salam." With this "knocking" the service proper began, moving away from Islamic practice and toward an Ewe religious sensibility with the introduction of the first call-and-response songs. As with the Ase songs performed the day before by the *bosomfowo* and *adehawo* (see p. 30), they were sung in free rhythm.

Kwasi raised the opening song of the *salah*, singing the Ewe version of the *takbir* (see ex. 2.2). "Kubaru" here is a transformation for purely melodic purposes of "Akbar." As they do in all these songs, the congregation responded in kind with the same verse and melody, but at the end of the response they broke out into vocal harmony. This African equivalent to the "blood harmony" of the American South is not learned—no one rehearses it—but considered to be born in the blood. It is a spontaneous, sensuous, and seductive practice, producing the kinds of organic harmonies that draw one into the core of a rich musical texture.

With the next two songs, *salah* seemed to be slipping further and further away from traditional Islamic practice into a full-blown musicality, while still utilizing key verses from the Qur'an. The first of these songs, sung in Hausa, calls for the gods to come and for people to pray (see ex. 2.3). Kunde and Tseriya, however, are conspicuously absent, because *salah*, whether done on Friday or Monday, is performed on their days of rest. Most of the women, once again, did not know the meaning of the words they were singing, including *illallah*, taken from the profession of the faith, the *shahada*. In this song it was just a filler that Kwasi threw in to fill out a musical line.

But in the second song this line from the *shahada* is the main focus, along with naming the gods. It is a phrase that has been developed into a textual leitmotif that can be found throughout the service in several different musical settings. It is obviously not the meaning of the line that is im-

Ex. 2.2. Allah Kubaru

portant for those who sing it, though most know that it is from the Qur'an, but the way the words roll off the tongue, their musical potential making them suitable for such variation (see ex. 2.4). The *adehawo* see and hear no contradiction in this mix of calling northern gods with the *shahada*; it is just not a matter of concern even for those who understand Arabic. For devout Muslims, however, not only is singing anathema to prayer, but calling out to the *gorovoduwo*, "idols" in Islamic eyes, while singing part of the profession of the faith, would be a blasphemy.

Highlighting the polyglot nature of lyrical practice in Brekete, the next series of songs was sung in a mixture of the Ga and Twi languages, again with few people knowing the meaning of the words they were singing. These songs generally are assumed to have come directly from Tɔsavi's shrine in Accra, where *salah* started and where Ga is indigenous to the area and Twi, along with English, a main lingua franca. The phenomenon of singing in languages not understandable to the performers can be found not only throughout Africa but worldwide and speaks directly against the overwrought linguistic analysis performed on the lyrical content of songs

Gediya zomuyisalah (Hausa)   Gediya, come let us pray

Ex. 2.3. Zomuyisalah (come let us pray)

Ex. 2.4. Illallah (1)

by most ethnographers, who invariably attribute direct agency to textual exegesis (Friedson 1996: 130–31).[12]

All of these free-rhythm songs were low key in both senses of the term. They had a relatively low pitch range, and the singing was somewhat subdued. It was the next song, with the introduction of the *atoké* bells and body concussion (the hitting together of two hands, which we summarily dismiss by labeling as handclaps), that things started to take off. Once again its lyrical content is based on the verse from the *shahada* and the invocation of northern gods. As Kwasi started the song, the two bell players sounded *abey*, the most popular style of Brekete music, with one bell playing a truncated version of the timeline and the other a steady four-beat cycle (see chap. 5). The tune is melodically concise and has a strong hook that is repeated and marked with three quick handclaps coinciding with the last three syllables of the line taken from the *shahada* (ex. 2.5). It is a joyous song that captures the musical imagination of the women, who during performance begin to shout "Salah! Salah!" along with ululations heightening the musical excitement, this last acoustic intensifier being a vocal sign of a northern soundscape.[13]

Ex. 2.5. Illallah (2)

Ex. 2.5 (*continued*).

This song seemed to be a kind of hinge, for it was at this point of the *salah* that *trɔsiwo* in the crowd started to become possessed. As I looked out over the mass of white figures seated on the mats, a woman here and there would suddenly spring up possessed, emitting the high-pitched "he, he, he" that Rouget cites as a near universal sound of possession (1985: 111). The *trɔsiwo* that were seized started spinning, but seeing that they were in a crowd of seated women, this caused quite a bit of confusion, with people scrambling to get out of the way. As the song continued, more and more women became entranced, the possessions taking off like a string of Chinese firecrackers. Once the initial possessions settled down, some of the *trɔsiwo*, while bending over in the classic frozen position of the possessed, began rubbing their hands together, signaling that they wanted the *senterwawo* (sentries, or handlers of the possessed) to bring them a *buta* (the Hausa word for the striped plastic kettle used by Muslims for ablutions, and in Brekete shrines as a container for the *amatsi*, the herb water of the gods). As the *senterwawo* poured water over their hands, the gods performed an abbreviated kind of ablution to purify the bodies of those whom they had entered. The *senterwawo* then escorted them inside the shrine by using the *buta* to lay a trail of water, which the *trɔsiwo* followed. Once inside, each *trɔsiwo* was dressed and adorned. They shortly emerged from the shrine, joining the other *trɔsiwo* who had been possessed since early morning and, during *salah*, mostly had stayed inside the shrine. All came out dancing, their elaborate and colorful dress highlighted against the sea of *salah* white.

When this song was finished, announcements were made and a short "sermon" was given exhorting the members to follow the rules of Kunde, not to fight among themselves, to trust in the gods, and so on. The mats were then removed from the dance area, and *salah* moved toward a full-blown Ewe musicality with the introduction of the *brekete* drums and the circle dance. Given the predominance of women, it was Ablewa's music (Ablewaza) that dominated as they formed a tight dance circle and jubilation set in.[14] Her timeline is different from Bangle's bell (see chap. 4) and the one used for *abey*, the fastest and most common music in most of Brekete celebrations. Although any Brekete song may be introduced at this time, there are a number of songs specific to *salah* that use this bell pattern. One of the most popular, not surprisingly, employs the line from the profession of the faith, but the response this time added the Hausa word *gobe* (tomorrow) (see ex. 2.6). This makes no textual sense when combined with the *shahada*; it is inserted here purely for the purpose of the dance. On this word the dancers turned toward each other and bumped

Ex. 2.6. Allah gobe

hips on the final syllable *be*, a most un-Islamic thing to do, to say the least, especially in a song that cites the *shahada*. These were women not worshipping Allah but celebrating their femininity in a most overt manner. It is precisely in these kinds of juxtapositions that *salah* is defined. There is no attempt here to reconcile Islam and traditional Ewe practices, to create a syncretism of two religious streams. They are merely juxtaposed, bringing together into close proximity separate religious tracts. If anything is reconciled, it is done within a musical context that is danced.

The singing and dancing continued for some time, with each song seeming to increase the level of excitement. Toward the end of the *salah* a special song was sung in Hausa for the collection of *sadaqa* (alms). In this song, sung to Bangle's bell, there was a correlation between word and action (see ex. 2.7). While the *adehawo* continued to dance and sing, a woman carried around a large calabash bowl for contributions. Every member was expected to donate some modest amount of money. At a *fetatrɔtrɔ* this money goes to the priest to help offset some of the considerable costs incurred when ceremonies entail a cow sacrifice. At the large monthly *salahgas* the money goes to a mutual fund for the purchase of such things as benches and, more recently, a sound system, something that has become de rigueur for all big celebrations.

Kasuwa, kasuwa	Market, market
Allah gobe kasuwa	Allah [help us] tomorrow with the market
Kasuwa, baba kasuwa	Market, father of the market
Allah gobe kasuwa	Allah [help us] tomorrow with the market

Ex. 2.7. Kasuwa (the market)

Bisi Kwasi, by the way, had sung all the above through a decidedly low-fidelity microphone fed through two metal horn speakers. The lower frequencies were totally lost, and the overall timbre was harsh and distorted, but no one seemed to mind. The overall consideration was that it was loud, whether distorted or not. This is not to say that distortion is a preferred aesthetic, as some researchers have suggested, citing that nearly universal feature of sub-Saharan music, a buzzed or burred timbre. There is no doubt in my mind that, given the choice and with enough financial resources, Ewes would consistently opt for a clearer and distortion-free sound, as long as it was loud. In fact, this is starting to happen at funerals,

Kunde yenkɔ	Kunde is going
Ablewa yenkɔ	Ablewa is going
Obiara numuse	Everybody should clap

Ex. 2.8. Kundea yenkɔ

as good-quality secondhand sound systems bought by entrepreneurs and rented out for such occasions become affordable. Not only has this resulted in a marked improvement in the quality of the sound, but also it has enabled a sizable increase in decibel levels. Unfortunately, improvement in sound quality has not yet reached *salah*. To reiterate, however, quantity ultimately trumps quality in these matters. What retains utmost importance, however, is the celebratory joy of making music together.

After *sadaqa*, the closing song of the *salah* was raised, as was the intensity of the drumming, singing, and dancing. It was as if the entire *salah* had been building to this climax. Exclamations of "Salah! Salah!" and ululations filled the air, and even some of the men yelled out "Fatihah! Fatihah!" as the women lifted their hands above their heads and pointed their forefingers toward the heavens, singing in the Ewe version of Twi (see ex. 2.8). Although in the other songs Kunde and Ablewa are not supposed to be mentioned, we find them in this closing song. People had no explanation for their presence, other than the classic "That's just the way we do it." For this song, unlike the previous ones in Twi, most people knew enough of the language to understand what it had to say, and it did what it said. As the women sang, the circle broke and, in sheer jubilation, they danced single file into the shrine.

With this danced exit, *salah* was over, and, after a short break, the serious war music of *agbadza* began, followed by the fast-paced *abey* until night set in and the *fetatrotrɔ* was over. Well, not exactly over. There was still one more piece of business to attend to. If you kill a cow and "break" its head, you have "washed all of your blood" and opened the door wide. All manner of gods and spirits, *voduwo* and ghosts, can come in, not just those who were invited. What brings them in is their desire for food and their unquenchable thirst. Blood attracts, and therefore blood must close the door, something that would happen the next Sunday, seven days after the cow was killed.

The Poured Gift   3

Of all the animals sacrificed to the gods, cows are by far the most significant and expensive. It is the only time when the gods are taken from their *kpomewo*, gathered into a large basin, and brought outside to be fed; it is the only time when they touch each other, not an insignificant occurrence; and, perhaps most of all, it is a time of great celebration and feasting. When the gods are well fed, they are happy, and when the gods are happy, the shrine and its members prosper.

A cow may be offered to the gods for many different reasons, not just at the triennial *fetatrɔtrɔ*. It may be offered as thanks (*akpedada*) for the prosperity someone has enjoyed and attributed to the helping hand of the gods. A cow may be sacrificed as a piacular fine for a serious offense such as committing adultery with another member's wife, practicing *juju* or accusing someone of doing the same, stealing, lying, or any of numerous other ethical breaches that violate the ten commandments of the shrine. It may be offered in order to clear one's path (*nuxexe*), the blocking of which was revealed in an Afa divination. Or it may be a matter of redeeming a pledge (*ataŋufe*), for example, if your children were dying or your wife was having trouble conceiving, and, after pledging a cow to the gods, you now have a healthy baby. This is not meant to imply that cows are falling left and right, being slaughtered in great numbers for the gods. Though animal sacrifices are common, a cow sacrifice actually is a fairly rare occurrence. It involves much more than merely supplying a cow, and, due to the heavy costs involved, most Ewes will try to put off such a sacrifice for as long as possible.[1] Even a *fetatrotro* does not always occur on its prescribed three-year cycle, for a *sofo* may have difficulty gathering the necessary financial resources to sponsor such an event.

My first cow sacrifice turned out to be none of the above, and, actually, didn't even involve a cow. A limited research budget excluded such a costly affair, so I did the Ewe thing: when the gods asked for a cow I pleaded for a reduction. Northern gods are sympathetic to the financial plights of their supplicants and usually are willing to listen to reason. Through cowrie divination, it was finally decided that I would be allowed to substitute a turkey instead, the logic being that it was the biggest fowl and hence equivalent to a cow. I agreed, and the date for the sacrifice was set. No one, however, was mistaking turkeys for cows, including the gods. It was simply a matter of postponement, a momentary reprieve for a debt to be paid. That debt was something I would not repay until years later, right before Anibra's death. Little did I know at the time that it would be one of the last sacrifices he would ever see.

It was during prayers at Sofo Kwamiga's that I first heard about the cow. I had just returned from Tosavi's shrine in Accra, where only a few days earlier the old man had placed my hands on the gods, a totally unexpected development. Not only had I never touched the gods before, but the noninitiated are not even supposed to receive the blessings of the gods straight from the *sofo*'s hand. It is customary for the priest to touch the *gorovodu* after someone prays and then shake the person's hand. But for a nonmember, instead of shaking hands, he raises his hand, palm up, and blows across it. And this was how I always had received the gods' blessings, that is, until I prayed at Tosavi's.

When I first met him he proudly claimed to be one hundred years old, and, although there was no doubt about his advanced age, I couldn't help being somewhat skeptical about his centenary status. I had seen more than one grave marker in Ghana claiming that the person buried had lived to be

125. It was common practice for the elderly and, after they died, for their relatives to exaggerate their age. Extreme old age signified a righteous life. My skepticism was soon overcome, however, when he showed me an official document with photograph dated 1934 identifying him as a certified healer by the Society of African Medical Herbalists. He told me he was in his late thirties when he got his license, and the picture seemed to confirm it. That would have made him at least ninety-five when I first met him in 1993.

Born and raised in Benin, a place known for its strong shrines, powerful medicines, and knowledgeable healers, he migrated to Accra looking for a better life. But these were troubled times in Ghana. The negative effects of colonization were intensifying, things were rough, and all kinds of people were looking for all kinds of ways to change their fortunes in life. His business was not going well, and his wife was having difficulty conceiving. When she did become pregnant, she couldn't bring the pregnancy to term, or the babies died shortly after birth. His medicines had not helped, and he began looking for more powerful remedies. He had heard rumors about northern gods that recently had been brought down to the south who might be able to help, and he went searching for them. He ended up finding Kodzokuma, the man who brought Kunde from the north. Judging him worthy of the gods, he helped Tɔsavi establish the first Brekete shrine in Accra. The *gorovodu* fetishes Kodzokuma had given him seventy years ago were still there and were considered particularly strong and powerful due to their connection to the original source of Kunde's power. It was Kodzokuma's son, the then current head priest, Kwasi Anibra, who first took me to see Tɔsavi.

It was a typical Saturday afternoon at Anibra's house in Accra. We were all sitting on the porch as a steady stream of Brekete members, priests, and assorted other people came to greet him, ask, complain, advise, and do a hundred other things that required the attention of the spiritual head of all of Lahare Kunde, the official name of the shrine. I was there because he had asked me to come to Accra to get away from what he considered to be the hardships of living in a village with no running water or electricity. He insisted on putting me up and paying for a fairly nice hotel near his house and assigned one of his cars and drivers for my convenience. It was a total reversal of the usual asymmetrical economic relationship between researcher and researched.

I had met Anibra the week before, when he had unexpectedly shown up at Kwamiga's shrine, which was located in a small village on the road north to Ho, the capital of the Volta Region. I was practicing *brekete* drumming in the courtyard in front of the shrine when an entourage of vehicles pulled up and a heavyset man, with the bearing of a chief, dressed in golden cloth dotted with sparkling moons and stars, stepped out of a truck marked Ministry of Agriculture. I was beginning to learn, and would continue to learn while in Ghana, that juxtapositions such as this, especially when it came to Anibra, would become a common occurrence for me. It turned out that he not only was the head of all the Kunde shrines, but also worked in the Ministry of Food and Agriculture as a financial consultant. Not knowing who he was at the time, I was curious, and somewhat confused, about why Kwamiga was making such a fuss over what I assumed to be a government official, yelling for people to get drink and gunpowder, both of which he liberally poured on the ground as Anibra walked in. The pope paying an unexpected visit was not an everyday occurrence. He had been in Lome, the capital of Togo, on shrine business and had decided to stop by to see Kwamiga, who was a senior committee chairman of the Lahare Kunde Association, to see how things were going.

Anibra went immediately inside the shrine followed by Kwamiga and other *bosomfowo* who happened to be around. When he reappeared about a half hour later, he called for me to come over. He asked who I was and what I was doing playing the drums. When he found out I was a professor doing research on Brekete, I was no longer a stranger but from then on merely "Prof." We briefly talked about university life—he had a bachelor's degree in accounting—and he invited me to come to Accra and relax, to take a break from the privations of village life. It is hard to turn down such requests, and, as was typical with Anibra, I really didn't have a choice. The next thing I knew I was in his car headed back to the capital.

It was a week later, during one of the rare pauses in the nonstop comings and goings of "porch" people, that he turned to me and said that if I truly wanted to learn about the history of Kunde, then I needed to meet this old *sofo*, a man who had walked with his father. So, as was Anibra's way, off we went in one of his many cars to meet Tɔsavi. It turned out to be not that far away, located near the Kaneshie Market, a bustling district in the western part of Accra.

When we arrived at the shrine, there wasn't nearly the excitement Anibra's visit had caused at Kwamiga's place. I assumed that he was a much more frequent visitor here. We were escorted into a reception hall, and, after drinks were poured and formal greetings exchanged, Anibra asked if the old man was around. A few moments later Tɔsavi appeared through a side door. Although obviously quite old, he had a spirit about him that belied his age. Anibra introduced us, told him that I was there to learn about the gods, and that he should feel free to tell me all. Shortly thereafter, Anibra left, and Tɔsavi and I spent the rest of the afternoon talking about the early days of the shrine, when he had "walked with Kodzokuma."

It was some time after this initial encounter that I found myself back in Accra and decided to pay Tɔsavi a visit. It was a Friday and I knew they would be doing *salah*, since his was the shrine that introduced such prayers as a formal rite (see p. 47). I wasn't disappointed and was pleased to see that Tɔsavi was still going strong, singing and dancing, though, given his age, it was now only occasionally. I had come not only to see the old man but also to say prayers and, therefore, had brought the customary offerings—kola nut, a special form of kaolin (white clay) called *alilɔ*, a bottle of foreign schnapps, and some money (all offerings involved money).[2] I asked Tɔsavi to officiate after the main part of *salah* had ended, which was taking place in the courtyard in front of the shrine.

As *salah* started to wind down, Tɔsavi motioned for me to follow him inside the shrine. I took off my watch and shoes, which is required be-

Fig. 3.1 Sɔfo Tɔsavi in "hunter's" tunic with talismans (Steven Friedson)

fore entering, and dipped my hand in the *amatsi* (herb water) that always sits in a basin before the entrance. Not exactly a holy water, it is more like a medicine meant to purify. If you recently have seen a dead body, or are a woman whose period has just finished, there are other herb waters you must be sprinkled with before you can enter the shrine. Once inside, Tɔsavi took his seat on the stool in front of Kunde's *kpome*, his house, and I knelt down holding a bowl that contained the kola (which also had been washed in *amatsi*), the *alilɔ*, and the bottle of schnapps. I put some money on top and started praying. It was still fairly early on in my research, but I had heard enough prayers to piece together a kind of stylized version, an approximation of what a prayer should be. One always begins by "knocking" three times at Kunde's door:

Agoo Kunde! Agoo Kunde!	
Agoo Kunde!	
Medogbeda srɔ̃nye kple vinye ta	I pray on the head of my wife and child
Mia nɔ sesiẽ	We should be strong
Na dzɔmianu za kple kele	You should guide us night and day
Mia ƒe dɔwɔƒe ne zɔ ɖe ŋgɔ	Our workplace should move forward
Nyi yomenɔla ka meɖe ne o	One who follows the bull never trips
Ma zɔ mɔ dedie	I should travel successfully
Ʋuƒoku nati ɖe akpa	Car accident, cast it away
Amɛadeke negatso mɔ na mi o	Someone should not cross our path
Ɖagbe neva na mi, ƒesi ƒesi.	Good fortune should come to us every year, every year.
Sempa	Finished

As you pray, the *sofo* punctuates your speech with another kind of "knocking." Using a knife, sometimes a stone, he strikes a hard surface, usually a piece of metal or a rock, which is sitting in front of the god. This "knocking" either is done in a steady pulsing rhythm or is struck when particularly important points are being made. Through this acoustical marking, the prayers are raised to an even higher level of discourse, requiring and demanding attention, sending them forcefully to the gods.

When I was finished praying, Tɔsavi took the offerings and put some of the kola and clay on Kunde, threw some into his *kpome*, and placed the money in front of the *gorovodu*. Although my prayer was directed to Kunde, one cannot, however, pray directly to him. Just as you cannot talk directly to chiefs, you cannot talk directly to the gods but must go through an intermediary, here the *sofo*, who, acting as a kind of *tsiami* (linguist), repeats what you have said. I was always struck by the matter-of-fact way *sofowo* addressed the gods, speaking directly to the *gorovoduwo*, the things sitting in front of them, not some ethereal entity before or behind. The *sofo* is not really praying so much as exhorting the gods to do their work.

When Tɔsavi finished, one of the *bosomfowo* who was assisting in the prayers (you always need an assistant) opened the bottle of schnapps and poured some into a tot glass that Tɔsavi was holding. As Tɔsavi poured the spirits on the spirit he said: "Wo aha enye esia, xɔ" (This is your drink, take it). After Kunde had been given his drink, Tɔsavi put his left hand on the fetish and blew blessings my way. Cowries, which have an open and closed side, were thrown to see if Kunde had accepted my prayers. Usually eight or sixteen are used, and if an even number land facing up or down, then the answer is yes; if an odd number, then no. Through the cowries it was revealed that Kunde had agreed: the prayers were accepted.

Tɔsavi then got up and moved to the stool in front of Ablewa, Kunde's wife, as I shifted over to my right to offer her my prayers. In her role as a nurturing mother, she may intercede on your behalf with Kunde, who is quick to judge wrongdoers, those who break the commandments. She tries to cool him down, pleading for understanding and forgiveness.[3] But if you cross her, Ablewa's punishment can be swift and severe. At least one *sofo* confided in me that she was a problem deity, difficult to take care of, and that the Dagarti and Ashanti were glad to get rid of her.[4] Tseriya, as she also is called, looks almost identical to her husband. Both are dark brown egg-shaped ovals each about a foot in length. What distinguishes them from each other is a knife blade protruding from Kunde's lower right side, and a hole on Tseriya's lower left side (see figs. 3.2–3.3). What might seem obvious to us—that this may relate to respective genital regions—when suggested to *sofowo* was totally dismissed. This, of course, doesn't necessarily negate this kind of understanding. These kinds of symbolic references may indeed be operating at an unconscious level.

Following standard practice, unless there is a compelling reason to do so, I did not repeat my prayers in full to Ablewa. After knocking on her door, but this time calling four times instead of three, I used the formulaic line "You already heard all and know what to do." This abbreviated prayer, however, did not relieve Tɔsavi of the responsibility of conveying to Tseriya all that previously had been said to Kunde. Having done this, he then gave kola, kaolin, and drink and blew her blessings my way, but this time with his right hand. Once again the cowries revealed that my prayers had been accepted.

We then moved on to the *kpome* of Sanya Kompo, god of the stone,

Tseriya's firstborn. Unlike the mother and father, she has the classic squared shape of a northern talisman, complete with attached cord so that it can be worn, and is covered with the reddish leather used by northerners when making these *tsilas* (fig. 3.4). (Northern talismans often have Qur'anic verses written on paper inside them.) Sanya is the messenger and secretary. He records all that you have done in your life, both good and bad. When Kunde and Ablewa are resting, it is Sanya Kompo who will carry an important message to them. Fitting the status of the messenger and scribe, and by implication translator, Sanya is a mercurial figure. Some *sofowo* say she is a woman, others a man, and still others both man and woman. As with Tseriya, I did not repeat my prayers but left that to Tɔsavi. After giving Sanya the offerings and me her blessings, Tɔsavi threw the cowries, and s / he also accepted.

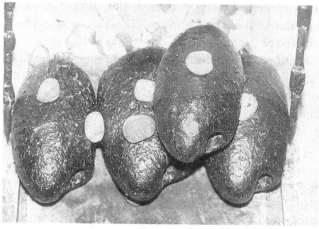

Next came Bangle, the second born, who is considered the most powerful god, even stronger than his father. For the son to surpass the father is
a deeply held ethos in Ewe life. Ketetsi, his Twi name, meaning "strong
man," is the warrior, soldier, protector, and avenger. His domain is *dzogbe*
(the desert), where the spirits of those who "died in the blood" (*vumeku*)
congregate along with other hot *voduwo*. Although he has the same oval
shape as his parents, he has a number of distinguishing features (see fig.
1.2). Coming out of one end of the oval is a metal bell, and, on the same
end, underneath the bell, is Bangle's beard, a black cow tail, marking him
as a wise and powerful man from the north. This relationship between
beards, foreigners, and the north can be heard in the rhyme any southern
child will yell when seeing a white man (*yevu*):

Fig. 3.2 (*opposite top*) Kunde
gorovodu fetish (Steven Friedson)

Fig. 3.3 (*opposite bottom*)Ablewa
gorovodu fetish (Steven Friedson)

Fig. 3.4 (*left*) Sanya Kompo
gorovodu fetish (Steven Friedson)

Fig. 3.5 (*bottom*) Wango *gorovodu*
fetish (Steven Friedson)

Yevu, Yevu, geyibɔ,	White man, White man, black beard,
Tamale	Tamale

This innocent taunt probably goes back centuries, referencing Europeans who came to this part of Ghana in pursuit of the slave trade. The calling of Tamale, the capital of the Northern Region, a more recent addition, also positions black beards with Islamic foreigners from the north. Inside Bangle, not visible to the naked eye, is embedded a knife, a further indication of his status as a soldier and warrior.[5]

When you pray to Bangle, unlike Ablewa and Sanya, it is like praying to Kunde; you have to say the prayer in full measure before the sɔfo repeats it. You are, however, not just praying to Bangle, but addressing a whole host of other gods that are clustered around him. Underneath Bangle, who sits on the circular cement stool of Sakra Bode, god of the land, is a retinue of lesser though still powerful gods, his troops, as it were, who help him in his work. The most prominent of them are Tsengé, god of the seven knives; Surugu, another soldier; and Gediya, the policeman, who is one of the most difficult gods to handle (see fig. 1.2). It is likely that these lesser gods associated with Bangle started out as powerful talismans that, through their effectiveness, eventually rose to the rank of gorovoduwo. Not all shrines have all these gods.

Once again kneeling down and holding the bowl of kola, kaolin, and schnapps, I knocked on Bangle's door and repeated my stylized prayer. Tɔsavi, who was now sitting on the stool in front of Bangle, heard my words and, after distributing kola and alilɔ to Bangle and the other gods under him, began to pray. As he said the prayer, he knocked on Bangle's door by using a knife to hit the bell that is part of Bangle's body. Once again, there is no set rhythm, rather phrases and words are punctuated and marked through this procedure. After pouring libations, he placed both his hands on Bangle, as is customary, and I waited for him to send me Ketetsi's blessings. But instead of blowing across his hands, to my complete surprise, he took my hands in his, right to right and left to left, causing them to cross, then left to left and right to right, thus crossing them again, and, finally, reversing the procedure one more time, finished by turning my hands palms up and then palms down. This was the traditional handshake of Bangle, the way members receive his blessing. He was not through, however, and, to my astonishment, he took my hands and proceeded to press them firmly on Bangle. The power of touching Bangle sent shock waves of energy through my body, giving me somewhat of a start. He then lifted both my hands and pulled me off the floor onto my feet, releasing my hands. As a *sofo* once told me, "Tɔsavi had blessed hands. When he gave you something you really got it."

After I sat back down somewhat in a daze, Tɔsavi asked Bangle through the cowries if he had accepted the prayers. But the cowries came up with an uneven number facing up and down—Bangle had refused. When this happens, the priest always asks first if it is a good fortune (*ɖagbe*), and Bangle said no. Was it something he did that offended? Tɔsavi asked, and Bangle once again said no. The usual suspects were then recited: Was it someone in the house, a member of the shrine, a person from another shrine, a *trɔsi*? Bangle said no to all until it came to me. When Tɔsavi asked if it was something I had done, Bangle said yes. Following a considerable list of things I might have done wrong, each one rejected by Bangle, Tɔsavi finally turned to me and asked if I chopped (ate) pork, one of the major taboos for shrine members. I said yes—after all, I wasn't a member, and I did particularly enjoy ham sandwiches and barbeque ribs—and he said "Aha! Stick out your tongue," which I did before realizing that he had picked up a knife used for sacrifices that was lying in front of Sakra Bode, the god of the land. A bit apprehensive, I was not really sure of what was going to happen next, when he proceeded to take the knife blade and four times scraped the slough off of my tongue and put it on the fetish, telling me: "You can never chop pork again." What my heritage couldn't get me to do, this West African god had imposed.

Still reeling from the fact that not only had I touched Bangle, but part of me was now, in a way, part of him, I have no recollection of what happened next. No doubt we prayed to Wango, god of the waters and roads (the only anthropomorphic fetish [fig. 3.5]), and poured the final libations for the ancestors, but I have no memory of these events, though I am sure they happened, for happen they must.

Turkeys for Cows

When I prayed at Kwamiga's a few days later and the gods asked for a cow, I was still very much in the mood of what had transpired at Tɔsavi's. As far as I knew, he was unaware of what had happened in Accra. I had only mentioned that I saw Tɔsavi and that he seemed fine. Kwamiga would always ask about Tɔsavi, for he was the *sofo* who installed the gods at his place. After praying to Kunde, as Kwamiga was getting ready to offer me blessings, I was caught off guard when he announced that he didn't care whether I was a member or not, that I had been to Kpando, knew more about the gods, and had seen more than most priests, and that he was going to shake my hand directly. All the gods use the right hand except for Kunde, the father, who does everything with his left, an unusual practice to say the least for a northern god with such a perceived close association with Islam.[6] But shake my left hand he did, after which he threw Kunde's cowries to see if my prayers were accepted. All eight landed face up, indicating a strong yes.

We then moved on to Ablewa, and, after repeating my prayers, not only did he shake my hand, but he gave me one of Tseriya's kolas and a piece of kaolin. When her cowries were thrown, however, she said no (*Ebe awo*). She had refused my prayers, and that is when I first heard about the cow. Now that I had touched them and had received their blessings directly from the *sofo*'s hand, it made sense to me that the gods would want more from me than the standard kola, clay, and drink. But when Kwamiga turned to me and asked if I accepted, and I explained that a cow was beyond my financial resources, he said, "Let's try a turkey instead." Of all the things I thought I would hear, a turkey was not one of them. In my many years of coming to Ghana and, before that, Malawi, I had never seen one, and had never exactly associated them with Africa. When I asked why a turkey, Kwamiga explained: "A turkey walks around all puffed out saying '*kpe, kpe, kpe,* I am bigger than a cow.'" He quickly added that if I couldn't afford a turkey then we could always beg Ablewa to accept a turkey egg instead. Metaphoric and metonymic relationships were definitely at work here. This substitutional calculus rested on the analogy that turkeys are the largest domestic fowl and cows are the largest domestic four-legged animal, and a synecdochical relationship: a turkey egg can, in certain circumstances, stand for a turkey. West African gods are decidedly this-worldly; you can bargain with them, cajole them, touch and be touched by them. Not wanting to push my luck too far, however, I settled on the turkey, and Kwamiga threw the cowries. Ablewa accepted my prayers; thus a sacrificial axis was put into play.

Before I left, it was mutually decided that the sacrifice would take place in two weeks, and that Kwamiga would take care of making the necessary arrangements, procuring all the animals I would need for the sacrifice. It was up to me to supply the drink: the aforementioned Henke Schnapps imported from Holland—foreign gods take foreign drink—and *akpeteshie* (local gin) for those who were there to help with the sacrifice.[7] Of course, I would be paying for all of it. Serving the gods, whether one is a member or not, can be an expensive affair—their service does not come for free.

Two weeks later, on a hotter-than-usual Saturday night, I arrived at Kwamiga's ready for my first turkey / cow sacrifice. Inside the shrine, as usual, and typical of most Ewe rooms, there was virtually no cross-ventilation. It was almost as if moving air were purposely avoided—who knows what the wind might blow in. Kerosene lamps lit the room, making it even hotter, and an abundant supply of mosquitoes seemed to have a particular affinity for me. Gods were not the only ones being fed that night. After formal greetings and the obligatory exchange of small talk, Kwamiga got down to business. "Bring in the cow," he said to no one in particular, and from somewhere outside a fairly large turkey was produced. I thought I was ready for all of this, but seeing a turkey in the confines of a *gorovodu* shrine, accompanied by my unavoidable cultural baggage of Thanksgiving and losers, was more than a bit strange; it verged on the comical.

A preliminary round of prayers ensued, after which I was instructed to take hold of the turkey's head and touch its beak to each fetish. If seeing a turkey in the shrine was somewhat strange, grabbing its head was downright bizarre. A turkey's head has no feathers, so when you grab it you are making direct contact with flesh. It felt like the wrinkled skin of a very old person. But whereas an old person's skin often feels cold due to reduced circulation, the turkey's head was hot, like a forehead burning with a high fever. I could feel the blood pulsing through its veins. The turkey definitely sensed something was up.

Once all the gods had been touched with the turkey's beak—three times for Kunde, as was customary, and four times for each of the other gods—one of the *bosomfowo*, dressed in his *adewu* (special hunter's shirt with attached talismans), took the turkey and cut feathers from the head (actually, seeing that it was a turkey, the back of the neck) and tail, putting them on each fetish. He then pulled back its head and summarily cut its throat, bleeding the animal directly onto the gods.

Seeing an animal sacrificed always reminded me of how far removed we are from the reality of eating meat. We buy our turkey either cut and sliced for sandwiches or dressed for Thanksgiving dinner. Americans consume a great amount of animal protein but are, for the most part, totally insulated from the killing ground required. If they are exposed to such killing at all, it often is at least one step removed from reality, usually presented in some kind of television documentary about the deplorable conditions in some holding pen. The overdetermined identification and empathy toward animals in the West is symptomatic of a disconnect between life and death. There was no disconnect that night, however, as the turkey, in full view of all of us, slowly bled to death.

None of this struck me as particularly violent.[8] It was all very matter of fact. The gods need to eat, and this was one way to feed them. They require a tremendous amount of energy to carry out their work—just watch them dance for confirmation of this fact—and thus they need constant feeding to maintain their presence in the world. Northern gods are continually hungry, forever thirsty. They make demands on their adherents because they are ultimately dependent on the actions of humans for their very survival (Barber 1981).[9] What is given freely will be returned a thousand times—the bargain they make with their devotees for a better future.

This was not the end of the sacrifice, however, for when Ablewa eats, everyone must eat. A dog was brought in for Kunde (dogs are considered a delicacy in the north; their meat is more expensive than cow, ram, or goat) and a cat for Bangle.[10] In addition to these animals, a goat must be given to Bangle and Wango. Turkeys and goats were, for me, in the realm of animals raised specifically for their meat; dogs and cats, however, were another matter. The former I could get used to seeing sacrificed, but I could never get around my cultural presuppositions about pets. Calling them a dog and a cat, however, is somewhat of a misnomer. Actually, they were a puppy and a kitten, which were cheaper and much easier to handle than full-grown animals, which, nonetheless, exponentially added to my discomfort.[11] If I was going to work with Kunde, however, there was no alternative.

When a dog is offered, as with everything else having to do with the senior god, it is done differently from the way other animals are sacrificed. As they do with the turkey, before killing the dog they first cut hair (instead of feathers) from its head and tail and put it on the fetish. But instead of slitting the throat, they cut the back of the neck, severing the spinal cord. After being bled on Kunde, the nose and upper lip, tongue, tail, left front leg, and still beating heart are cut out and put on the *gorovodu*. What remains of the dog is placed on a ram skin and slid on the floor, making sure the body never leaves the ground, then taken outside and buried. Kunde's food, including his kola, is never eaten.[12] However, the parts of the dog that are placed on Kunde are dried and ground up with herbs and gunpowder to make his medicine, a powerful curative for all kinds of problems.

The cat offering to Bangle was also unusual and, for me, even harder to witness than the dog. The cat's head was cut off straight away and placed on top of Ketetsi, its eyes wide open and mouth still moving. The lungs were then cut out in one piece and placed in the cat's mouth. This is considered to be a highly spiritual and powerful act. It was explained to me that this was done to counteract *juju*: that the *juju* should come back on whoever would try to do something to the one offering the sacrifice. The cat, one of the hottest of animals, ends up eating itself.

It is at moments such as these that an ethnographer has to come to terms with some deeply held sentiments that are diametrically opposed to those with whom he works, a cultural ethos that confronts an uncomfortable reality. Is it cruel to kill a kitten, inhumane to sacrifice a puppy? Where I come from, there are laws against doing such things.[13] Yet, for most Ewes, dogs and cats, puppies and kittens are like chickens and turkeys, goats and cows, all to be used for human needs.[14] Different animals may serve different purposes—dogs for hunting, turkeys for eating—but they are all animals. Africans—and I am purposely using this term here in its essentializing form—hold that there is a great divide between human and animal. This is more than a widely held belief; it is part of an African ontology that is anthropocentric through and through.[15]

The last animal to be offered was the goat, which, to my relief, was not an animal that had a particularly emotional significance for me, other than that a goat's cry can sound remarkably like a baby's. Using basically the same procedure as the turkey, the *bosomfowo* removed the goat's hair from its head and tail, slit its throat, and bled it directly on Wango first and then Bangle. The goat, as is the cat, is considered to be a hot animal—if you have ever smelled a male goat you may already know why—and its head also was cut off and placed on Bangle. Drenched in blood, with severed heads sitting on him, Ketetsi's visage was a powerful and, at least to my Western eyes, a disconcerting image.

With the sacrifices finished, gin and schnapps were passed around—I definitely needed a few tots—and the talk turned to how things went. The general consensus was that the sacrifice had gone well and that the gods were pleased. Kwamiga informed me, however, that there was one more piece of business to take care of. In seven days I needed to return to the shrine with a dove in order to close the door. For this ritual, unlike the sacrifice of the turkey, I needed to buy the bird myself. His only instructions were to make sure the dove was large and completely white. At the time I thought, "great," after watching a dog, cat, goat, and turkey being killed, in a little over a week I would get to come back and sacrifice the symbol of peace.[16] But you can't put off closing the door. You never know what else came in when you opened it. Blood attracts all kinds of visitors, not just the gods it was intended for.

Seven days later, on a night that was even hotter than the one a week before, I showed up at Kwamiga's with a pure white dove. These kinds of nights are particularly stifling. Usually a breeze picks up around sunset only to die away into an oppressive stillness as night descends. We went inside the shrine, where, just sitting there, I started sweating profusely. I wasn't particularly looking forward to watching what for me was this carrier of olive branches, the consummate symbol of peace, get its head wrung off and bled on the fetishes, as I had seen happen before with a dove. Add to the mix that mosquitoes were once more biting me mercilessly, and all I could think of was how quickly I could get this over with and leave.

Once again we made a round of prayers and offered drink, kola, and clay to the gods. And, once again, I was handed the dove and told to touch its beak to the *gorovoduwo*. But before doing this, I was instructed to whisper into the dove's ear all that I wanted to happen in my life. After I did this and touched the dove's beak to the fetishes, Kwamiga took the bird, stood up over Bangle, and told me to come forward. Holding the dove with outstretched arms, he held it over my head. It started beating its wings, and a cooling breeze that was beyond refreshing came over my body. Maybe it was the juxtaposition of being so hot, but I had never quite felt anything like that before. He passed the bird over my body three times and, then, to my surprise, instead of killing the dove Kwamiga told me that we were going outside to set it free, something very unusual for closing the door. But priests have a certain leeway to improvise and vary the rituals they perform, though certain things, like giving Kunde a dog, are fixed.

It was a moonlit night, seemingly perfect for such an event. It had even cooled off a bit outside. We moved to the center of the courtyard in front of the shrine, and Kwamiga handed me the dove. I was told to hold it above my head and let it go. It was a welcome reprieve: instead of being responsible for its death, I was going to be the agent of its release. I did as I was told, and watched as it flew off into the night. I guess it had been cooped up for quite a while, and, as a result, its wings were still stiff, even though it had just gotten some exercise as my personal air conditioner. The dove, however, only made it about ten feet into the air when it fell with a thud and crashed on top of the roof of the shrine, not exactly the vision I had in mind, though it actually seemed much more fitting of the moment, as if to remind me that gods really are this-worldly. Whenever my ethnographic musings verged on the romantic, the gods always seemed to have a way of pulling me back to earth, and this was no exception.

Sacrifice and Libation in West Africa

Ewe religion is sacrificial to the core. Hardly a day goes by without someone sacrificing something for one reason or another. If not offering a cat for Bangle, then a dog for Kunde; if not a sacrifice for one of the *trɔwo*, then one for Afa, the god of divination, or to blacken a chief's stool, or to remember an ancestor. So ingrained is it in Ewe life that they even have an onomatope for the sound of blood dripping from an animal's throat: *tsrolotrsolo*. Far from being displaced by a globalized horizon of televisions and CD players, internet cafés and computers, billboards and Benzes that have begun to seep into the Ewe landscape, sacrifice is still part and parcel of the everyday lifeworld. I am not suggesting, of course, that Ewe fishermen on the Guinea Coast who barely make the equivalent of a dollar a day are actively engaged in this consumptive call, but, nevertheless, they are exposed to it on a regular basis.

How then do we understand everyday cultural practices so removed from the possibilities encountered in our lifeworld? What do we make of a religious praxis—sacrificing cats and dogs—that so offends our sensibilities, is so "experience-distant" (Geertz [1983: 57], quoting Kohut)? To condone such sacrifices misses the point; to justify them already assumes their guilt. The comfort of cultural relativism has long since passed its prime, unable to support the failings of a tired neutrality. Explaining it all away in the social security of paradigmatic chains—hot and cold animals, projected upon the plane of the sacred and the profane—may tell us something about how minds work, but has nothing to say when it comes to confronting the sway of such powerfully felt persuasions. Sacrifice, particularly in Africa, has long been the grist for the structural mill, an example of the ritual bastardization of mythic thought, the categorical slippage of a primitive people. Through the substitution of turkeys for cows, or, as in the famous case described by Evans-Pritchard (1937) for the Azande, cucumbers for cows, sacrifice becomes a matter of substitutional flow, a syntagmatic working out of sacrificial need generated from the binary structures of the sacred and the profane. But it is precisely this slippage, this communicative potency of the victim, that moves along an axis of concentric circles of sacralization and desacralization bounded by rites of entry and exit. The sacrificial object, acting as an intermediary between divinities and humans, the sacred and profane, loses its solidity, its opaqueness, becomes transparent, ultimately disappearing in the sacrificial act. This transformation into invisibility is what brings the gods near. Yet, try though it may, this consolidation of mass disguised through a discourse of desire cannot penetrate the density of the sacrificial act. It defies explanation, thus carrying a heavy burden of delayed expectations. While much ink has been spilled over sacrifice—and gifts—it is time to recover these acts from the theoretical limits of the sacred and the profane, and reinstate them within a horizontal understanding of everyday experience. And though poststructuralist centering of decentered masters may be a needed corrective to self-assured tales, it, too, fails to penetrate the density and opacity of the sacrificial act. What is needed is a return to that very density and opacity, the things of sacrifice themselves, not in order to explain them away as figments of a collective imagination, symbols standing for something else, but to bring into question what such things are in the first place.

What is given first and foremost in sacrifice is not a dog or a cat, a turkey or a cow, but what dogs, cats, turkeys, and cows are given to. Ask any Ewe what these things are, what blood is given to, and, whether he is a traditionalist, Christian, or Muslim, whether he thinks it is a gift from the north, the work of the devil, or false idols, he will tell you animal sacrifices are given to "fetishes." If ever there was a word that conjured up the dark heart of Africa with all of its negative connotations, it is this. But Ewes come by the word honestly. It was from the shores of the Guinea Coast that this term became common—and now not-so-common—currency in the West. When Portuguese sailors came to the west coast of Africa in the fifteenth and early sixteenth centuries, they applied the term *feitiço* (from the Latin *facticius*, "artificial" or "made by art") to these substances and treated them "as the heathen equivalents of the little sacramental objects common among pious Christians" (Pietz 1987: 37). They must have seen something in these strange-looking things and how they were treated that reminded them of their own religious practices.

From this initial, more neutral identification with powerful things capable of important effect, the word "fetish," like the objects it referenced, accumulated material from the negative accounts of missionaries, traders, and travelers, which found their way into early ethnographies and from there into Marxist theory and psychoanalysis. Fetish as a term became a fetish, the avatar for a moral discourse of other minds, mystification, and pathology. Whether the fetish was a talisman or Christian amulet, or more mundane things such as shoes or money, fetishism was cast as an archaic and unhealthy fixation with things not real. Shoes and money are, of course, "real" things, in fact overdetermined things in the classic notion of fetishism; they are just not the things users make of them: substitutes for missing penises; symbols of value, power and control; ultimately a search for some kind of security. And while Freudian analysis may have something to tell us about disavowals and desires (a shoe fetish works from the bottom up in the hopes of filling an absence), and Marxist theory about the obfuscating nature of capital (money *is* a powerful illusion), when applied to other realms in other worlds such analyses lose their ability to speak. Even more recent reworkings of the concept—it all can be explained as another example of the universal process of concretization, animation, and the conflation of signifier and signified (Ellen 1988)—tell us something about categorizing and representing minds, but still very little of what a fetish is as a thing. What is lost in this attribution of motive, this causative privation, is the things themselves. Fetishes lose their opacity, their thingness, becoming transparent supports for other more intangible effects. In this transparency, things collapse; everything becomes equally close, equally far.

But *gorovodu* fetishes are not objects once removed, thus twice thought. They are not empty vessels that northern gods inhabit, lifeless matter animated by outside forces. For those who offer sacrifice and libation, *gorovoduwo* do not re-present, nor are they symbolic of, something else. Fetishes are there, in the world, in particular places and locations. You can see them, smell them, touch them, and be touched by them (something I found out at Tɔsavi's). Explaining away this presence as a direct result of the deeply held beliefs of adherents—that it's "real" to them—adds nothing to our understanding of fetishes as Ewes think of them. This weary subjectivism merely acts as a placebo, assuaging our concerns with the reality that confronts us. *Gorovoduwo* have a solidity to them, a density that cannot be penetrated. Whatever else may be made of these gods, they are no more or less than what they purport to be: they are first and foremost things.

As things, they have ontological priority in the lifeworld of the shrines. Before a wife of Kunde or Bangle ever appeared in southern lands, there were the fetishes, potent things Kodzokuma brought from the north. He may have brought down the fetishes, but he didn't bring the knowledge of how to make them. If they were going to be transformed from individual *voduwo* handed down from father to son into a medicine shrine that would spread throughout West Africa, he would have to learn. He sent for help and, according to the lore of the shrine, the Dagarti sent him Mama Seidu, a Hausa, to teach him how to make and take care of the gods, knowledge he passed on to such *sɔfowo* as Tɔsavi. The history of the religion was close at hand, for I was dealing with the first generation of priests. Not every *sɔfo* can make the gods, however. He has to have received the power either directly from Kodzokuma or from the home shrine in Kpando. This has led to an amazing consistency in the look of the gods. All Kundes have a knife and all Bangles a beard, whether in a shrine in Nigeria or one in Côte d'Ivoire. Once I asked Anibra how there could be so many of the same fetishes at the same time. Without dropping a beat, he asked me what happens when you put two atoms of hydrogen together with an atom of oxygen. It is the same for the gods. When the right combination of material is brought together under the necessary ritual conditions you get the gods.

What then are these fetishes, these god-things that Kodzokuma learned to make? If we take these man-made things as merely things, then aren't they just three-dimensional objects, a particular configuration of matter and form that can be described, measured, and weighed, and all the rest mere superstition? As a corrective to this extreme positivism, do we then take into account a "system of symbols," to quote from Geertz's (1973: 90) famous definition of religion, "which acts to establish powerful, pervasive and long-lasting moods and motivations . . . [which] seem uniquely realistic," and attach this reality to these objects, rendering them religious artifacts capable of being read in a multiplicity of ways?

But already we can sense that the *gorovoduwo* as things begin to disappear under this kind of questioning. They become interpreted things, thick with meaning but void of substance. The gods are not floating above the surface of things, in suspended animation, waiting to descend into the world under the appropriate conditions, whether they be the beliefs of people or the analyses of anthropologists, psychologists, and other interested parties. *Gorovoduwo* are already, down to their very fiber, of this world. As things of this world they have an existence, a standing forth, that cannot be captured in such thick readings of what are actually extremely thin surfaces. Their immense facticity overwhelms. God-things are not, however, frozen objects in space and time. They are always-already on the move even as they sit unmoving in front of their *kpomewo*. Stare at the gods, and you will never see them. Catch them in the continual round of sacrifice and libation, and you might get a glimpse of their dwelling in-between. In this fleeting glimpse, this blink of an eye, we may begin to see the simple unfolding of what these things are as things, to borrow a notion and an etymology from Heidegger's ontology, what the ancient Indo-European word "thing" originally meant—a gathering (1975: 153, 174). Heidegger's notion of what is gathered as a thing, which he understands as the staying of earth, sky, mortals, and divinities into a single fourfold, seems to parallel what Ewes mean when they say Kunde is a fetish.[17]

The Brekete fetishes are medicines of this earth. From underground comes their outer skin, made from a large wild tuber; within are numerous plants and medicines made thick with the blood of animals. They *are* the sheltering and concealing earth brought forth into the world. This concealment is part of their destiny, a density that no amount of analysis will ever open up. Dwelling "on the earth," fetishes are "under the sky" (Heidegger

1975: 149). Made of things nurtured by the sun, the fetishes already have the sky as part of them. But as opaque is the earth, transparent is the sky. Things invisible become a refracted presence reflected off the impermeability of the earth, each mirroring the other. Shaped by the hands of priests, mortals who combine elements in a particular way, the gods are allowed to show themselves from themselves as things. Divinities depend on men to depend on them, each thus mirroring the other, living the other's death, dying in the other's life (Heraclitus's dark formula). This fourfold "mirrorplay" of the fetish, each reflecting the other, thus each in the other, gathers in its own particular way. This gathering does not happen in the interior of the fetish, nor is it contained within its surfaces—oppositions of inside and outside are not operative here. Neither does this gathering congeal into something fixed, an object ready-to-be-used, or present-at-hand, persisting through various subjective articulations. Rather, the thingness of fetishes, the fourfold of earth, sky, mortals, and divinities, happens in the consecrated outpouring of sacrifice and libation, "the poured gift"(Heidegger 1975: 172); it is what makes northern fetishes a site of the *trɔwo* (the gods). At this gathering we may begin to understand fetishes as fetishes and, in doing so, retrieve sacrifice from the metaphysics of violence inherent in the binary oppositions of the sacred and the profane.

When pouring a libation to the *gorovoduwo*, schnapps is poured into an ordinary tot glass and then poured directly onto the fetishes. There is nothing special about this glass, its material or design. It is like any other found in the numerous drinking bars that dot the landscape in the Volta Region. But when it is used to pour a libation to the gods, it becomes a consecrated vessel, one that is capable of giving out the "authentic gift" (Heidegger 1975: 173). During cow sacrifices, however, the priest doesn't pour schnapps into a tot glass, giving it measure, but pours it freely onto the fetishes directly from the bottle, fitting for the general excess inherent in such sacrifices. It is a "strong outpouring flow" (173) similar to what happens when the jugular vein of the bull is cut and blood gushes out all over the fetishes gathered in the bowl. This consecrated outpouring is not a more benign form of sacrifice, as it is so often portrayed; sacrifice is instead a form of libation.

However, the pouring of blood from the throat of a turkey or cow is not the same as the pouring of schnapps, whether from a tot glass or a bottle. Blood is not first poured into something then poured onto the fetishes; it is given directly from the veins and arteries of animals. What does the holding here? What is taken in and what is kept? Where is the void that gathers the gift of blood into an outpouring? We may posit a sacrificial animal metaphorically as a strange kind of vessel, but animals, as long as they are alive, do not have a void in the same sense as a glass or bottle.[18] There is no empty space in their interior into which to pour something, no opening from which to pour it out. A bottle of schnapps may need to be opened in order to pour out its contents, but it does not need an "opening up" to become a vessel. Turkeys and cows, on the other hand, do. All such vessels as vessels, by their very nature, are made to pour through an opening, which, as do all openings, creates a liminal membrane.

But animals are another matter. To give them an opening, throats must be cut, veins and arteries severed. In this cutting, the sacrificial act releases the animal into the void, and it is through this opening up that the animal's essential holding and keeping of life becomes the strong outpouring for the gods. The poured gift brings the gods near, transposed in close proximity to those who can die, to go along with them, to be by their side. Wherever this consecrated gathering occurs, whether it is at a shrine in Africa, in the precincts of a Catholic church, or in the words of a poet, it is a cause for celebration.

Cows for Turkeys

When I finally paid my debt to Ablewa and offered a real cow, it wasn't a decision I made entirely on my own. Afa (see chap. 6), the god of divination, had to remind me of that unfulfilled promise. A lot had happened in the ensuing years, and I know this wasn't the only thing the gods had asked of me and had not yet received. I visited many shrines, and it was sometimes hard to keep track of all the requests. It was during an Afa divination that a *du* (cast) appeared indicating that one of the kola-nut gods wanted something from me. It turned out that Tseriya was calling for her due; it was time to pay the debt owed to her. No bargaining this time, for she was adamant about her request. If I wanted to clear the way, a cow was to be given or things would start going wrong for me. Gods may be patient, but they do not forget what is owed them. Eventually you will pay one way or another. Giving a cow was infinitely preferable to the alternatives, especially when it concerned Ablewa.

In the years since I had sacrificed the turkey, I had offered many animals in many different situations, but I had yet to give a cow. I informed Kwamiga of what Afa had said, and he was pleased to hear that a cow would be sacrificed at his shrine. Apart from any positive spiritual benefits that would accrue to the shrine, and there were many, a cow sacrifice was always good for business, for it was one of the most powerful demonstrations of a successful shrine, itself indicative of being right with the gods, which in turn was a good recruitment tool. We mutually decided that the cow sacrifice would take place in one month, which would give me plenty of time to make the necessary arrangements. He insisted that we invite Anibra, which I already intended on doing. I was planning to go to Accra in a couple of days anyway, and that would give me the opportunity to invite him personally.

I arrived in Accra on the following Monday and found Anibra in his office at one of the government blocks overlooking the huge garbage dump near the arts market. I never did get used to seeing Anibra in his other capacity as a government official, often wondering if the Ministry of Food and Agriculture had any idea of who one of their financial consultants was in his off hours. But we had known each other for some time by now, and sitting in his office in downtown Accra, I found the idea of inviting him to the cow sacrifice totally normal. Time and repetition have an uncanny ability to familiarize. He seemed pleased but was worried about the expense. Anibra was always concerned that I not be taken advantage of, and that what was asked of me not be exorbitant, another refreshing reversal in the usual asymmetry of being-in-the-field. Early on in my research he called a meeting of priests in Kpando, introduced me, and told them that I was here to learn about Kunde and they should open their doors to me. I was their stranger, an important classification in the ethos of the shrine, for I was not the only stranger there. Northern gods might have been "Eweized," but they have never lost their status as foreigners. Therefore, they should be careful in how they greeted me. Everyone got the point. There was other business on the agenda and he quickly moved on, but that short speech made a tremendous difference in my research. Years later he was still looking out for me, and I appreciated it. But I assured him that giving a cow was something I wanted to do and it would not be too much of a financial burden for me. When I asked if he would be able to attend, he said that he thought he would be in Lome on business the weekend of the sacrifice and would try to come but could not promise.

Unlike the arrangements for the previous turkey sacrifice, this time things were left in my hands. Although Kwamiga had offered to help, this was something I wanted to do on my own. I had been in Ghana long enough, knew enough about the system, and had offered enough animals to be able to take care of things. The drinks were merely a matter of buying sufficient schnapps and *akpeteshie* for the sacrifice and festivities to follow. Buying the animals, however, was a bit more complicated. Getting a goat, a ram, and fowls was no problem—they were readily available at the

Agbozume market—but procuring a cow was another matter. Beef may be sold in the local markets off the hoof, but live cattle are not. For that job I enlisted the aid of an Islamic friend (most butchers in the markets are Muslim) who knew the cow trade. He assured me he would be able to get a cow for a good price and have it delivered to Kwamiga's the night before the sacrifice.

With that taken care of, I went to the market in Agbozume, where I often had bought goats and rams. The "*yevu* tax," that inevitable raising of prices for white men, was somewhat ameliorated due to my long-standing and ongoing relationship with several of the sellers. After a little de rigueur bargaining, I purchased the rest of the animals, that is, except for the dog and cat. I always had refused to buy these animals directly, explaining to *sofowo* that in my culture we considered these to be pets (I had to explain pets), and didn't condone the killing of these animals, that I needed to respect that cultural injunction. They seemed to understand my predicament but always insisted that, nevertheless, Kunde and Bangle had to have their food or "there would be big trouble." So, as usual, it was understood that I would make a donation to the shrine and that they would take care of that end of things.

On the day before the sacrifice I sent the goat, ram, fowls, and drink to Kwamiga's. The cow was to be delivered late in the afternoon, and I thought that everything was set. No need to get there too early, so I planned to come around 10:00 p.m. for wake keeping. Anibra, who was in Lome, was due to be there the next morning. I was looking forward to seeing him and to the sacrifice, that is, except for the dog and cat.

When I arrived at Kwamiga's around 11:00 that night, the first thing I saw was the cow tied to a tree next to the shrine, and I immediately knew there was going to be a problem. To say that what I saw was a cow, however, is a bit of a stretch, for actually it was more like a large calf, at best, barely a juvenile. In the interest of getting me the best deal, something my friend always prided himself on, he ended up trading size for price and in the process sacrificed maturity. I sat down and knew what was coming. After water was offered and traditional greetings exchanged, Kwamiga turned to me and said: "The ram for Ablewa is fat and a good color, and the goat for Bangle is good and so are the fowl, but the cow, that cow is an embarrassment! You can't offer a mere child in the place of a bull." With absolutely no hesitation I agreed completely, which surprised him because I think he was expecting me to put up a bit of an argument. I asked him what we were going to do given the fact that it was 11:30 p.m. on a Friday night and no cows in sight. It was about this time that I started taking double tots of gin.

Kwamiga didn't have any answers, but my friend who was with me said he would go to the border town of Aflao, about a fifteen-minute drive from the shrine, and see if he could find someone in *zongo*, the Islamic section of town, who could help, but he held out little hope of actually finding a cow this late, especially on a Friday night. Just as he was getting ready to leave, someone from Kwamiga's shrine, who had just arrived and had heard about the trouble, remembered, as if he had been told by Ablewa herself, that he had an uncle who might own a cow he would be willing to sell. He wasn't sure how big it was or how much it would cost, but was sure it would be better than what we had. Looking for a cow in the middle of the night in an African village definitely puts one in a seller's market, and we immediately sent him off to contact his uncle. Some two hours and several tots later, back he came, to everyone's relief, with a large bull in tow.

By the next morning, and with me still fairly drunk from the night before, everything was finally coming together as we all waited for Anibra to arrive. I had had nothing to eat and was trying to stave off throwing up, thus thankful that he was late. Finally at around 10:30 a.m., when I was feeling somewhat better, his entourage appeared. Almost as soon as he arrived, Kwamiga, anxious to get on with the business at hand, ushered all of us into the shrine and the sacrifice got under way. Anibra did me the honor of presiding over the prayers, repeating what I said and sending it on to the gods. What had been asked for was now being paid. We were opening the door wide, for "when one eats everyone sits at the table."

As was always done for a cow sacrifice, after the initial prayers, all the gods were placed together in a large enameled bowl and carried outside. All, that is, except for the male part of Wango, who never leaves his *kpome*. It is the female part, called Adzinɔ, who is covered in cowries and sits in front of him (see fig. 3.5) who is put into the pan and brought outside. Bringing the gods together in such close proximity, with them actually touching each other, exponentially increases their power and thus their danger. This was not merely a collecting together of things in one place; it was simultaneously a gathering and a clearing. Things must be done carefully in order to maintain this clearing where sacrifice happens, and not to offend those who are gathered together. This does not mean that there was a prescribed set of actions requiring a strict fidelity to rules. There always is a certain amount of confusion surrounding a cow sacrifice. I have never seen one performed without some kind of argument over exactly where the cow should be positioned, who should do what, and so on. Killing a cow for the gods is rather somewhat like the play of *brekete* drums; it is a set of approaches the very structure of which invites variation and elaboration.

When we came out of the shrine, someone was drawing a large cross representing a crossroads inside a circle with kaolin powder. As the *trɔwo* were brought out in the pan, gunpowder, which had been poured on the four corners of the crossroads and in the center, was set off. The gods were placed in the middle, and six *bosomfowo*, dressed in their hunting shirts, brought in the cow. It looked even better and bigger in the light of day. It was a hefty bull with a sizable set of horns. Anibra turned to me and said, "Well done." (If he only knew.) The bull took a good ten minutes to die, a testament to its life, a death worthy of the gods. Anibra stayed to help divide up the meat, which I later found out was something he didn't usually do. It was an honor that was not fully appreciated at the time, though of course I thanked him for doing it. He told me he had to get back to Accra and couldn't stay for the celebration. We said our good-byes. It would be the last time I would see him alive.

It was a week later that we got the news of Anibra's death. He woke up in the morning, was taking his blood pressure, as he did every morning (he was being treated for hypertension), and collapsed. By the time they got him to the hospital he was dead. All the priests were shaken up. If it could happen to Anibra, the spiritual head of all of Lahare Kunde, it could happen to anyone. But it was the will of Mawu, the supreme deity, and we just had to accept it. The initial shock of his death wore off eventually, but the sense of loss and sadness seemed to hang over the shrines for quite a while. I remember the day at Sɔfo Peter's when Anibra's death was officially acknowledged in a very poignant way. At the end of prayers, while pouring libations, Peter called Anibra's name and told him he could no longer drink with us but now had to take his with the ancestors.

About a month later, as a thank-you for the cow sacrifice, Kwamiga brought members from his shrine to my compound on the beach to celebrate *brekete*. Several other *sɔfowo* were invited; there was lots of drumming, singing, and *trɔsiwo*, but it all seemed somehow sad with Anibra gone. In the middle of the proceedings Kwamiga grabbed my arm and pulled me up to dance, something I always enjoyed doing with him, but this time it felt different. As we moved across the dance floor, it was as if we were dancing our sadness, though this was something felt more than

Fig. 3.6 Sɔfo Kwasi Anibra
(Steven Friedson)

thought. When we sat down, I turned to look at Kwamiga, but he turned
away with a tear in his eye, a different kind of poured gift.

It was shortly after this that a finely dressed woman decked out in gold
jewelry and high heels walked into the compound. I was impressed, especially with the high heels (the overwhelming majority of women wear
some kind of sandal), for it is at least a half-mile walk, much of it in the
sand, to get to our place. She was quite striking, and everyone turned
around to look at her as she came over to me. All I could make out over
the drumming and singing was that she wanted to talk to me, and that
the sɔfowo also should come. We all went inside the reception hall, and
she proceeded to tell me that she was Anibra's daughter and wanted me
to know that her father had often talked of me, that she knew he wanted
me to have the gods, and she had come to fulfill his wishes. Taken aback, I
could only get out that it was too great a gift and I could not accept it. With

that she fell down on her knees and took my two hands in hers, crossing them as in Bangle's blessing and started to weep as she kept repeating *akpe, akpe, akpe* (thank you, thank you, thank you). At this point all of us, including the *sofowo*, had red in our eyes, and the color wasn't from anger. The next thing I knew, she got up and walked out the door. If she was Anibra's daughter, no one had ever seen her before. To this day no one knows who she was or where she came from. The general consensus among the *sofowo* was that she was one of the gods.

Anibra was buried on the 6th of October 2001 in Kpando, the home of the shrine. I was in the United States and couldn't make it to his funeral, but I heard that sixteen cows were slaughtered that day.

Eku, eku gbidi.
When you die, you die forever.
—*Agbadza* drum language

Deadland   4

Anibra, as Sɔfo Peter reminded him, now drinks with the ancestors. Having crossed the river to Tsiefe, he dwells with the
dead in a land from which no one returns.[1] Ancestral souls,
the *dzɔtɔwo*, may return to be reborn in succeeding generations, but this is not equivalent to the return of the unique
human being that was and is now no more. That person, as
the *agbadza* drums say, is dead forever.[2] And since no one
has returned to report on the matter, no one is quite sure
what Tsiefe is like. Some Ewes say it is a dark, mirrored image of existence on earth, a village where life carries on in a
shadowed form devoid of material substance. If you were
a chief in this world (*kodzogbe*), you are a chief in the next;
a fisherman here, then a fisherman there, plying the waters
of the underworld.[3] Others, however, dismiss the question as
unanswerable, thus any reply mere speculation, idle chatter.

Typical of Ewes and frustrating to ethnographers, there is little consensus on this or many other details concerning traditional notions of death. Everybody, however, seems to agree on the direction—Tsiefe is down there somewhere. That is why you pour libations on the ground, and no one doubts its importance to the world up here. Ancestors become more powerful in their deadness, in their ability to protect and punish.

Sometimes, however, it is hard for the recently departed to let go, especially when their death is unexpected, as Anibra's was, and that is why they need to be reminded that *kodzogbe* is for the living. Not only do family and friends grieve for the dead, but those who have died also grieve for those they have left behind. And since the living are not keen on joining the dead, as they sometimes may want them to do, loneliness and despair may set in for the deceased, grief turning into something more problematic. Envious of the living, the dead become more resentful the longer they hang around, and the more resentful they become, the more trouble they can cause. Ancestors are venerated, called during libations to come take their drink; ghosts (*ŋoliwo*), are to be avoided at all costs. There is a whole repertoire of remedies to send the dead along their way, mortuary rites not the least of them. One of the last things done at a burial is to take the casket around the old haunts of the deceased to say one last good-bye and, in the final ritual, *yofofo* (literally, "beating the grave"), when part of the fingernails, toenails, and hair (significantly, the parts that seem to keep growing after death) are interred some days later, the dead are told in explicit terms that this is their final farewell and it is now time for them to move on to Tsiefe.[4] But if this final ritual is not done, or for some reason the dead refuse to accept their fate, they are caught in between this world and the next, becoming troublesome specters.

Not to say that Anibra was one of these disaffected souls, though it seemed he was far from ready to go. Everyone, including him, figured he'd be around for many more years to come, especially given the spiritual forces surrounding him as pope of Lahare Kunde. Powerful priests (Tosavi comes to mind) tend to live long lives, and Anibra was only sixty-two when he died. When I last saw him at the shrine of Kwamiga, who himself recently turned eighty, there was no indication that anything was wrong. Anibra seemed as healthy and alive as ever. In fact, he had told me just the month before he died that, since he was now in the process of being "retired" from the Ministry of Food and Agriculture, something not of his own choosing but as a result of the change of administrations in the last election, he could devote his full time to the shrines and was looking forward to making some needed reforms. He wanted to standardize practices, and this included establishing "rules for *trɔsiwo*" (controlling their unpredictable behavior was a continual problem for a religion that was trying to codify experience); improving hygiene and sanitation (by building tiled altars, for example, that could easily be washed down after sacrifices); and, in general, increasing regulatory control from the top down. Brekete had outgrown its current structure, and it was becoming increasingly difficult to keep tabs on shrines as geographically dispersed as those in Abidjan and Lagos, and on new ones that had begun to form in Gabon. Most troubling was the fact that some people were making the *gorovoduwo*, or what they said were the fetishes, on their own and installing them in shrines outside the purview of Kpando. He was determined to reign in this perceived disarray but died before he could carry out his plan.

No one knows the workings of Mawu, and, although certain things could be ascertained through such procedures as Afa divination, other things were destined to remain a mystery. Anibra's death was one of them. *Juju* was immediately ruled out, for there was no *juju* in the eyes of the members and priests that could overcome Anibra's power, and to think that he had committed some transgression serious enough to warrant death, whether against the *trɔwo* or the ancestors, was out of the question. This is not to say that such things don't happen to *sɔfowo*, even important ones.

The Priest of Kpando

A case in point was that of Sɔfo Baniba, the priest entrusted with the care of Kodzokuma's shrine, who died suddenly a few years before Anibra at the relatively young age of forty-four. I had met him on my first visit to Kpando and had seen him off and on over the years, but really got to know him when I spent most of the summer of 1997 living there and hanging out at the shrine. I wanted to see what went on at the Brekete equivalent to Mecca on a day-to-day basis.

That summer in Kpando gave me a fairly solid grounding in the daily workings of a shrine, thanks largely to Baniba. I would regularly get up with him at four o'clock in the morning to wake the *trɔwo*. Ata, the senior drummer, a true virtuoso, was also usually there, playing the praise names of the gods on the *brekete* drum as Baniba poured them water, gave them a small bit of tobacco, and threw cowries to see how they awoke.[5] If there was something wrong, then it was up to him to find out what it was and rectify the problem, which could be as simple as offering kola or as complicated as resolving a serious dispute between members. The rest of the day was devoted to dealing with who and what kinds of things came to the shrine. It was during this period that I began to realize how important healing was to the everyday practice of a *sɔfo*. There is a reason members are referred to as *atikeɖeviwo*, children of the medicine. A large part of Baniba's time was taken up with medical problems of various kinds. But here, as among the healers in Malawi with whom I had worked, what was considered an illness and appropriate medical response was a much more inclusive category than the Western biomedical model takes under its purview. Medicines were applied to all kinds of "illnesses," not just those that resulted from dysfunctional physical states.

Sɔfowo are expected to have command over a large number of plants, an extensive pharmacopoeia to address a wide range of problems. It takes a considerable amount of knowledge to identify the appropriate plants and understand what to do with them. Leaves are just leaves until you take them and transform them into *amawo* (herbs), and this always involves more than merely manipulating and combining the pharmacological properties of different plants. You often have to know their secret names, for example, to be able to activate and gain control over their power, or other esoteric knowledge that renders the medicine efficacious. Some of this knowledge has been handed down from *sɔfo* to *sɔfo*, some from father to son, in other cases it has originated in dreams, and in still others it has been taught to priests directly by the *trɔsiwo*. In addition to this plant-based pharmacopoeia, priests must know how to administer the kaolin and kola that have been transformed into medicinal substances through their offering and contact with the *gorovoduwo* and, most important, how to make the black powder of Kunde, a mixture of parts of dogs who have been sacrificed to him, along with gunpowder, herbs, and other compounds. It is some of the strongest and most powerful medicine available to a *sɔfo*.

Along with his duties as a healer, Baniba was also in charge of the upkeep of the shrine: waking the gods, putting them to sleep, making sure that they were fed and given drink on a regular basis, that the ancestors were called and similarly taken care of, and that all of the taboos associated with this care were strictly enforced. Significantly, seeing that this was Kpando, he also was responsible for making the gods for new shrines and occasionally renewing old ones. In that respect, given the rapid growth of Kunde, Kpando was a virtual god factory. Although Kpando was the spiritual headquarters of Lahare Kunde, it wasn't the political one; that rested in Accra with Anibra. However, serious cases of infractions by members, and *sɔfowo* in particular, were invariably brought to the attention of Kpando and thus Baniba. If a priest was found guilty, and the charge was serious enough, the fetishes could be and sometimes were collected and deposited at Titibigu, Kodzokuma's compound in Kpando where the shrine was located.[6] Baniba oversaw all of this too. Taking care of Kodzokuma's shrine was a heavy responsibility, but Baniba took it lightly, not in the sense that he didn't take it seriously, but as the Ewes understand the phrase, he took things "coolly" (*blewu*). Although easygoing, as with most *sofowo* he had a seriousness of purpose and a certain charisma that was compelling.

It was the following year that I heard that Baniba had gone to Benin to officiate at a *fetatrɔtrɔ* and suddenly been taken ill. Rumor had it that he had committed a serious offense and had "fainted straightaway." Word was sent to Anibra, who immediately rushed to Benin. Finding Baniba in a coma, he pledged a cow to the gods if he was allowed to get him back to Kpando alive, which he did, but Baniba passed away as soon as they arrived. When I heard the news, I was shocked and saddened. Although people weren't saying much about what had happened, I was told by more than one *sofo* that he had allowed palm oil to be served at Kodzokuma's "table," a strict taboo. In most shrines there is an altar dedicated to Kodzokuma, often located in a separate room from where the *gorovoduwo* are, a kind of shrine within a shrine. That was the way it was in Kpando, except that Kodzokuma's was set up in the outer hall of the shrine, covered by a curtain of white calico. On the table, as it is on all these altars, was a photograph of Kodzokuma in his northern smock, watch prominently displayed on his right wrist, with his unique white double beard. Several of the *sofowo* have commissioned this photograph to be painted on the fronts of their shrines, and it is starting to take on the status of an icon (fig. 4.1). I have often wondered how future generations will understand this image of its founding father. Will they start reading the watch as something more than a tool for reading time, or his unusual double beard as some kind of sign of a double existence, with one foot in this world and one in the next, as is the case literally with the picture of Amadou Bamba, the Sufi saint of Senegal, that is plastered all over Dakar (Roberts and Roberts 2002)?

At the end of prayers to the gods and pouring of libations to the ancestors, a special libation always is given to Kodzokuma at his table. Along with gin he also is given *pito*, if available, the fermented millet drink that is a favorite of northern peoples. During a *fetatrɔtrɔ* he also is given some of the food that has been cooked, but it must contain no *tadi* (hot pepper) or palm oil of any kind. This serving of food is called *kplɔɖoɖo* (setting of the table) and, according to the *sofowo*, this is what got Baniba in trouble.

Fig. 4.1 Painting of Kodzokuma on a shrine wall

The food that was prepared at the *fetatrɔtrɔ* for Kodzokuma turned out to have had palm nut that had been crushed, thus palm oil. To me death was an extreme price to pay for what seemed like a rather minor infraction, but it was explained that serving Kodzokuma palm oil was tantamount to giving your father poison. From what I knew about Baniba, it just didn't make any sense. Why had he allowed it to be served knowing full well it was such a serious taboo? "He was testing Kodzokuma's power, thus that of the *trɔwo*," was the inevitable response, "and you don't fool with these gods." Baniba was gone, his death explained, and that was the end of it.

Nudedzitɔ

My time in Kpando made a big difference in my research beyond learning the ins and outs of daily practice at the center of Lahare Kunde. For the people in the southern shrines—regardless of what I thought I was doing—I had made a pilgrimage north to Mecca to learn the ways of the gods and was on my way to becoming a *sofo*; but I wasn't even a member, which became an issue during my stay. At that time some of the first generation of Lahare Kunde was still around. Nudedzito, the first *bosomfo* of Kodzokuma's, who was with him for more than fifty years, was still alive and, although living in Togo, was staying in Kpando that summer. He was barely able to walk, and at that only with the help of a cane. But this rather frail-looking man gave me nothing but grief virtually the entire time I was there over not being a member. Regardless of what Anibra had said about opening up Kunde to me, Nudedzito kept insisting that I shouldn't be in the shrine, learning all of these things, when not only was I not a *sofo* or *bosomfo* but I hadn't even been to *dzogbe*, Bangle's realm, where only the initiated could go.

I steadfastly had refused to join because I knew that membership would change my relationship with Anibra and everything else about the shrine. My research agenda was on a trajectory diametrically in the opposite direction from such a move—you can't be in-between if you are a member. By the end of the summer, however, after deciding that I was indeed serious, Nudedzito had somewhat softened his stance and actually started inviting me to dance with him during Brekete gatherings on Sunday. Whenever he did, I was always amazed at how gracefully he could move without his cane, though he could barely walk with it.

One Sunday morning in particular stands out, though it didn't have anything to do with dancing except for the fact that we had just finished. As Nudedzito and I were sitting down, two of the gods grabbed a six-month-old baby and started playing catch with him. They were about five feet apart and people rushed to try to get the baby back, pleading with Tseriya and her daughter Sanya to put the child down. But the *trosiwo* would have none of it. In the middle of all of this, Nudedzito stood up and threw his cane at the *adehawo*, yelling at them that the gods knew what they were doing and should be left alone. He complained that people these days just didn't have faith and trust in the gods like they used to. The *trowo* continued to throw the baby back and forth for some five minutes—the baby, by the way, was smiling throughout the whole thing—before giving him to one of the *senterwawo*. Although these are serious gods, they always seemed to have a playful spirit about them, though sometimes this manifested itself in rather unusual ways. The history of the shrine was close, and I felt privileged to have been able to dance with men who had walked with Kodzokuma. Nudedzito died in 2003, having outlived both Baniba and Anibra.

Old Words

Anibra's death, unlike Baniba's, was taken as part of Mawu's plan and, in that sense, was in no need of human explanation, or rumor for that matter. It was a "natural" death, though he should have lived at least into his nineties, as had Nudedzitɔ. But as the Ewe proverb says,

| Agbenɔnɔ kakaka megbɔa yɔme | Even a long life does not lead |
| ŋuti yina o. | past the grave. |

Anibra, along with everyone else, must cross the river to Tsiefe. That is why a few coins are put inside the grave, so that the dead can pay the boatman to ferry them across.[7]

Although Anibra's death was unforeseen, it was something that he himself had predicted (as Baniba and Nudedzitɔ had their deaths) before he was ever born. Every Ewe tells the bomenɔ, the old woman who is the caretaker of souls, what kind of "wares" they will bring into the world to sell—in other words, what kind of work they will do, who they will marry and how many children they will have, whether they will have a cool or hot temperament, lead a relatively smooth or troubled life, and so on.[8] Some say it is said to a room full of clay Legbas, and still others directly to Mawu, the supreme deity, or Se, the god of destiny. Last but not least, all Ewes will speak of when and how they will die, whether it will be from a massive stroke, as was the case with Anibra, an auto accident in the prime of life—an all too frequent occurrence in Ghana these days—or from serving palm oil to the picture of an old man. When you are born, however, and cross the threshold from the bome into kodzogbe (this world), all is forgotten, nothing remembered.[9] But one is held to his or her gbetsi, as these final words before birth are called, and, though certain things can be negotiated through sacrifice and libation, when the appointed day arrives the prophecy is inevitably fulfilled.[10]

Life and death for Ewes is in this coming and going: from an embodied presence of flesh and bones in kodzogbe to a disembodied mirrored existence in Tsiefe; from this wisp-of-the-wind substantiality in deadland to the purified "kernel," as Rosenthal (1998: 176–77) calls it, the seed of a particular life force that waits in the bome to be reincarnated (amɛdzɔdzɔ; literally, "person-born-born").[11] Reincarnation, however, is not to be confused with the rebirth of an individual who once lived on earth. That this soul is not coterminous with the individual is obvious when one considers the unique gbetsi spoken before each and every birth—in a previous life a fishmonger, in the one to come a queen mother; in one life dead at thirty, in the other at ninety-five. Each person is a unique combination of forces and energy that come together in that particular way only once. This points to the high value placed on individuality in Ewe culture, which belies that old notion of collective minds for collective souls. What an ancestor bequeaths to the newborn is but a part of who that particular great-grandfather, great-grandmother, or great-uncle was when he or she was alive (it always skips at least two generations). That is why an ancestor can be in Tsiefe, *kodzogbe,* and the *bome* at the same time.

It is said by some that after sixteen journeys to this world—the number undoubtedly refers to the sixteen original casts of Afa divination (see chap. 6, pp. 165–66)—the *dzɔtɔ,* no longer interested in partaking in the round of birth and death, retires to the lowest part of the underworld, a place called Agɔkpo (Westermann [1928] 1973: 77). I would like to think that a part of Anibra was one of these old souls who was ready to retire, the weight of his accumulated existences sending him deep into deadland, his name enshrined along with his father's in every libation poured in every shrine of Lahare Kunde. When the *sofowo* pour such a gift, they call into those depths for him to once again draw near and come take his drink.

Libation for Anibra

Tɔgbuiwo medo agoo, medo
    agoo zi etɔ
	Grandfathers I knock three
	    times

Ame vɔwɔtɔ, ame vɔwɔtɔ	The evildoers, the evildoers (the sunrise is for you)
Miatɔe nye fiẽsi fiẽ miaa	Yours is the sunset, the cool sunset
Tɔgbuiwo medo gbe na mi	Grandfathers I greet you
Sɔfo Kwasi Anibra, Meyɔ	Sɔfo Kwasi Anibra, I call

—(Free translation of a *tsifofodi* [libation])

Calling brings closer what it calls.
—MARTIN HEIDEGGER, *Poetry, Language, Thought*

When the final words of his *gbetsi* came to pass and Anibra died, it took three months before he was buried. This was not going to be any ordinary funeral, and there was much to be done before the shrine would be ready to say farewell to its pope. In the "old days," before the advent of refrigerated mortuaries, most people were buried within three days of their death, no matter who they were—no mystical or religious explanation is needed here; the pragmatism is obvious.[12] The fact that a corpse could be preserved for even three days in those conditions is a testament to local knowledge of herbs and natural preservatives. Nowadays, since the dead can be kept "on ice," time is no longer an issue when the unrelenting equatorial heat works its entropic effect on dead bodies. Anibra's family could take its time—his body was being kept in a mortuary in Accra—to organize a funeral befitting the passing of the equivalent to the paramount chief of all the shrines.

When the burial and funeral finally came to pass, it was a grand occasion lasting four days, and no expense was spared.[13] Thousands of people from all over West Africa and beyond descended upon Kpando, where Anibra was laid to rest. According to all accounts, by Friday afternoon Kpando, a sleepy town located in the hills above Lake Volta, was bursting at the seams. Virtually every cooking pot was working overtime to try to feed the multitude, and every spare room and veranda appropriated so people would have a place to lay down their heads, though no one got much sleep.

The official proceedings began the day before, when the gods were formally told of Anibra's death and pending burial. A dog, ram, goat, cat, and dove were sacrificed, and a branch of dried palm leaves was placed across the entrance to the shrine signifying that the door was "closed." The gods were in mourning for their dead *sɔfo*, and no one could enter the shrine, nor would the *trɔwo* leave their *kpome* for seven days or take any food or drink, kola or kaolin until the period of mourning was over. As a result, none of the cows that were slaughtered over the next few days were offered to the gods, no blood poured on the *gorovoduwo*, no heads broken, no eyes given. The killing of these cows, as opposed to what happens at a *fetatrotrɔ*, was strictly utilitarian, with nothing overtly spiritual about it. They were killed to feed the many people who had come for the funeral. *Trɔsiwo* also were discouraged from manifesting the gods. If someone did become possessed he or she was immediately taken by the *senterwawo* to be washed in the special *amatsi* that sends the *trɔwo* on their way. Possession rarely, if ever, occurs at funerals anyway. I have never seen a possession at a wake keeping, burial, or funeral outside the context of a shrine.[14] Ewe ancestors simply don't tend to possess their progeny, something that, if it happened, would probably be considered close to incestuous.

Friday afternoon Anibra's body arrived in an ambulance from Accra. A huge crowd had gathered to meet it, playing *brekete* drums and singing, following it as it made its way slowly through the streets of Kpando to

Titibigu, the home of the shrine. Ironically, it sits almost directly behind the large stone EP (Evangelical Presbyterian) church with its tall bell tower dominating the townscape of Kpando. If you didn't know that the shrine was there, however, you would miss it altogether. There are really no distinguishing features about the compound giving the uninitiated any clue that it is the spiritual center of Lahare Kunde. When the ambulance arrived at the shrine, elders came outside and poured a libation for Anibra before it continued a short distance to his house (built after he was enstooled as head *sɔfo*), where the coffin was taken inside and his body laid in state on a bed specially prepared for the occasion. Throughout Friday and Saturday, until the room was closed to get the body ready for transfer to Titibigu, people came to view the body and pay their last respects.

Things, however, really didn't get under way until Friday night with the start of wake keeping (*ŋudɔdɔ*), when the *agbadza* drums held sway throughout the night. This is not to say that other "drums" (here meaning a style of music) were not played; some were, such as *ade*, the hunting drum, which is a much more important music for northern Ewes than in the south (hunting always has been a more significant activity in the northern Volta Region due to the surrounding forest), and, of course other *brekete* styles such as Ablewaza and *abey*. But it was *agbadza* that dominated the night. For the southern Ewes this is the paramount mourning music, its themes of war and death resonant with the matters at hand. And since southern Ewe musical styles define *brekete* music, it is no surprise that *agbadza*, which is also Bangle's drum, was played in a northern Ewe town where it is not part of funeral traditions. There is something about this music that has the sound and feel of the ages, and no southern funeral or Brekete *fetatrɔtrɔ* would be complete without it.[15]

I remember the first time I went with Anibra to a wake keeping and experienced Bangle's music in its proper context. It was for a *fetatrɔtrɔ* at a shrine located on the back road to the University of Ghana at Legon. Typical of staying with Anibra, I had no idea we were going to a shrine for such an event until we actually got there. It was during my first visit with him, and everything was still fresh, not weighted with the inevitable sedimentations that come with repeated experience. It started out around dusk, as usual sitting on the porch, and with no notice the next thing I knew we were being driven to what seemed like the middle of nowhere. Because I didn't know where we were going, and was still in that inevitable naïveté that accompanies the early stages of fieldwork, I was envisioning all sorts of esoteric rituals in some far-off shrine. After about a forty-five minute drive, suddenly it was no longer countryside but a huge new development of middle-class duplexes, each with a postage-stamp-size front lawn complete with grass, something I had never seen before in front of a home in Ghana, where, for the most part, the swept-earth policy was still in force. It was quite a vision, just not the one I was expecting. It turned out that we were there to visit one of his wives (most priests have several wives), who was a nurse. We stayed for about an hour, and most of the conversation revolved around a low-fat diet she had put him on and how his blood pressure was doing: not exactly the ritual I was expecting either, though even popes have to deal with the mundane details of existence. By the time we left it was dark, and we headed back into the city so that he could take care of some business. We pulled up in front of a nondescript building, and he went inside while I waited in the car seated behind tinted glass windows—I could see out but no one could see in—watching the nightlife pass by illuminated by the kerosene lamps of the street sellers. It was a rare chance to see Accra at night without being the only *abruni* (Akan for "white man") around. After a few more stops, including getting a bite to eat, we finally headed to the shrine at Legon around 11:00 p.m.

When Anibra arrived with his entourage, which I guess now included me, a shout went up from those who had gathered for the wake keeping, gunpowder was set off, and, in general, a great fuss was made. We were seated under a canopy of woven palm leaves that had been erected in front of the shrine, and after the obligatory greetings I settled in for what I assumed would be a long night. I had spent many of them previously in Malawi (Friedson 1996), but this night was under West African stars, a whole different constellation. The *agbadza* drums, which had been playing and had temporarily stopped when Anibra arrived, resumed along with the singing and dancing of the *adehawo*. The dance area, as always, was circumscribed by benches on three sides, with members sitting to the left and directly facing the shrine on the far side; the *awukuwo*, the drumming group, to the right; and *sɔfowo*, *kpomegawo* (administrative heads), and special guests sitting directly in front of the shrine on chairs, the whole making a square where everyone could more or less see everyone else.

As is typically done at such affairs, people would usually dance in pairs, or sometimes three or four together. Although people danced together, it was always as individuals. No one faced anyone else, nor did the Ewe do a version of a line dance. Someone would get up and grab a person's arm, inviting him or her to dance. If more than one person was invited, or others spontaneously joined in, which often happened, and there was a mix of male and female, protocol demanded that there always be a woman between two men or vice versa. This choosing and accepting the invitation to dance reinforced friendships, reconciled strains, affirmed kinship ties; its refusal could exacerbate grievances, prolong a feud, break off a budding romance, and bring to public attention other cleavages. Dancing together meant something, not the least of which was the fact that bodies were moving together in poetic ways.

With everyone facing the same direction, people would begin with a simple "waiting" step until *sogo*, the master drum for *agbadza*, signaled with a roll for the dancers to break into the dance proper and move across the floor in the classic backbreaking Ewe style (see www.remainsofritual .com for video footage).[16] When they reached the other side, they would turn and perform the waiting step once more until *sogo* signaled for them to dance back to the starting point. The dancing finished at both ends with a hip shake to the right and then to the left, a bend back and then finally forward from the waist, with the arms being thrown forward "giving" the dance back to the crowd. Often this closing move would be extended, allowing people to display their individuality and sometimes virtuosity. Throughout the night various combinations of people would get up to dance in such a manner, simultaneously several different groups dancing in different directions. Unlike the wake keeping at Anibra's funeral, this one featured *trɔsiwo* all over the place, freely moving in and out of the shrine, dancing and singing among the *adehawo*.

As we sat there, people were continually approaching Anibra, including the *trɔsiwo*, to say hello and pay their respects. I was intently trying to make sense of what was going on with all that music coming from those three relatively modest drums and wasn't paying attention to much else when Anibra grabbed my arm and led me to the dance floor, something he had never done before. You do not turn down an invitation to dance from the pope. As we walked out in front of where we had been sitting, all of the *adehawo* immediately came off their benches and knelt down as we stepped back and forth waiting for the signal from the *agbadza* drums. Anibra smiled, I smiled, the energy of the drums and singing turned up a notch, and when *sogo* gave the signal, we danced as women fanned us from behind with wraps of white calico. I did not have a habitus of dancing *agbadza*, to appropriate Bourdieu's (1977) term, the sedimentation of hearing, seeing, and feeling this dance since I was a baby being borne on my mother's back. But I had been to enough funerals, had already provided enough entertainment for those who were there while I learned to dance in a very public way, to have been able at least to do a credible job, with feet, arms, and torso roughly in the correct relationship with themselves and the drums. We turned and began to dance our way back, but in that turn something happened. I don't know if it was from watching Anibra dance, as I had been doing out of the corner of my eye, or it was something else. Actually I have no idea how it happened, but I experienced a complete reversal of effect: what was once up was now down. The relationship between hands and feet, drums and bell, remained constant, but what was now felt as a rising up had been a step down. In this reversal, this turn, my body relaxed and what had seemed an effort was now at ease. When we had danced our way back to our starting place, with the *adehawo* cheering and women throwing the calico wraps around our shoulders, Anibra grabbed me with both arms in an embrace and led me back to my chair. It is only now and then that I have been able to recapture that feeling of reversal when I dance, and when I do it feels as if my body is floating with a buoyancy that is nevertheless firmly rooted in the earth. When it happens, I invariably feel Anibra somewhere nearby, dancing in the corner of my eye.

Around 1:00 a.m. Anibra got up to leave, but he told me to stay, and I would see him in the morning. It was quite a night, for every time the many *sɔfowo* who were there to celebrate the *fetatrɔtrɔ* got up to dance, I was invited to join along. To not only dance *agbadza* that night but be there at four in the morning as an old man leaned back at the end of his dance, stomped his foot to the ground, and cut the air with his hands, was to understand something about wake keeping and mourning, war and death, that only *agbadza* could say. And it could say this only in that particular way late into the night, as people, making music together, sacrificed their sleep for what was to come.

By the time Anibra's car showed up the next morning, I couldn't believe it had been that long since he had left. It was Sunday, and the shrine was packed. As soon as he arrived, he was escorted inside a house nearby and sent word for me to join him. Food was brought in, and he invited me to share a meal of smoked fish with fresh *pepe* (raw tomatoes and onions), not exactly what I had in mind for a breakfast after a night of dancing and drinking, but, to my surprise, it seemed to be just what I needed. I hadn't realized how hungry I was. When we finished eating, we all went inside the shrine and Anibra prayed to the gods. When he finished, the *gorovoduwo* were brought outside, and, as was always done, placed on a crossroad that was drawn in the middle of the dance floor. The cow was led in by the *bosomfowo*, who, as usual, had an extremely difficult time lifting it over the basin, but after several minutes of yelling at each other about what to do and how to do it they finally got the bull on its side, hoisted it up on a few benches, pulled back its head, and the gods were fed. There was something about staying up all night, a sacrifice of sleep, that seemed to fit the occasion. Anibra stayed for another few hours, and then we all got up to go. I ended up back at his house and slept for the rest of the day.

No such luxury was had according to reports from his funeral in Kpando, where by Saturday morning, after a night of dancing, drumming, and drinking, things were just getting started, since there were three more days to go. As daylight broke, the *bosomfowo* killed several of the many cows that had been bought for the occasion, each one a visible testament to the wealth of the shrine and the feasting that was to ensue. But no gods would participate in this meal, for their door was closed. The only one who got blood that day was the hole that was dug in the ground over which the cows' throats were cut.

Later that morning a small *salah* was held, after which *agbadza* was played once again, but this time with the *brekete* drums taking the lead, for this was *agbadza* in its guise as Bangleza (Bangle's shrine music). A short break ensued, and then the fast-paced *abey*, the celebratory music of Brekete that defines the shrine more than any other style (see chap. 5), took over. The gin and *akpeteshie* flowed, kola was freely distributed, and the *adehawo* (now thoroughly lubricated in more ways than one) sang and danced for the rest of the day.

As the afternoon wore on and *abey* kept getting faster and faster—there is an almost continuous acceleration with tempos easily reaching a density referent of 560–600 eighth-note pulses per minute—the drumming, dancing, and singing began to coalesce into a long, extended crescendo that reached a peak when the equatorial twilight set in and Anibra's casket was carried down to Titibigu and taken inside a special burial room, the yɔxɔ (literally, "grave room"), so that the body could be prepared for the final funerary rites. As is done with chiefs and other important elders, he was buried secretly later that night inside the room next to his father Kodzokuma. Leaving him buried in a graveyard was way too dangerous. Someone could easily dig him up some unsuspecting night and make off with parts of his body. A priest such as Anibra had accumulated much spiritual power in his life and, because there is no mind-body duality operative for Ewes, his physical body, its bones, flesh, and viscera, his ŋutila, had retained something that not even death could take away. With bodies such as this, care must be taken that parts not be stolen to make powerful *dzoka juju* (literally, "fire rope *juju*"). That is why there is someone always watching over the body at wake keepings to keep the dearly departed company, whether chief or commoner, and to make sure they leave in one piece to rest in peace.

Much else happened during those four days as well: more cows were slaughtered, people feasted, rituals both public and private were carried out for and on Anibra, speeches were made, eulogies and homages paid, prayers said, and the politics of the shrine discussed both formally and informally among members and sɔfowo alike. After all, there was, at least temporarily, a vacuum at the top. On Sunday there was even a service at the Catholic church near the shrine.[17] Anibra, in his younger days, once had been a member. When he was growing up in the 1940s and 1950s, if you wanted an education, you were more or less forced to go to a mission school and be baptized. But that was not the only reason he told me. His father had encouraged him to explore other religious traditions so that he could find out for himself the truth of Lahare Kunde, something he had done with his own children, several of whom were now Christians. The last major organized event was a huge salah held on Monday morning. Jesus, Allah, and Kunde all during one funeral made for a decidedly ecumenical affair. On Sunday and Monday tables also were set up to receive donations and contributions. One young sɔfo told me that, although he didn't witness it himself, he heard that some of Anibra's relatives from England brought ten million cedis (local currency) and just threw them up in the air for people to take.[18] Whether true or not, as with the number of cows actually offered, this, too, became part of the legend that already was starting to form around Anibra's final farewell.

But lest we lose sight of what happened during those four days, what took place most prominently, and what the proverbial observer from Mars would have noticed first and foremost, was that people were making music together. From wake keeping on Friday night and continuing virtually nonstop until late on Monday, the drums and voices of the adehawo could be heard resounding throughout Kpando. As they mourned they celebrated Anibra's life through music. For Ewes there is no difference between the two.

Killing Time

When sogo, the master drum for agbadza, says "[When] you die, you die" (Eku, eku), and kidi, the main response drum, responds "forever" (gbidi), it is left to kagaŋ, the small high-pitched support drum, to say what the pragmatics of burials are really all about, "They are going to throw sand [in your face]" (Woyi ke dege [ŋku nε]).[19] Burials impress upon dead bodies the finality of it all—having sand thrown in your face is hard to ignore. And thus the agbadza drums tell us something that is fundamental about

Ewe death and thus Ewe life, something ontological, not only in what it says but in the very musical structure of how it is said.

All Ewe drums, not just those of *agbadza*, have this ability to talk, to impart the distilled understandings of generations through proverbs, to praise the ancestors by calling out their special drinking names (Anyidoho 1997: 128–30), to critique and criticize the living, and to do such mundane things as asking for a beer during a performance (Chernoff 1979: 75; Alorwoyie, n.d.).[20] This is nothing more than the iconic "talking drums of Africa," a phenomenon that has been recounted ad infinitum in traveler and missionary accounts, was a favorite of Tarzan movies, and occupied the imaginations of a few anthropologists (Rattray 1923a, 1923b; Peek 1994), some ethnomusicologists (Blacking 1973; Nketia 1974), and various others, including at least one botanist (Carrington 1949), and one professor of English (Ong 1977). To understand this phenomenon as a kind of transformational grammar, irreverently appropriating Chomsky, which projects the deep structure of what is said into the aesthetically charged surface of what is played, is to miss the point entirely.[21] These are musical sayings, not linguistic events translated, transformed, transliterated, trans-anything into something else, which is not to say mimetic considerations are not in play. Rather, it is something said by *agbadza* musically, powerfully, and poetically. This "something" is said in no small measure through the constitution of cross-rhythmic surfaces, the very fabric of what the drums have to say.

African cross-rhythms, based on polymetry, are the site where at least two rates of motion are present at all times, always available for rhythmic elaboration. Meter in this sense is not equivalent to "measure" in Western musical terminology, with its implied structure of strong and weak beats (see Kolinski 1973; Arom 2006). Simultaneous multiple rates of motion are a synchronic scaffolding defined by streams of unaccented neutral beats composed of pulses (usually either two or three per beat, or their multiples) upon which drummers, dancers, and singers engage in a particular kind of musical experience.[22] It is an ontological structure, a musical way of being-in-the-world in multiple ways, a fundamental feature of a widespread and historically deep African rhythmic praxis (see chap. 5).

When the *agbadza* drums speak of death, what are deceptively simple parts based on two-syllable words are complexly related in relationship to the bell's timing, an asymmetrical timeline usually played on the *gankogui* (iron-forged double bell) to which all parts of the ensemble relate (see chap. 5).[23] The entire *agbadza* drum phrase as actually played (*Eku, eku, eku gbidi*) is eight syllables long and distributed over one cycle of the bell, which spans twelve pulses (ex. 4.1). The tonemic influence is minimal, all

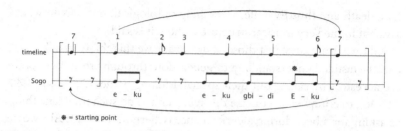

Ex. 4.1. Eku, eku gbidi

syllables spoken with a neutral or midtone, except for the last (*di*), which takes a high tone. There is no question that it is the rhythmic movement that gives the phrase its linguistic identity. *Eku* is said by *sogo* with two open hand strokes, and it may or may not play the finish *gbidi*. This is usually left to *kidi*. Played with sticks, it always supplies the existential hook. By not "speaking" the final word, *sogo* creates an absence that brings forth the word from *kidi*, thus in a sense marking it. In addition, the entire phrase moves toward this word, emphasizing it first in the delayed completion (it takes the third repetition to complete the phrase), and second by the filling in, as it were, of the two empty pulses that follow the first two repetitions of *eku*. *Gbidi*, this final word, literally this last word, also gives the phrase the position of its first word (*Eku*), thus making it a sentence and marking its specific starting place in the timing of the bell. In other words the phrase has a beginning and an end that are not arbitrary but fixed within themselves and their relation to the bell pattern.

What I am labeling stroke 7 is, in the literature, often taken as stroke 1. Agawu (2006), among others (Zabana 1997; Chernoff 1979), simply assumes that it is the beginning first stroke. (Locke [1982: 225] shows both starting points.) *Gankogui* bell players do often play what I am labeling stroke 7 on the low bell. The marking of this event on the low bell, however, does not mean that it is the beginning of the pattern. Virtually all Ewes with whom I have discussed this issue say, if anything, it is the ending of the timeline. In keeping with Ewe ambiguity, here the end *is* the beginning, and the beginning *is* the end. Usually, however, bell players do start on what I am labeling stroke 1.[24] Jones comes to the same conclusion by way of his discussion of a "jingle of nonsense syllables" that represents a resultant pattern of a combination of clapping and the "standard pattern": "He [the African] hears the resultant as *ending* on the first beat of the gong-gong and therefore as starting on the gong-gong's second note" (1959: 54; italics in original). Marking of endings is typical of much African music, which seems to privilege endings over beginnings (Blacking 1973). This gives the timeline a propulsive force heading toward the final stroke on the low bell. Instead of thinking of this as a movement forward in a straight line, a more cogent analogy would be a curving or falling downward back to stroke 1.

Sogo, as always in *agbadza*, initially gives *kidi* its part, resulting in both drums playing virtually the same thing. Sounded over and over, the sentence folds back on itself and, in doing so, defines a particular kind of musical space; in essence it becomes a riff, the essence of which is repetition. An undertheorized musical phenomenon, repetition is perhaps not the right signifier for what actually goes on.[25] It is much more a retrieval, continually recovering and bringing forward that which is left behind, the acoustic equivalent of what is visually present in the popular *adinkra* symbol *sankofa*, which is a bird with an egg in its mouth turning backward. This bringing forward, which is precisely a reaching back, builds on itself, layering reoccurrences on top of one another, creating a stacking of sonic material that seems to suspend forward motion and linear sequencing.

Paradoxically, riffing sustains a static rhythmic base maintained by *kidi* from which *sogo* explores melo-rhythmic and metrical possibilities. What *sogo* elaborates on is not so much a rhythmic pattern as a cross-rhythmic site located in a standing field of intense motion. The resulting pattern, however, itself is made from auditory points that must maintain their individual identity in order to create the cross-rhythmic effect. In this stacking effect of the riff, there is both a thickening and simultaneously an opening up of sonic space. This is not merely an acoustical phenomenon but a bodying-forth-in-the-world.

The riff carves musical space out of the timing of the bell in one and only one way. If you are not exactly right with the timing, most Ewes can hear it instantly and will not hesitate to tell you so in rather emphatic terms.[26] It is almost a visceral reaction, as if playing it wrong is for Ewes what grating fingernails on a blackboard is for us. But when everything is in its place, when the parts are so tight they are loose, so heavy they are light, so dense they are transparent, against but with each other, then the music lifts up and back over itself, falling in a continual round of the same.

To be in the right place at the right time, the phrase must begin on the pulse between the fifth and sixth strokes of the bell, with the second syllable landing on the latter (see ex. 4.1). The next repetition of the word *eku* aligns with the first stroke of the bell two pulses later (a key anchoring point), and the last repetition of *eku* two pulses after that, followed by the hook *gbidi*, with the last syllable falling on the fifth stroke of the bell, which takes it back to the beginning. The timing and the phrase are, and are not, two separate entities. The rhythm of the words, in essence, is woven into the texture of the bell just as the timing of the bell is woven into the structure of the riff, resulting in something akin to the pattern in a fine single-weave *kente* cloth, the design of which is created out of both the warp and weft threads (see Thompson [1983: 207–22] for a discussion of "rhythmized textiles").

Of course, drummers and bell players do not count out pulses to figure out where things go: they just play, feel the correct timing. And this takes us to the fact that the three repetitions of the word *eku* are equidistant, a not insignificant detail in regard to this "feel." This equidistant articulation results in a phenomenal metrical pattern of three beats, each beat made up of four pulses. A 3-beat meter (1 beat = 4 pulses) covering one cycle of the timeline is the metrical structure from which *sogo* and *kidi* construct their basic riff. Understood in this way, however, the part could become a rather boring cliché. But when interlaced with the bell and the clapping patterns of the *adehawo* (see p. 142), it takes on a whole new life. Beyond its obvious cross-rhythmic relation, the word *eku* significantly starts at a different place in the bell than the various clapping patterns, giving it a much stronger feel of crossing. Upon first hearing, it seems almost alogical as it floats above *and* below the clapping and the bell. This is especially true when sometimes the *sogo* plays only one stroke (the first syllable of *eku*), which seems like he is merely marking metrical time. We are dealing here with a rhythmic virtuosity that is part of an everyday cultural currency.[27]

Not everyone, however, hears what the drums have to say; fewer and fewer people do these days (a common complaint of the elders about the youth who don't seem to be interested in such things). But for those who do—and here that old warhorse still applies—the medium is the message. Within the very structure of cross-rhythms of *agbadza* drumming is an ontological understanding—the multiplicity of Being—that can be interpreted only through a musical experience that says something.

But what does *agbadza* say that bids both farewell and simultaneously conveys the pulse of celebration? Can the answer be reduced to that tenacious mystification of music as emotional empathy masquerading as catharsis? When will we let Africa finally disabuse us of such strange ideas? The kind of musical experience I am referring to here is not an action of subjectivity, but a release from it. And when this happens, we don't play music, it plays us.

If *agbadza* is not primarily a means of emotional expression, discharging tensions, unblocking the flow that has been stopped up in the emotions of loss, essentially the plumbing theory of mental health—if it is something more than merely an entertainment, amusement, or diversion to pass away the night during a wake keeping—then what exactly is it about this music that makes so many people spend so much time and energy in playing it? And it does take a lot of energy. One only has to look at the sweat pouring from a drummer's body to confirm that fact. Is it just a matter of people feeling good as a result of expenditure, a kind of runner's high that releases endorphins? Catharsis and enjoyment are no doubt an important part of what goes on and might explain part of what happens, but this brings us no closer to an *understanding* of music *as* mourning. *Agbadza* does something more than expend energy—whether it releases grief, joy, or endorphins—it makes it. Like a cold fusion machine, that so far unattainable dream of technology, more energy comes out than is put in. That is one of the reasons why people can go on for days at a funeral, or an old man can throw away his cane and dance throughout the night. What Victor Turner has to say about spirit possession seems to apply: it is a "meta-power," a "social arousal . . . unlocking energy sources in individual participants" (V. Turner 1986: 43). Beyond exhaustion, before physical limitations, when there is nothing left, music is there to give something more. Needless to say, this is not true of all funeral music. The closest thing we have in the West, not surprisingly, can be found in black churches or the second line of a New Orleans funeral. The musical energy of the crossroads not only survived the Middle Passage but colonized the music culture of the entire Black Atlantic.[28]

This energy-producing structure is a very particular and specific way of people making music together. It is not floating above the fray, as it were, in a metaphysical ether, but is down on the ground, where motion and sound happen, where gods are fed and feted. Playing such music is being there before subject-object distinctions, beyond social dialogue, communication, even intersubjectivity; it is an experience where there is participation in a whole that has no parts. This is something that is hard for us to conceive of, for it seems to defy logic. A "musical whole with no parts" must be analogy, metaphor, hyperbole, anything but a reality. Of course there are parts, separate people fulfilling interactive roles in communal experience, producing tonal rhythmic patterns that can be pointed to, talked about, analyzed, even frozen into some kind of notation, though ethnomusicologists are still trying to figure the last one out. Playing Ewe music, however, is not how individual parts fit into a whole, just as dancing is not an attempt to align one's body with some kind of underlying and regulative dance beat, regardless of how obvious this may seem to the naked eye of the beholder. That was Agawu's (2003, 2006) mistake.[29] Nor does this lived musical experience fall into the old adage that the sum (*agbadza*) is greater than its parts (*sogo, kidi, kagaŋ*; call-and-response singing; backbreaking dancing). There is only the whole, every part, every movement but a different refraction of that reality, not contributing to it but coming out of it.[30] And each player—drummer, dancer, and singer—takes out more than is put in. This excess of musical energy at a wake keeping is the balancing of accounts between life and death, the restoration of the *force vitale* (Tempels 1959) which is lost when someone dies.[31] It is nothing less than the rhythm of the crossroads inscribed in the flesh of the world.

Kpando Rerun

A year after Anibra died, I returned to Kpando to offer the gods a cow in his honor. It was something I had been planning on doing since I had realized I couldn't make it to his funeral, something I still regret.[32] I had heard that Kokokri, Anibra's younger brother, had been installed as the new pope, and when I came back to Ghana in the summer of 2002 I contacted Kwamiga to see about setting up a meeting with him to make arrangements for the sacrifice. He had been enstooled the year before, shortly after the palm branch was removed from the shrine door in Kpando, and a dog, ram, goat, cat, and dove were offered to the gods to mark the end of their mourning, as they had been the week before when the door was closed. On the day that they "opened the door" the *sofowo* also consulted Afa, the god of divination, to make sure that the path was free and that there was nothing left to do and, more important, to confirm that Kokokri, the last-born son of Kodzokuma, was indeed the person to succeed Anibra, as Anibra himself had indicated the year before he died. According to Afa the funeral had gone well and nothing more needed to be done and indeed Kokokri was to be the new pope of Lahare Kunde. Sometime that week after Anibra was laid to rest in his ancestral home at Titibigu, Kokokri was taken into the shrine and was seated on Kunde's stool seven times, and thus was to have his life transformed as he became the last *sofo* in a direct line from Kodzokuma's blood.

Two weeks after I arrived in Ghana, on a Sunday afternoon in Aflao, I met with Kokokri, his older brother Kofi (who had been passed over as head of the shrine), and Kobla, one of Anibra's sister's sons, the *sofo* of the second-most-important shrine after Kpando. It was the shrine Kodzokuma had established when he had fled Kpando during the troubles in the 1950s over whether the northern Volta Region, then called the Trans-Volta, would be part of Togo or incorporated into the newly independent Ghana (Amenumey 1989). Kodzokuma had been on the Togo side of the debate, tensions had been high and positions entrenched, and when his side had lost, he had had to flee Kpando, and that was when he had set up his new shrine in Kɔndome, a district in Lome.

I hardly knew Kokokri or Kofi, but had known Kobla for some time, since whenever Anibra was in the area, Kobla was always with him. The first few times I had seen him, I had thought he was something like Anibra's bodyguard. He was a big man, though not particularly tall, but had the presence of someone you did not want to mess with. He always wore sunglasses and never left Anibra's side. I soon found out, however, that Kobla was not his bodyguard, at least not in the physical sense of the term, but was something akin to the shrine's spiritual enforcer. It was widely said that he knew more about the gods than anyone else, including Anibra, and if someone was threatening one of the shrines and it was serious, then Kobla was the *sɔfo* to turn to.

After expressing my condolences and regrets about not being able to attend the funeral, I explained that I wanted to offer a cow in Anibra's honor at Kpando. Everyone agreed that it would be a fine gesture and they would make the necessary arrangements. Kokokri was a soft-spoken man, probably in his early forties, and seemed to still be adjusting to his new position as pope and didn't say much. In many ways he seemed just about the exact opposite of Anibra, who had an outgoing, bigger-than-life personality. More unusual, Kobla barely said anything either. It was Kofi who did most of the talking. He said that they would take care of all the details, and all I had to do was provide the cedis (money). When Anibra had been around, I wouldn't have questioned the amount Kofi called for; he always made sure that I made minimal contributions to whoever or whatever I was asked to give to. But Anibra was gone, and, although I knew the amount that was mentioned was beyond somewhat suspect—cow sacrifices were expensive but not that expensive—I didn't say anything and agreed. It was decided that the sacrifice would take place in one month's time, and they would get back to me for the exact date after they checked with Kpando. I heard back the next week through Kwamiga about the date and made plans to travel to Kodzokuma's shrine.

We arrived in Kpando on a Saturday afternoon, and, after settling into Anibra's house, where I had always stayed when I was in Kpando and where he had been laid in state, I made my way to the shrine to see how things were going. It was the first time I had been back to Kpando since

Anibra had died, and it all seemed somehow sad, though it was good to see old friends. When I got to the shrine, we immediately went inside to make prayers so that I could inform the gods that I was giving them a cow in Anibra's name and that they should accept this offering freely. Anibra's sister, Kobla's mother, a rather large, tough woman, was still around, as was the old *bosomfo*, the man with no fingers (probably lost to leprosy), who was always sitting in the shrine, and Tse, a cousin of Anibra's who was the caretaker of his house and a senior member of the executive committee. We sat inside and talked for a while, mostly about the funeral and how it had been a grand event they would be talking about in Kpando for years to come. They were sorry I had missed it but were glad I had come to Kpando to pay my respects to Anibra. I left after about an hour to go back to the house and relax, because I knew it was going to be a long night. As I walked out the door I told Tse, who was leading me back to the house, that I wanted to see the cow. He explained that it wasn't here yet but was due any minute and I would be able to see it later that night, when I came for wake keeping. This seemed a little strange, but I didn't inquire any further.

After getting some rest, we headed back to the shrine around 10:00 p.m. where there were already quite a few people, though *agbadza* had just gotten started. After we exchanged traditional greetings and sat down, I asked to see the cow. Tse, a bit reluctantly, took me around to the side of the shrine where the cow was tied to a post. With no small amount of irony, as had happened the year before, to call it a cow was a bit of a stretch. It wasn't much bigger than the one that my friend had bought and that had caused all the fuss at Kwamiga's. Was this the best they could do? But Tse said that this was what Kofi had sent, that cows were hard to get around Kpando, and that I should "take it lightly [*hodzoe*], not to worry, that all would be fine." What Kwamiga had said the year before—"That cow is an embarrassment!"—came to mind, but I kept my peace.

In spite of all of this it was a fine wake keeping. Ata, the master drummer I had met when I first came to Kpando, was playing the drums, and *agbadza* was particularly "sweet" that night. A steady supply of *akpeteshie* and schnapps, and plenty of kola, contributed to the mood. And, in a repeat of that other time, I got more than a little drunk and was suffering the next morning when the cow was offered. The *bosomfowo*, however, didn't have nearly the struggle they had had the year before trying to lift the cow and hold it over the basin. We stayed for a while after the sacrifice, but with Anibra gone, things just weren't the same, in more ways than one, and we left for the coast in the early afternoon.

As we were driving back, winding our way through the cool, shaded forest roads found in this part of the Volta Region, my mind wandered to the night before when, after more than a few tots had come my way, I got up to dance. It wasn't a conscious decision, nor was it a particularly inebriated one, but merely a manifestation of the fact that one doesn't really dance in such situations, one is danced. When I stood, several *sɔfowo* joined me and, as always happens when priests dance, the *adehawo* knelt down and women were fanning us with lengths of calico. *Sogo* waited, we waited, and Ata, the shrine's master drummer, in what was at least for me the perfect moment, sounded that distinct roll of *agbadza*, the call to dance. As I danced I remembered the first time Anibra and I had crossed the floor. It was as much a feeling as a memory, more of a blessing than a thought, as if his presence were hovering on the edge of my peripheral vision. In that moment, as before, the dance was both heavy and light, and, once again I was somehow in-between, a tear in the intentional fabric of the world, and tears came to my eyes, though I don't think anyone noticed. Anibra had taught me something about joy that night that I hadn't really grasped at the time, something that Kwamiga taught me about sadness when he and I danced at my compound. These were not lessons to be learned and remembered, but musically experienced anew, each time, and there are really no words for that, only music, only dance.

And is not repetition itself a kind of resurrection of the dead...?
—PAUL RICOEUR, "Narrative Time"

The Rhythm of the Crossroads 5

That day I first met Anibra at Kwamiga's shrine, I was standing in the middle of the courtyard with a *brekete* strapped across my shoulder, working on the drumming for *abey*. Although *agbadza* dominates the wake-keeping night, it is *abey* that rules the day. There is a concentration of forces in and around this music that makes it the gravitational center of activity for shrine members and gods alike, who spend an extravagant amount of time dancing, drumming, and singing to its fast-paced groove. During celebrations it is played for hours at a time with no break, one continuous reverberation made up of hundreds of different songs.

Abey is the most technically demanding of all *brekete* drumming, the site where the virtuosity of a master drummer is released and displayed. Thus it was with no small amount of trepidation, given the complexity involved and the fact that I was coming to this musical practice relatively late in life, that I had picked up the double-headed metal drum made for me the week before. Any used metal barrel about two to two and a half feet long will do—mine had stickers on it picturing an umbrella with raindrops and the warning "Dangerous When Wet"—as long as it can produce the requisite sound. What is significant about a *brekete* drum is the fact that it has been consecrated, thus activated. The drum I was playing had been given drink, had been fed with the blood of several chickens, and contained Kunde's kaolin and kola. That is why you are never supposed to let it touch the ground, though, as figure 5.1 makes clear, this sometimes happens. A ritual *brekete* is something like a fetish, a *gorovodu*, with an animated existence beyond the intentions or beliefs of the one who is drumming. *Brekete* drummers don't impose their will upon the drum, but rather release the sound inherent within it.

We were playing in the courtyard because Kwamiga had decided early on two things about my drumming apprenticeship: (1) if I was going to learn drumming, then I needed to do it in the proper place; and (2) I needed all the help I could get. The second reason was intimately linked to the first, because playing in the environs of the shrine would attract the

Fig. 5.1 *Brekete* drummers (Elise Ridenour)

support of the gods, who are inexorably lured to the sound of the drums, which is, of course, why they should be played at the shrine in the first place. And, since I was in the beginning stages of learning, if I wasn't playing correctly, surely the gods would want to help for the sake of their own aesthetic sensibilities.

A good *brekete* drummer, using only one bentwood stick typical of the kind used on northern talking drums, can unleash a torrent of sound that impresses upon those who have gathered—shrine members, spectators, gods, and those whom they ride—something that is not only heard but physically felt, a vibration that penetrates the boundary of the body's flesh. It goes without saying that this proficiency was not something on my immediate horizon when Anibra's entourage arrived and I was playing *brekete*, still struggling with exactly how things sometimes fall apart when you are doing your best to bring them together. But some of this, thanks to a passing remark by Anibra, was soon to change. On the way to Accra later that day he mentioned that, if I was really serious about learning *brekete*, then I needed to look up Kpesusi, a legendary drummer and old friend of his.

The Wife of Kpesu

Some people are born to play drums, and Kpesusi was one of them. At an early age he displayed a fascination with drumming matched by an aptitude for playing that was truly impressive. A child prodigy and no doubt the reincarnation of an ancestral drummer—how else to explain his prodigious talent—he was playing the lead *brekete* in the shrine of his maternal uncle Sofo Zigah by the time he was thirteen. By his early twenties he was an admired master drummer, recognized for his classical style, the elegance of his line, the nuances of his rhythmic sense. Not as flashy as that of other drummers, his playing had a refinement that impressed those in the know. He was a drummer's drummer.

Mawuko, as he was known back then, was part of a long and distinguished line of great drummers associated with Zigah's shrine, the oldest and one of the largest on the Guinea Coast. It was Zigah who had first received the gods directly from Kodzokuma's hand, even before Tɔsavi, and it was largely from his shrine in Aflao that Kunde's fame initially spread in the south. Part of this had to do in no small measure with the fact that he was responsible for the innovation of utilizing used metal petrol containers to make the *brekete* drums. He was a soldier at the time, had access to these metal barrels, and decided to adapt them for use as drums (wood was scarce and expensive on the coast).[1] The resulting sound was striking—gods with music like this must be strong—and people flocked to his shrine to hear this new style of drum.

As Mawuko matured from adolescent to young man, Zigah, as maternal uncles sometimes do in patrilineal societies, took his nephew under his wing. It was a nurturing relationship unlike the more strict formality of paternity. He taught him the way of the gods: how to take care of them, pray to them, offer sacrifice and libation, eventually even how to make them. He became Zigah's most trusted *bosomfo*, to the consternation of the *sofo*'s sons, not only helping to take care of the gods, but also aiding Zigah to install them in more than one shrine. It was understood that one day Zigah would give him the *gorovoduwo*, to place him on Kunde's stool, a rare event, for drummers hardly ever became priests. If they do, ironically, they no longer drum. Zigah took Mawuko deep into the tradition as the tradition took him deep into drumming: the more he learned about one, the more he understood the other. When he played, the depth of his knowledge was evident to all who had the ability to truly listen to what his drumming had to say.

By the time I met him, however, he was no longer playing drums, having "retired" years before. *Brekete* drumming is, for the most part, a young man's game, and men rarely carry on the practice past middle age regardless of their passion for the art. He was then in his early sixties, and, in addition, he was now a *sofo*, and priests virtually never play the drums, their status as heads of a shrine precluding that option. How can you carry out all the duties of a priest and play drums at the same time? But neither age nor being a *sofo* had put an end to his drumming career; rather, it was Zigah's death that had precipitated the event.

After being a priest for over sixty years, Zigah died a peaceful house death at the age of ninety-six, one more example of the long life of *sofowo*. His son Bibio took over the shrine, and Mawuko was more or less left out in the cold. Bibio always had been jealous of Mawuko's relationship with his father, and now that Zigah was dead and he was head of the shrine, Mawuko was forced into a kind of internal exile. He drummed less and less; his heart was heavy, his mind no longer on it. By the time of Zigah's grand funeral, which took place two years after his death, he had, for all intents and purposes, quit playing. The grand funeral, in fact, was the last time Mawuko drummed in public, paying one final tribute to his deceased uncle. Though he stayed on at the shrine for the next eight years helping his cousin take care of the gods, little came his way. Those years were a struggle for him and his family—he was now married with several children—and finally in 1992 he left the shrine he had grown up in, drummed in, eaten kola in. It was a hard move, but Mawuko was determined to establish his own shrine. Anibra finally made that possible, personally installing the gods Mawuko himself had made.

They were more or less age-mates (Mawuko was slightly older), and whenever Anibra was in the area, Mawuko was always by his side. When Mawuko came to him about starting his own shrine, he was more than ready to help both financially and spiritually. After Mawuko made the gods, Anibra arranged that they be sent to Kpando to receive the power from the source. At Kodzokuma's shrine the gods were put on the seats in front of each *kpome* of the home shrine, and Bangle and his entourage were taken to *dzogbe* to be fortified in the desert of hot deaths and *voduwo*. The requisite sacrifices were done, part of the substantial financial burden incurred to become a *sofo*, and the gods were brought back to Mawuko's shrine in Aflao, where another round of sacrifices was performed to formally welcome the gods. Anibra himself placed Mawuko on Kunde's stool, fulfilling the promise made by Zigah years before. Mawuko the drummer was now Sofo Kpesusi, a duly installed priest of Lahare Kunde.

His given name was Mawuko (literally, "only God"), his day name Kwami (a male born on Saturday), and his Christian name Paul (to attend school back then you had to be baptized), but, when I met him everyone knew him as Kpesusi, the name of the Mami Wata god he had found in the sea; actually, to be more accurate, the god had found him. He was standing in the surf helping some fishermen pull in their nets one day when he suddenly felt something hit his foot. It was a sharp sting that tattooed three black marks on his insole, which are there to this day. He didn't pay much attention to it, but a few moments later he was stung on the other foot, with the same results. This time, however, he reached down into the surf and picked up a large stone carved with animals and other strange figures. He was baffled by what he had found (it looked "European" to him), so he took it to the owner of the net who had this strange thing sent to his compound, but as the stone moved inland the sky turned black and a strong storm erupted. If you have ever experienced one of those quickly formed and powerful thunderstorms along the Bight of Benin, then you will understand why there is no doubt that there is a thunder god, whom the Ewes call Xebieso. The net owner, wanting no part of someone else's potential Mami Wata god (thunder and water go hand in hand), immediately gave it back to Mawuko.

The problem with being found by a Mami Wata god is having to figure out how to take care of her.[2] She may be demanding, but serve her well and she can bring good fortune. Fail to understand her needs, however, and it can lead to fatal consequences. More than one owner has gone mad trying to satisfy her desires. The liquid nature of water is part of the liquid nature of Mami Wata gods in all their various forms, for they always come individuated. There is no one Mami Wata, but she is always a multiplicity of effect. For Mawuko, dealing with Kpesu, a name Afa divination finally revealed, has always been problematic. Not only was he responsible for his own set of *gorovoduwo*, he also maintained a special shrine to Kpesu, and he became known as Kpesusi, wife of the god (the radical *si* indicating betrothal). Gender seems to be a fluid issue in Ewe culture (pronouns are not gender specific), and wives can indeed be males, at least linguistically.

Although many people knew who Kpesusi was, not that many people knew where he lived. He was a private person, not seen often in public, and, in addition, his shrine had only a few members and wasn't that active. After some initial inquiries I finally found him located in that labyrinth of back streets off the main road that runs through Aflao. The border with Togo was only a stone's throw away from his compound, as was the *zongo* quarter with its large Islamic population. The area had become choked— no city planning, only contested land rights—and the many narrow alleyways that zigzagged back and forth gave the place an air of intrigue. Kpesusi's shrine was at the end of one of these passageways, built on his father's land. Significantly, Zigah's shrine, now headed by Bibio, was also close by, something that partly might explain why he was having trouble recruiting members, since Zigah's shrine was still very active and one of the largest in Aflao.

When I entered his compound, to my surprise, Kpesusi said he had been expecting me, not that he knew I was coming or even knew who I was. But his Mami Wata god, according to him, kept sending "European" things his way, including the occasional *yevu*. For example, there was the book from the Korean Central Historical Museum (1979) that mysteriously showed up in the mail one day. He had absolutely no idea who had sent it, but for Kpesusi it was foreign and all things foreign were, in a sense, European. One of the items pictured inside was a statue of a Buddhist Goddess of Mercy made in the period of the Koryo Dynasty (935–1392 CE). Kpesusi decided that this was a picture sent to him by Kpesu in one of her many forms and promptly had the picture painted on the outside wall of her shrine (fig. 5.2).

Books were not the only thing "European" to find Kpesusi. It turned out I wasn't the first *yevu* to study drumming with him. In the early 1970s a young American researcher and musician who was working on his mas-

Fig. 5.2 Kpesu in the form of a Buddhist Goddess of Mercy

ter's thesis in ethnomusicology had found his way to Kpesusi and lived with him for a year, studying drumming and hanging out at Zigah's shrine. But after that year and a few letters, he never contacted him again. One of the first things Kpesusi asked me was about his former student: if I knew him, was he still alive, why had he never returned or at least written again? Our shadows are long in the field and sometimes we don't realize how long they last, especially for young ethnomusicologists.

When I told Kpesusi that I wanted to learn *brekete* drumming and that Anibra had sent me, he decided we needed to go into the shrine house to continue our discussion, because we were talking about spiritual things concerning the gods. I took off my watch and shoes, as usual, put some *amatsi* on my forehead and chest, and entered. Kpesusi's aesthetic sense of a certain refinement in his drumming carried over into a visual acuity that gave his shrine a unique look. Unlike the typical cement gray or dark blue *kpomewo* of other shrines, his were painted a bright yellow. On each end of the cement rooms of the gods were carved lions, and in front of Wango's home was a carved crocodile. The fetishes all had a highly polished blood sheen; their spiritual weapons were well fashioned. Nothing seemed haphazard. Each god's home formed a special tableau, a particular arrangement of elements—weapons, talismans, fetishes, kola, kaolin, cowries, and knives—cohering into a whole. And along the back wall was a veritable history of the shrine in framed photographs: Kodzokuma as a young man in his hunter's shirt covered in talismans, next to the iconic picture of him quite a bit older, with the double whitebeard and wrist-

watch; Mawuko as a young man sitting behind Bangle (the soldier); Zigah and Mawuko holding Tsengé (god of the seven knives). It gave the shrine a presence, a visage of great *sofowo* who were watching over us.

As we sat in the shrine, I told Kpesusi of my travels to Kpando, my work with Kwamiga, and my stay with Anibra. Hearing all of this, he provisionally agreed to take me on as a student but decided that we first needed to make prayers and hear the gods' response to my request to learn their music. Anticipating this possibility,—nay, inevitability—of asking the gods, I had brought along a bottle of Henke Schnapps. Kpesusi sent for kola and kaolin, I put some money on top, and, under the gaze of those ancestors pictured across the back wall, we prayed to the *gorovoduwo*.

I knelt before Kunde's *kpome* and "knocked" on his door three times: "Ago Kunde! Ago Kunde! Ago Kunde!" Kpesusi seemed pleased that I knew the protocol. As we went down the line of gods and threw the cowries, each one agreed, that is, until we got to Wango, the god of the waters and roads. Given Kpesusi's affinity to gods of the water, not surprisingly, it was the *trɔ* with whom he had a special connection. Wango's cowries repeatedly rejected my prayers, and Kpesusi's inquiries of why this was

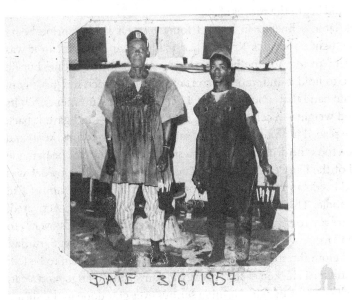

Fig. 5.3 (*opposite, top*) Kodzokuma young man / old man

Fig. 5.4 (*opposite, bottom*) Mawuko as a young man, sitting behind Bangle and holding spiritual weapons

Fig. 5.5 (*above*) Zigah and Mawuko holding Tsengé of the Seven Knives so revealed nothing; every question was answered in the negative. Suddenly, and only for a brief moment, Kpesusi went into a trance (not possessed like a *trɔsi*), spontaneously divining what Wango had to say. I was surprised—I had never seen a *sofo* do this—and what he was saying was in a language I could not understand. Whatever Wango had told him Kpesusi felt no need to explain, other than to tell me that, although he had been given the okay, there were some serious rituals in store for this god in my future. With this final okay from the gods, there was now no doubt in his mind that, although his former student had not literally returned, I had come back to make good on what he had left undone.

At the end of the prayers, after the customary libations to the ancestors, Kpesusi informed me that we were now ready to proceed, but, before we could begin drumming, the first thing he needed to do was make me a drumstick. This was not to be just any piece of wood used to beat a drum, something that could quickly be fashioned from a branch of a tree for immediate use. It had to be heated and bent into a very particular shape, sanded smooth. Not only that, but it also had to be activated, to put Kunde's spirit inside, and that would entail more than instrumental skills. Kpesusi told me to come back in a week with another bottle of schnapps, and we would begin the process.[3]

A week later, schnapps in hand, I found myself in the shrine being handed the bentwood stick Kpesusi had made. That didn't mean it was being "given" to me, for the necessary rituals remained undone, but he wanted me to hold it and, more important, for it to touch me, have contact with the hand that would wield it. I held it for a few moments, felt its balance and weight—nicely made but nothing special—and gave it back to him. He placed it on top of Kunde, said prayers, gave drink, kola, and kaolin, then took the drumstick and, in a small hollow that had been made in the end of the handle, filled it with Kunde's medicine. Gunpowder was also stuffed inside and set off, sparks shooting out of the end almost like a Roman candle. This was turning out to be quite a drumstick. Activated, it was now ready to be put in Kunde's *kpome* (literally, "Kunde's oven") to be "cooked" for seven days. As I left, Kpesusi told me that on Saturday, three days before the stick would be "outdoored," the gods had to be fed: a dog for Kunde; a chicken each for Ablewa, Sanya, and Wango; and a cat, dove, and chicken for Bangle. Nothing serious ever gets done in the shrine without the shedding of blood.

Kpesusi is slight of build. He has a lightness about him that gives him an air of moving easily through the open vortexes of daily life, but when he slaughters an animal for the gods a weight sets in, a solidity, a finality that cannot be overcome. On that Saturday afternoon inside the shrine, Kpesusi, slightly crouched with one foot in front of the other, offered animal after animal with swift deadly cuts. The gods were well polished that day, and I had a new understanding of the priest-drummer with whom I was to work.

On Tuesday, as instructed, I returned to the shrine and found the stick where I had left it, still sitting inside Kunde's *kpome*, but now it was dedicated, medicated, and ready to go. Before it was handed to me, Kpesusi prayed:

Ago Kunde, Ago Kunde, Ago Kunde

Kunde, I knock three times

Adza Kunde, Omalan Kunde, Dagarti Kunde, Kodzokuma Kunde, Kɔwu Zigah Kunde

[Priests of Kunde]

Meyɔ! Meyɔ!

I call! I call!

Nyatefeɛ, edze xɔlɔ. Xɔlɔ ŋkɔenye Agɔsu.

Truly, you made a friend. The friend's name is Agɔsu.[4]

Xɔlɔ la dzesi Kodzokuma ƒeme le Kpando.

That friend knows Kodzokuma's house in Kpando.

Eva tsom le afisia be ye be yasrɔ wo brekete ƒoƒo.

He crossed me here that he wants to learn *brekete* drumming.

Nyatefeɛ, Nyea nye megbe o.

Truly, I have not refused.

Kunde ameɑɖeke menɔa ŋgɔgbe nawo o. Ewoe nɔa ŋgɔgbe ye ameɛ kplɔ na do.

Kunde, nobody stays at your front. You alone stay in the front and the person follows you.

Nusi dim amɛgbetɔ le la, yenye agbe, agbe yomea ega, ega yomea susu, susu yomea, nyatefeɛ, srɔ kple viwo nanɔ asiwo.

What a human being searches for is life, after life money, after money knowledge, after knowledge, truly, you should have wife and children.

Meɖe kuku nawo Kunde be alesi nena brekete lem meƒom keke vinyewo ha wo ƒo mea, nafia brekete ma Agɔsu woa ƒo ʋua abe alesi wo Kunde nedi lãme nam meƒo nɛ ene.

I beg you Kunde that as you let *brekete* catch me and I play it, teach *brekete* to Agɔsu to play the drum just as you Kunde put it in me and I play it.

Wɔava me nenema pepepe.

It should come through exactly.

Egbe, me agblɔti sia dem asinee.
    Na geɖe lãme ne—naɖo lãme.

On this day I hand over this *agblɔti*
    (curved stick) to his hand. It should
    enter his body—possess his body.

Eye nunana si wɔava nawo
    Kundea wo ŋutɔ ye tsɔge akpi
    nɛ wɔa va nawo Kunde. Metsɔ
    ɖesiaɖe de asiwo me.

And whatever gift he shall bring to
    you Kunde, it is you yourself who
    will give it to him to bring back to
    you Kunde. I put everything in
    your hand.

Na kpe ɖe eŋuti.

You should help him.

Nye ha matsi agbe. Eyaha natsi
    agbe.

I also should live. He also should live.

Miaha kafu ŋkɔ na Kodzokuma,
    Kɔwu Zigah tso mavɔ heyi
    mavɔ me.

Together we will praise the name of
    Kodzokuma and Kɔwu Zigah
    forever and ever.

Yesu Kristo nede asiɖe edzi.
    Yehova nena wɔava eme
    tegbetegbe. Amen.

Jesus Christ should make it come
    through. Jehovah should make it
    happen everlasting. Amen.

Kpesusi was an ecumenical priest. Alongside the symbolic prominence of
the crescent moon was the cross—a rosary sits above Sanya's house and
Jesus' Sacred Heart is painted on an outside wall. All of this, however,
ultimately coheres into the patrimony of Lahare Kunde, as Kpesusi made
clear as he finished the prayer:

Oh! Lahare Kunde Sempa. Tɔgbui
    Kunde, nyatefe, evuya ʃom
    melea, wo Kunde ʃe vue.

Oh! Lahare Kunde the words are
    finished. Grandfather Kunde, truly,
    this drum that I play, it is you
    Kunde to whom it belongs.

Ati sia eɖo xɔme nawo.

This drumming stick has entered your
    room.

Nunana si wɔana, mexɔe le esi.
    Wɔawoe nye avu ɖeka, koklo
    wɔame ene, dadi, kple ahɔnoe.
    Bisia ya li, aha dze edzi.

The gifts that he should bring, I
    received from him. They are one
    dog, four fowls, a cat, and a dove.
    The kola is here, drink is added.

Esi mekɔ atsi sia de asi nea, wo
    Kundeɛ dem asi nee loo.

As I hand over this stick to him, it is
    you Kunde who puts it in his hand.

Mefia ho dzedo, ho dota, ho yixɔ,
    Yeve le ʃome, Agegbetɔ
    Agegbenɔ

I show it to the sunrise, the zenith, the
    sunset, thunder god in the sea,
    the god of the bush, male and
    female.

With these words he held the stick in his two hands and pointed it to his left, above his head, and to the right, and then invoked the following deep Ewe saying, the meaning of which was left unexplained:

Dzinukugba, dolisa.[5]   The moon breaks and the hole takes it.

With that he touched the stick to my hand three times, saying:

Mefiawo bo. Mefiawo   I showed your power. I show your
    agblɔʋu.   drumming stick.

Then he commanded:

Ɖo asi ɖaa!   Display your hand!

I held out my left hand, and, as he counted, he touched it with the stick seven times and handed it to me with the following blessing:

Nafo breketea—menye ekutɔ   Henceforth, play the *brekete*—not the
    me o, menye dɔtɔ me o.   death one, not the illness one. Beat
    Nafo breketea natsi agbe,   the *brekete* and live long, get money,
    akpɔ ga, awɔ nunyui ne   do good for Kunde and Tseriya!
    Kunde kple Tseriya loo!

He told me that the spirit of the gods was in the stick so that the drumming would go inside me, and I would start dreaming the rhythms of *brekete*. That was it: no other prayers to the other *gorovoduwo*, no offerings, nor cowrie divination; now just the hard work of drumming, and it was hard work, as Kpesusi never tired of reminding me.

To say that things proceeded smoothly, that I picked up the drumstick and magically overcame a lifetime of not playing, of course, would be far from the truth. Rituals and magic, despite lingering childhood fantasies, don't really work that way. This is not to say that nothing happened. When I first started drumming with the stick, it just didn't feel right; my earlier assessment of its weight and balance seemed suspect. It was appreciably heavier than other *brekete* sticks I had used, the padding on the handle seemed too short, the curve too acute. Frankly, it just felt wrong, uncomfortable to hold, let alone to beat the drum with, but there really wasn't much I could do about it—I certainly wasn't going to ask for a new one—so I tried to adjust the best I could.

The first few days of drumming were total frustration for both Kpesusi and me. His gentle spirit did not always carry over into his teaching. I heard "YOU'RE LATE" so many times about the melo-rhythmic figures I was trying to learn that I began to feel as if I were the rhythmic equivalent of that infamous Ghanaian sense of clock time. This was followed, thankfully, by a few days of kind of "getting it" which, unfortunately, were followed by days of not getting it at all. Kpesusi had no clue at all why one day I was clueless and the next on the way toward actually playing. Neither did I, and I was starting to get depressed, when something began to happen. It was not exactly the broom in *The Sorcerer's Apprentice*, but the stick did start taking on a life of its own, seeming to "talk" to my hand: "Hold me like this, not this. Don't grab so tight." The stick began to settle itself in the V of my palm between the lower part of my thumb and forefinger, and I started to have a greater sense of control. Holding it in this way allowed my fingers to release on open strokes and close around the handle for stopped ones. The differentiation between these strokes is absolutely crucial to playing the melo-rhythmic figures correctly, for they are defined by the resulting timbral difference, the first having a low booming sound, the latter a sharp crack that is focused. The two strokes quickly alternate and require an agility that had been a total mystery to me. The free stroke is fairly straightforward to play, but the stopped stroke is technically more difficult. The edge of the rounded end of the stick is pressed against the head, which I found difficult to do without tensing up. I had been trying to do this by lifting and turning my wrist, which caused it to tighten. But when I started to feel the stick being controlled in the V of my palm, the free fingers grabbing the handle for stopped strokes, it had the secondary effect of turning the end of the stick automatically, producing the required sound without tensing. This breakthrough in technique allowed me to physically (and rhythmically) relax, and all of a sudden I was able to play patterns I thought I never could. What I was learning was not so much an intellectual or auditory understanding of the music as a bodily one, a dance of the hand, and the first dance I learned, not surprisingly, given all the blood that was spilt over the making of the drumstick, was that of sacrifice.

The *lātsovu* (literally, "animal-cutting-drum") is played for the *lātsohawo* ("animal-cutting-songs") sung after major sacrifices such as a *fetatrɔtrɔ* (see chap. 1). These songs are considered some of the most powerful music in all of Lahare Kunde, as is the drumming. Kpesusi was taking me directly into the tradition—no preliminaries here, a movement from a stripped-down and simplified rendition for beginners, progressing to more and more complexity. It was the drumming equivalent of being thrown in the water and either sinking or swimming. There was something essential about this music, as I was soon to find out.

The first figure he showed me was the opening *brekete* call for Kunde. I use the term "show" intentionally, because that is how I initially learned. Kpesusi would drum a phrase, I would watch, then repeat it until I could play it with him. Audition, of course, is crucial, but the visual aspect, especially in the initial stages of learning, should not be underestimated. This also applies to the way those born into the tradition learn. Young boys watch drummers and try to emulate their bodily movement, at least as much as they listen to them, and I did the same with Kpesusi.

Although I could pretty much follow the sequence of open and stopped strokes that defined the figure and play it by itself, I was having trouble trying to figure out how the pattern fit with the timing of the bell—as was mentioned in relation to *agbadza*, all parts relate to the bell pattern in one and only one way—so I asked the bell player (one of his sons) to slow down. But Kpesusi reminded me, as if I were a bit dense on the uptake, that if the bell slowed down, then we wouldn't be playing *abey*, but *agbadza*. The bell's timing for *abey* has the same seven-stroke configuration of short and long values as that for *agbadza*, and, as far as I was concerned, "Same structure, same bell." It wasn't that Kpesusi was unaware of this fact. Naturally, the bell patterns for *agbadza* and *abey* are the same, that is a given, but the bell for *agbadza* is not a slow-downed version of the bell for *abey*, nor vice versa. They are two different kinds of groove, and that was precisely his point. This difference is not incidental, but fundamental. It speaks to a concrete musical experience that absolutely refuses to be reduced to abstraction. This is not a reflection of the inability of Kpesusi, or Ewes in general, to abstract, as an older discourse would have it, but a tenacity in holding on to what is actually there, and what is always there is the bell, whether for *abey*, *agbadza*, or numerous other Ewe musical styles, as drummers never tire of telling those of us who have trouble keeping track of such things. Exactly where the bell's timing begins and ends, however, is open to interpretation, a fact that has been of concern to more than one outsider trying to learn this music.

Even Odds

Ask an Ewe drummer "where one is"—that inevitable question asked by Western musicians when encountering this music for the first time—and he will tell you, "Listen to the bell." For *abey*, as it is for *agbadza*, the bell's timing is the hinge of a suspended musical world around which all else

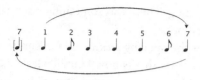

Ex. 5.1. *Abey* timeline

turns (ex. 5.1). We really don't have an equivalent term for this phenomenon in Western musical practice. It is something in between a meter and a rhythm, something that at once defines a rate of motion and gives that motion a life of its own. Heard from womb to tomb, this seven-stroke asymmetrical line covering the span of twelve pulses has assumed the contours of a naturalized aesthetic, a part of a musical physiology that embodies a deep Ewe sensibility.[6] More than merely an acoustical phenomenon, the bell's timing is held in the body of every drummer, singer, and dancer, because it is part of the body, the source from which it came and the destination of its specific realizations.[7] It is precisely as body that each refraction of the musical texture has the possibility to rehearse the bell in a different way.[8] When asked where "one" is, Ewe drummers tell you to listen to the bell because there is no "one."

Listening to the bell, however, can be a daunting task for a musician enculturated into a rhythmic approach that privileges a unilinear metrical scheme. For those who have come to this music later in life, for whom the bell's toll is not of the body, the timing doesn't seem to want to stand still. Logically we know that it is one phrase, one particular distribution of rhythmic elements, but the fixed pattern of the bell, at least to a newcomer, suddenly and spontaneously may shift its perceptual position, and, try as one might, one cannot seem to get it to go back to where it had been. Once this new perception becomes somewhat familiar and stable, it may suddenly shift its position once more back to that original perception, all done outside the realm of intention. It is something akin to the experience of seeing a drawing of a transparent Necker cube spontaneously shift (see fig. 5.6). First one may see the cube tilted downward, the next upward, something that initially occurs outside purposeful intention, though over time one can gain a certain amount of conscious control over the shifts.[9] In the timing for *abey*, what seemed entirely logical at the start—Aha! so this is how it works—sounds totally strange and out of place in the middle, only to end up the same at the end.[10]

This "wildness" has been mastered by the Ewes, domesticated, if you will, giving rise to a rhythmic imagination that is truly impressive from

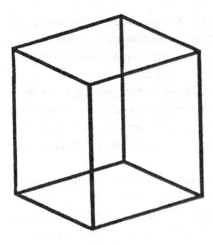

Fig. 5.6 Necker cube

any musical perspective. The imagination is, itself, an experienced sense of how things fit together while each part still maintains individual identity, thus forefronting cross-rhythmic contours. Cross-rhythms, however, are something quite different from merely playing two rhythms together, regardless of their degree of complexity. Genuine cross-rhythms do something—they cross—and this crossing is possible only within the parameters of a polymetrical framework, when at least two contrasting meters based on streams of unaccented beats of varying duration are present (see chap. 4, p. 113).[11] Everything else is mere syncopation, which is what African rhythm is often reduced to in Western eyes and ears, thus masking its rhythmic vitality and, more important, its ontological significance. Ewes have developed this rhythmic sense of crossing into an art that permeates not only musical life, but the very way people experience the world and each other. There is no one absolute stable ground to point to and from which to posit a world; rather, there are always multiple shifting grounds that are equiprimordial. Relationships, both social and cultural, physical and metaphysical, don't calcify into rigid formulations, closed and unwavering, but are continually opening out to that which is not there, thus a moral order fixed in absence, an exponential curve into possibility.

The bell's timing can readily be felt in a 2-pulse or 3-pulse beat, with the inherent possibility of these beats combining into additive and divisive arrays, namely, what Rose Brandel (1959) calls the African hemiola.[12] This African understanding of the musical potential of the primary binary opposition of even and odd, that six pulses can be arranged into a ratio of 3:2 (i.e., three groups of two [1 2 / 3 4 / 5 6] or two groups of three [1 2 3 / 4 5 6]) is not a mathematical formula acoustically realized, but an embodied ontology that is a fundamental attunement, a way of being-in-the-world that simultaneously entertains multiple rates of motion, gaits, to retrieve the equestrian metaphor. Just as the difference between a horse trotting and a horse galloping is more than a matter of speed, the difference between a 2-pulse and 3-pulse beat is not merely the former moving faster than the latter. For both, the difference is not only quantitative but qualitative. Along with Brandel, I want to rescue the term "hemiola" from its moorings in Western musical praxis and rethink its potential within an African context.

The work the hemiola does in Africa is not the same work it does in the West. In Western parlance, hemiola refers to a musical device used "for giving rhythmic variety" (Rushton 2001: 361–62). For the most part, this has been merely a rhythmic technique and has had no particular structural significance.[13] The African hemiola, on the other hand, is not some occasional rhythmic device, but something that runs deep in much of African musical life. It is as structurally important to musical thought as the authentic cadence is to functional tonality in Western art music.[14] Evidence is everywhere: in the drums of affliction found throughout southern and eastern Africa, where spirits are heated through specific drum rhythms grounded in the polymetrical principles of the hemiola (Friedson 1996); in the melodic threads that weave the *zar* spirits as well as the *bori* into a divine ride (Besmer 1983); in the dances of the !Kung Bushmen of the Kalahari (Marshall [1955] 1995); in the many shrines of West Africa and the diaspora (Wilcken 1992; Amira and Cornelius 1992); and so on.

A particularly striking example of the deep-seated nature of the hemiola can be found in the film *Baka: People of the Forest* (1988). In a remarkable scene two Baka men are fanning a fire to smoke out edible termites. One of the men begins beating on the ground with a bunch of leaves and the other joins in. Instead of beating the ground in a random rhythm or in synchrony with the other part, he immediately settles into supplying the other side of a hemiola. This impulse toward rhythmic complementarity invites participation in ways that resonate beyond the acoustical realm; it is a way of being-in-the-world that has profound moral and ethical dimensions (see Chernoff 1979 and Bebey 1975 on the importance of musical experience to African sensibilities).

In *brekete* drumming, hemiola brings forth the possibility of being-there-and-away by players and dancers who freely interact with each other in complex ways through and in multiple layers of cross-rhythmic elaboration. The fine grain of Ewe musical experience is inscribed in these delicate balances between metrical movements. It is the grace of this musical complexity to leave enough of a trace that a hint of the genius of this deep Ewe play can be had. Without it we would be describing only what we thought we had heard. Tracing this hint, however, perforce takes us into linguistic formulations of musical phenomena, always a problematic move. How do you describe that which is the gift of no language in language? Even the simplest of musical utterances seems to escape language's ability to take hold of what is musical about musical being, the musical thing, Charles Seeger's "linguo-centric predicament" (1961: 78). The best we can do is point the way, in the direction of where on the horizon it can be found, moving on the periphery of its limits where cross-rhythms both happen and cease to be. This place, always in motion, refuses to stand still for the analytic gaze of inquiring minds, its tracks and pathways open only to a type of phenomenological description that respects such movement. This is not a vicious circling, doubling back on itself, but the very movement that defines the center of attention. The moment this circling stops, the center is lost.

Nowhere in Brekete is this movement more clearly seen, heard, and felt, the principles of cross-rhythms and polymeters placed in bold relief, than in the clapping practices of shrine members, a musical phenomenon that deserves more attention than it usually gets.[15] Within its straightforward presentation the ambiguity of the timeline is clearly foregrounded, thus marking rhythmic paths that cross.

Akpefofo (Thanks-Beating)

Clapping (akpefofo), far from being the inconsequential accompaniment that most of the literature would lead you to believe, is, other than singing, the most direct way for a majority of people at a shrine event to participate in music making. (Only a relatively few have the technical facility and aural imagination to master the brekete drums, or, for that matter, interest in doing so.) The deceptively simple musical structure of clapping brings forth basic principles of Ewe rhythmic construction and is an important aspect of embodied musical experience. Within its confines we can begin to grasp the lived experience of an "ekstatic" musical time, a palpable sense of what it is like to be there in multiple ways, hence music's ontological significance. But first, we need to start with the actual physical act of clapping, something that has been totally overlooked in the scant literature on this subject.

Not everyone claps the same, either rhythmically or in kinesthetic terms. Most Westerners clap one hand against the other, with the dominant hand usually hitting at an angle against the weaker hand. Although this is not an answer to that famous Zen *koan*, it does result in "one-hand clapping." Most shrine members, on the other hand, clap with both hands parallel to each other, with flattened palms hitting together simultaneously. This tends to counteract the dominance of one hand, creating a rather sharp and loud percussive sound that engages the hands equally.[16] The potential of body concussion is brought forth not only in its increased decibel level but also the tuning of the body into a rather specific timbric band. This is to say nothing of the fact that we musically clap to the same beat, or at least try to, while Ewes always have the possibility of clapping to several different beats suggested by the structured ambiguity inherent in the cross-rhythmic texture of the music. Cross-rhythmic clapping is as "natural" to an Ewe as clapping synchronously is to us. As Jones (1959: 102) points out, "If from childhood you are brought up to regard beating 3 against 2 as being as normal as beating in synchrony, then you develop a two-dimensional attitude to rhythm which we in the West do not share."

In Brekete some people clap four times to one cycle of the bell (4 beats each composed of 3 pulses), other people clap six times (6 beats each composed of 2 pulses), and still others may freely mix the two, usually in a 3-beat (2 pulses per beat) + 2-beat (3 pulses per beat) pattern (ex. 5.2). In *abey* the 4-beat clap is clearly privileged—most people do clap it, along with a second *atoké* boat-shaped bell that also plays a steady four beats to one cycle of the timeline—but this does not mean that only one ruling meter predominates and the other parts play against it, as Chernoff (1979), Locke (1978), Agawu (2003, 2006), and others have suggested for similar Ewe styles that utilize this bell pattern. It would seem to make perfect sense that those who clap in 4, of course, hear the bell in a 4-beat metrical scheme. But quantity here does not trump quality, nor does it necessarily

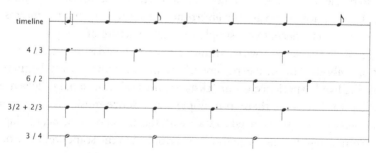

Key: number of beats / ♪ pulses per beat

Ex. 5.2. Clapping patterns

impart a squared metrical base to the timeline that all other parts relate to. And this gets to the crux of the debate. When people *are* clapping in 6 or a combination of 3 + 2, is this just a syncopated figure pressing on the 4-beat metrical structure, or are they actually hearing the bell in a different meter? If the latter, then the answer must be that they are hearing the bell in a 6-beat or 3 + 2-beat pattern (i.e., structuring their clapping to be isomorphic with the perceived meter of the bell) at the same time as others were taking the exact same timing and hearing the bell's timing in a 4-beat metrical form. This would result in polymetrical clapping, some people clapping and hearing the bell in 4 while others were clapping and hearing the bell in 6 or 3 + 2.[17] While I believe this to be a more cogent interpretation than the notion of a continuous syncopation, there is still another possible explanation that may be more in keeping with Ewe sensibilities.

If an abiding principle of Ewe rhythm is that there are always at least two different kinds of beats going on at the same time—and there is plenty of evidence for this—then the bell would not be isomorphic with the clapping, whether in 4, 6, or 3 + 2 beats, but in *cross-rhythmic relation to it*. In other words, if you clap in 4, then you would hear / feel the bell in 6 (or in 3 at fast speeds) and vice versa. This also holds for the 3 + 2 clapping; you would then hear the bell as 2 + 3. It is a cognitive shift that foregrounds a fundamental difference in approach to rhythmic praxis. From childhood, Ewes have been trained to hear and feel the other. This is not just a musical technique, but a specifically African approach to rhythmic life, a way of being-in-the-world that gives it energy and force. Instead of striving for similitude, difference is sought; homogeneity gives way to complementarity and relationality, the hemiola principle at work.[18]

From an African perspective the trick is to hold all of these metrical possibilities suspended in the body at the same time. This is not to say that all are realized at the same time, which is one criticism leveled against this kind of analysis. Just as Gestalt psychologists say you can't actually see both figures in a multistable illusion simultaneously (the figure-ground argument), the same could be said about acoustical illusions, implying that one can't actually hear two metrical patterns at the same time.[19] (Personally, I am not convinced that Ewes and other Africans cannot do this.) Regardless, you don't have to hear two things at once to have such possibilities in hand. Having both ready-to-hand gives the music a buoyancy, an uplift that is not a subjective occurrence felt inside but happens "out there" in between the players even when there is only one person involved, for cross-rhythms are always-already a being-with. This "condition of weightless balance," as Gadamer (1976: 53) puts it in his ontology of play, is an "absorption into the game . . . an ecstatic self-forgetting that is experienced not as a *loss* of self-possession, but as the free buoyancy of elevation above oneself" (55; italics in original). This buoyancy is what I am referring to here as rhythmic suspension. To enter the world of cross-rhythmic suspension is to enter the bodily realm of maintaining multiple beats in the body at the same time, something African dancers do as a matter of course (see Friedson 1996, chap. 4).

The suspension granted through this rhythm of the crossroads is not some kind of mental construct caught in the structural bones of a Lévi-Straussian binary opposition, but inscribed in the viscera of bodies that are both here and away. This bodily knowledge cannot be fully grasped except through the medium of its offering. It has particular contours and grooves that can be approached only through a bodily practice. This bodily feel is, following Geurts's (2002) idea of cultural senses, part of what Ewes call *seselelãme*, an attunement, a feeling tone of the body.[20]

In keeping with the synesthetic nature of this phenomenon, let me suggest that this suspended feeling is somewhat akin to the bodily sensation one gets when juggling. Tossing a ball into the air and catching it is not juggling, nor do we enter that domain when two balls are kept in the air, though both of these actions could be juggling in the hands of someone who can actually juggle. You always can work competence down. It is only when three objects are kept in motion by our two hands, which I take to be the essence of juggling, another kind of physical hemiola, that we break into that realm. This act of motional balancing grants suspension, a particular kind of attunement, an uplift—anyone who juggles is familiar with this phenomenon. What I am suggesting here is that there is something fundamental about the binary opposition of odd and even, twos and threes, which is rooted in the bilateral symmetry of the body, hence the power of the hemiola. In the music of Brekete this suspension is the cold fusion of receiving more energy than you put in.

Playing In-Between

Abey, as with *agbadza*, is shot through with hemiola not only in the bell and the clapping, but on all levels, including the drumming parts of the *kagaŋ* and *kidi*; the former is based on a metrical pattern of three, the latter on a metrical pattern of four, the two parts together forefronting the polymetrical possibilities of the bell's timing. I had learned these parts early on in my training, but Kpesusi insisted that I continually engage them during my apprenticeship, for, along with the bell and clapping,

Ex. 5.3. *Abey* supporting parts

these drums form a kind of macro-cross-rhythmic riff from which the lead drumming takes its cue.

Kidi in *abey* style, by itself, is simple and straightforward: two repetitions of the *kidi* part cover one cycle of the timeline, dividing it into two equal parts, which in turn are each divided into two equal parts (two dotted eighth notes followed by a dotted quarter note), producing a strong 4 feel in line with the main clapping pattern (ex. 5.3). (A simple variation that is often used is changing one of the dotted quarter notes to two dotted eighth notes.) What is of prime interest here is the fact that the pulse itself changes. 2 pulses of the *kidi* cover the same span as 3 pulses of the bell, a hemiola one level lower or higher depending on your analytical point of view. This results in 8 pulses being substituted for 12 pulses of one cycle of the bell and here strongly argues for a divisive rhythmic approach due to the change of the pulse. This "slowed-down" pulse has a particular flavor to it, especially given the incessant nature of the 12-pulse structure of the timeline, and offers evidence that drummers have a feel for a musical space that cannot only be additive but also be divided or carved in different ways. One could also, of course, analyze this as a change at the beat level—that is, a doubling of the 4-beat motion to 8 beats, the dotted eighth note taken as beat. But if we follow the definition of beat as a grouping of pulse, then this still would necessitate a change in the pulse (now to a dotted sixteenth note), thus a "pulse hemiola" (4 dotted sixteenth notes to 3 eighth notes of the timeline eighth-note pulse).

Cutting across the 4-beat feel of the clapping and the 8-pulse structure of the *kidi* is the dry, loud crack of the *kagaŋ*, playing a simple 2-pulse figure aligned to the 12 pulses of the bell, repeated three times to one cycle of the timing (see ex. 5.3).[21] Although one of the simplest patterns, *kagaŋ* beautifully illustrates cross-rhythmic principles. It always can be correctly timed by beginning on what I have labeled the first stroke of the bell (ex. 5.1). While I had known cognitively that one stroke of the *kagaŋ* synchronized with this stroke of the bell, the feel of the pattern escaped me. The *kidi* I could play, even with its change in pulse, because all I had to do was track the 4-beat clapping pattern, but the *kagaŋ* was a completely different matter. I couldn't "feel" how the three repetitions of the *kagaŋ* fitted with the timing of the bell, that is, until one day, while I was working on a *brekete* phrase, the *kagaŋ* player leaned over to take a drink of water and had only one hand to play his part, reducing it to the first stroke of the two-stroke repeating pattern, and all of a sudden the arterial that *kagaŋ* traveled revealed itself to me. These understandings that divulge themselves on the periphery, as it were, are not to be taken lightly, for they often speak of things immediately in front of our face that we neither see nor hear. I immediately stopped playing the *brekete* drum—I had learned long ago to not let such serendipitous moments pass unexplored—and asked the *kagaŋ* player to repeat what he had done. And, not surprisingly, he gave me a puzzled look and started to play the entire *kagaŋ* part. After no small amount of explaining, and a fair amount of reluctance on his part—the roll of the eyes syndrome that every researcher gets from his interlocutors in what must seem such strange requests—I finally got him to repeat the one-hand-*kagaŋ*-take-a-drink action. Playing only the first stroke, he was beating what seemed to me to be an offbeat timing, here the back part of a 3-beat (4 pulses per beat) meter (i.e., the third pulse of each beat). What had been so difficult—trying to fit the *kagaŋ* part with the bell—suddenly became easy when I concentrated less on the fit with the bell and let myself feel the offbeat timing of the *kagaŋ*. This, in essence, meant paying more attention to the metrical feel. This offbeat structure of *kagaŋ* suddenly gave the other layers of the ensemble a dynamism that enhanced their polymetrical potential. *Kagaŋ* was, as drummers say, like the salt in a stew, bringing out the individual flavors of the other parts (Locke 1978).

As the bell's timing began to take on a naturalized effect for me, feeling it on my skin as much as hearing it, and I felt more secure playing *kidi* and *kagaŋ*, I started shifting back and forth between the two drums during practice sessions, trying to gain a proficiency in changing rhythmic perspectives. This shifting from the strong 4-beat feel of the *kidi* to the offbeat threes of the *kagaŋ*, initially somewhat jarring, slowly turned into a reinforcement of both parts; one seemed to invite the other, calling to the other. Somewhere in the process—I am really not quite sure when—instead of hearing the part I was playing, I began feeling the other, and somehow it seemed that I was playing more than I actually was. How I was doing this I have no idea, but I soon realized that one part could not really exist without the other, for it was the play in-between the two that really mattered, generating something more than the sum of its parts.

Playing in-between this ontological riff—the drumming of *kidi* and *kagaŋ*, the timing of the bell, the clapping of the *adehawo*—is the virtuosity of a *brekete* drummer, the soaring of a human being in total control, "in the flow," to appropriate Csikszentmihalyi's (1990) terminology, his abilities exquisitely matched to the task at hand. Needless to say, this was something I was still struggling with as Kpesusi began teaching me Kunde's call.

Ghost Notes

As I watched, intent on following the asymmetrical pattern of open and stopped strokes that define Kunde's drum, I slowly began to realize that there was something else going on besides the obvious strokes of the right hand, something that was happening in its absence. In all of my concentration on the drumstick, first my own and now Kpesusi's, I had entirely forgotten about the left hand, Kunde's hand. Kpesusi's was almost always in motion, playing on the short end of the drumhead behind the snare. He seemed to be filling in the empty pulses, creating a steady stream of eighth notes, something Western-trained percussionists refer to as "ghost notes." The notes still sound but are sotto voce. In other words, in the opening ten-stroke phrase of Kunde (ex. 5.4), in which each stroke is based on a 2-pulse beat, every other pulse was being filled in by the left hand. I started to follow suit, and, once I engaged my left hand, the timing of the figure (and its variations) with the bell's timeline became much more secure and exact. The "you're late" mantra went from capital letters to lowercase and started to fade away altogether.

Both hands now working together, I became somewhat competent in playing Kunde's words, for all the rhythmic figures for *lātsovu*, the drumming specific to sacrifices, are defined by timbral changes that talk. Kunde's drum speaks Hausa, and, not surprisingly, given the ethos of the foreigner, it speaks of strangers:

> Bako mei geri me bebe ido bei   Stranger with the big eye cannot know
>   geni yafi me kesa.   all that the owner does.

In relation to Kunde it speaks of the fact than no Ewe will ever know all there is to know about the gods. They came from the north, and those in the south, who currently have the gods, are only their caretakers. This well-known Hausa proverb is translated into the drumming and Eweized understanding of Hausa as

Kaka mako_, mako mangari
to to to ta ta to ta to to ta

yafi di yai benza mugu ya[ro]
ta ta ta ta   to ta ta ta ta

(Drum vocables: to = open; ta = stopped)

In *brekete* music, Twi, Hausa, and Dagarti are almost always approximations, interpretations by people who do not speak the language.

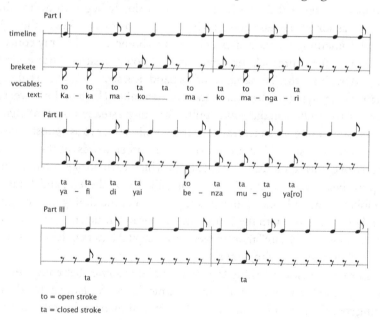

Ex. 5.4. Kunde's *lātsovu* (drum motto for animal sacrifice)

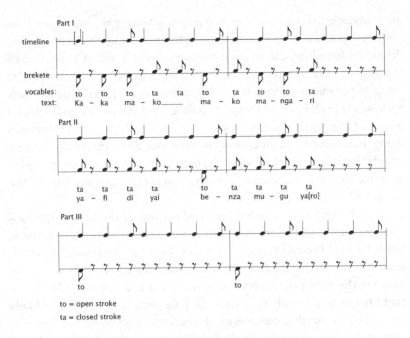

Ex. 5.5. Ablewa's *lātsovu* (drum motto for animal sacrifice)

The entire figure is composed of three distinct parts, taking six repetitions of the bell to play. It is timed in an obvious 6-beat meter that cuts across the strong 4-beat feel of the clapping (in *abey* this pattern is forefronted), the second *atoké* bell, and the *kidi* support drum. The opening ten-stroke phrase starts on the last mark of the bell, and its highly asymmetrical arrangement of open and stopped strokes obviates a feeling of regularity, seemingly meant to destabilize. This asymmetry, however, is counterbalanced with what follows: a four stopped-stroke pattern that is repeated, though slightly altered, with the addition of one open stroke, and the third part, which merely plays the first stroke of the timing twice (ex. 5.4). Tseriya's drum, sonically reflecting the fact that she is married to Kunde, is exactly the same, except for a change in the third part (ex. 5.5). What is ontologically significant here, to make the point one more time, is neither the figure, nor the fact that it talks of strangers, but the fact that it creates a sense of crossing, creating a timbral and rhythmic space in-between.

With this figure more or less in hand, a curious thing started to happen: what had been random sounds in the environment began to take on musical meaning. The first time I noticed this I was walking by the local maize-grinding machine when it suddenly gave out three loud knocks. I spontaneously heard this as the three opening strokes of Kunde's drum and found myself, without thinking about it, filling in the rest of the phrase. This was not the only time such a thing had happened. The soundscape was, in essence, becoming rhythmized—I was hearing *brekete* everywhere in all kinds of things, including my dreams. The gods took on an aural presence that was pervasive in its absence. In fact this rhythmized being-there became so all encompassing it was a bit unnerving. To give this rhythmic life some kind of outlet became a virtual necessity if I didn't want the sounds to totally overtake my existence. Drumming seemed like it was no longer an optional activity.

Over the next several weeks I learned the rest of the *lātsovu* figures—those for Bangle and his retinue, considered the most powerful drumming fitting for a soldier, and Wango, the god of the waters and roads (see www.remainsofritual.com for transcriptions)—and simultaneously was introduced to the appropriate ways of elaboration. It was also around this time that I began to seriously start chewing kola. *Brekete* drumming and kola seemed to go together, the energy of one feeding off the other. There is, I was to find out, nothing quite like playing *brekete* after chewing kola and having a few tots of gin. Regardless of the political correctness of all of this, we should not underestimate the power of these substances to alter consciousness in a way favorable to musical performance. Psychoactive substances have had a long relationship with music in many different cultures, and, although there may be many cogent sociological, cultural, and psychological explanations for this phenomenon, there is, also, a musical reason that should not be overlooked.

As I continued my drumming with Kpesusi, the process pretty much remained the same. He would show me a figure and I would repeat it, but the learning became foreshortened (I was getting things much quicker), allowing for more material to be introduced. As I tried to play more complex and extended variations, however, I had more difficulty getting these more complicated parts straightaway, and the dreaded refrain of "Listen to the bell!" began to reappear. By now, frankly, I was sick of hearing this phrase and paid little attention to it. Of course I was supposed to listen to the bell, but that magic formula sometimes just didn't seem to do the trick. One day while I was struggling with a particularly difficult variation, accompanied by that incessant command, it suddenly crossed my mind that I was assuming something about what Kpesusi was saying that was not really being said. It was not exactly a new insight but more a remembering of something I had forgotten. It occurred to me that maybe he was not telling me to play *with* the bell, to figure out how the part fit with the timing, as I had been trying to do, but, rather, to listen to how the drumming rubbed up against the bell, as it were, played against it, what kind of cross-rhythms it created with the particular perception of the timing pattern. I was suddenly rediscovering a lesson I previously had learned about supporting drum parts but now applied to the *brekete*. With this realization an audible and bodily felt "click" happened, as if the cogs of a wheel had come together and an interior space in *brekete* opened up, a depth to the music, a still place that was riding right on the surface of things, where everything was happening, where paths crossed.

In this musical experience of crossing, no part, no rhythm, is a thing unto itself. To exist in such a time one has to be at least aware of what is crossing with what, and thus *brekete* drummers somehow must also maintain, or be engaged in, pay attention to, a doubled existence, one that is precisely a playing-in-between. And with this we also reach perhaps the limit of language's ability to speak of what is phenomenally happening, and the musical body takes over.

Dancing at the Crossroads

Sometimes, when things seemed to be going particularly well, when I felt I was playing more than my hands would allow, Kpesusi would spontaneously begin to dance, giving me the opportunity to experience in some small way what it is like to drum for a priest. When a *sofo* dances, something of an elegance lays hold, and there was no more elegant a dancer than Kpesusi. There is an inward grace about his style that radiates outward. One only has to look at the smiles on the faces and the nods of the heads of those who watch him when he dances for confirmation of that fact. Light on his feet, his body seems to float over shifting surfaces. One doesn't learn to move like that, one is born to it.

This was especially true when he danced *abey*. Unlike the classic backbreaking style of *agbadza* for which the Ewes are famous, *abey* dancing involves more foot and hand movements, many of which are iconic, at least when performed by men. Crossing the hands with outstretched palms and straight fingers in a quick cutting motion is symbolic of slitting a throat, whether of an animal for sacrifice or an enemy in war; or bringing one's crossed arms close to the chest is indicative of an embrace by the *sofo* of his members, a symbol of love. Foot movements are always done softly, like those of a hunter stalking his game, except for the occasional emphatic stomp on the ground at heightened moments, perhaps indicating a kill.

Some of these movements were adapted from celebrations for Tɔgbui Zik-pui, the war stool, when dancers would demonstrate their power with cut-ting motions, and stomping their feet; others from the *ade* hunting dance of the northern Ewes, who, it seems, were in turn influenced by Ashanti dancing, especially the funeral dance of *adowa*; while still others seem to have originated uniquely with Brekete.

Dancing *abey*—consistent with the timing of the bell, drums, and clap-ping—is itself a polymetrical exercise. Danced bodies, by their very defini-tion, are always musical ones, and what has been said about the ontology of cross-rhythms also applies here, though, as with the acoustical evidence of the percussion ensemble, the sheer physical movement may be mislead-ing. The core movement of the feet figures a strong undercurrent of a duple beat based on a walking step, each step subdivided into four equal pulses. The left foot lifts out on the fourth pulse and then steps back in place on the first pulse, followed by the right foot in a short step on the sec-ond, ending with another left step on the third pulse. This sequence is then repeated, leading with the right foot, with the whole movement covering one cycle of the timeline. This produces a basic kind of shuffle step that is accompanied by a free swing of the arms that follows the natural inclina-tion to cross our bodies when we walk (i.e., right arm swings out as the left foot is put forward on pulse four). While this movement of the feet and arms is clearly articulated when women dance, for men the shuffle steps in between the main lift and step are often suppressed, creating a more walk-like dance. This seems to free the hands for more elaboration of the iconic movements mentioned earlier, something the women do not do.

Once again, there is no doubt that the rhythmic structure of this dance easily can be analyzed in a simple 4-beat meter, something that on the sur-face of things makes perfect sense; and, once again, the ontological depth of this phenomenon will be missed, a case of mistaking, to invoke Geertz invoking Ryle (Geertz 1973: 6), twitches for winks.[22] The foot movement is a 4-beat feel *in cross-rhythmic relation* to the possible 6-beat feel of the bell. This cross-rhythmic relation is forefronted further at the level of the pulse: 12 pulses for the bell's timing and 8 pulses for the feet, as in the *kidi* part. Following cross-rhythmic principles, danced bodies also rub against the various beats of the music in complex and shifting ways. Dancers them-selves instantiate and embody the principle of the crossroads.

In drum and dance the crossroads are distilled into temporal flows elaborated across the metrical possibilities of the African hemiola, an ontomusicological structure that always-already calls out to the other. This is not a matter of three *against* two, or two *against* three, as it is usually stated, a stance that flattens this rich musical world to a single rhythmic perspective, a mere semblance of itself. The African hemiola, rather, is not against anything; it embodies a deeper duality, one where both sides of the ratio are continually and equally responding to each other's call. What is primordial in this calling response, however, is neither one side nor the other, even or odd, but what dwells in-between these primary boundaries; it is where the roads cross. This in-dwelling is the phenomenon of shifting granted through the suspension of polymetrical possibility, the lifeblood of a musical way of being-in-the-world that is precisely in-between such nodal existence. Happening in the in-between, musical experience makes a claim on those who are there by way of those who are away. It is first and foremost in musical experience that the varieties of religious experience, to invoke an ancestor closer to home, take hold.

I call mother earth, that which one cannot jump over,
Land where fathers and mothers are buried
—Invocation by an Afa diviner

Burials 6

The ritual performed by Kpesusi, the remains of which can be seen on the front cover of this book, was both a blessing and a protection (see pp. 4–5). During morning prayers Wango, the god of the waters and roads, had warned him that trouble was on its way. Somehow it was all connected to Anibra's death and the woman who came in gold and high heels the day Kwamiga and I danced (p. 95). Kpesusi had been in the room when she had offered me the gods, but, unlike the other *sɔfowo*, he had always thought that she was a Mami Wata. After all, I lived on the beach. Regardless of who she was, one thing was for certain: the rituals he had seen in my future were coming due.

When Anibra's daughter, or whoever or whatever she was, offered me the gods and I refused, I thought that was the end of it. But, as with most things having to do with the shrine, it turned out to be not that simple. It seems the gods were coming my way regardless of whether I planned on getting them or not. Of course I hadn't planned on having my life threatened, either, or being caught up in what eventually took on the contours of a grade-B movie complete with characters named Baba, Blackie, and the Rastaman (at least that is what most people called him), the last of whom was "going to get macho men from the rasta mafia in Lome" and kill me and my wife in the middle of the night. I had been in the United States for the past nine months, and, to say the least, this was not exactly my idea of a warm homecoming. But this threat set in motion a field of ritual action that ended up with Sakra Bode, the god of the land, being buried in the center of our compound.[1] And when you get Sakra you get all the *trɔwo*, because a part of each is in him.

The Case

On the surface it was all about walls and sea views—I built the former and the Rastaman wanted the latter—but we were merely bit players in a long-standing feud between an uncle, who was the ostensible head of a lineage, and his nephew, the stool father, who, given the convoluted polygonous kinship patterns in this part of Africa, was actually the older of the two. The uncle was a junior brother of the nephew's father; thus he, along with all such patrilineally related nephews, called him *tɔɖia*. Both were well over seventy-five and had been at each other's throats long before I ever stepped foot in Ghana. For decades they had been taking each other to court, usually over land disputes, with nothing ever seeming to get resolved.

Spiritually, the nephew was considered more powerful than the uncle, because he controlled the stool house where the war stools, thus spirits of the ancestors, resided. One does not choose to become a stool father; rather it is the stools themselves (i.e., the ancestors) who recruit the one who will take care of them. He seemed well suited for the job, having been a soldier in the Royal West African Frontier Force in World War II (the scars were still visible where he was bayoneted in the side during the Burma campaign), a policeman for the British administration of the Gold Coast, and eventually a security guard at the University of Ghana. He was a serious man, not someone to be fooled with. When he decided to retire and return to his hometown of Adafienu on the eastern coast of Ghana, however, he did not consider himself a "traditional" man at all, and though he respected tradition, placed little credence in the old ways.

But within six months of settling into his new house he started catching glimpses, fleeting images, of old people dressed in white cloth who were calling out his name. Whenever he greeted them, they would disappear, and when he went looking for them, they were nowhere to be found. He also began having disturbing dreams: the ancestors were berating him because they wanted something, but he would invariably awake before he could figure out what it was. Try as he might to ignore all of this, the intensity of the sightings and the anxiety of his dreams increased to the point that he thought he was going to lose his mind. He eventually consulted an Afa diviner, though it was against his nature to do so, given his mind about tradition at the time, and it was revealed through the casts what to everyone else was obvious: the stool house wanted him as its father, and he must either respond to the call or go crazy and die. The nephew, if nothing else, was a pragmatic man and, regardless of what he believed, knew he had no choice. He abandoned his new house and moved into his ancestral home, where the stool house was located.

When I finally met him in 1997, he had been stool father for over ten years, and for those ten years he never once had left the house on Wednesdays, even to attend court cases involving his uncle. Wednesday was the day he attended to the stools, which meant he could not have sexual relations the night before, could not leave his compound regardless of the reason, and could only wear a knee-length waist wrap of white calico, nothing else. It was on that day that he entered the stool house to talk to the ancestors, offer them drink, and find out what they wanted.

The stool house is serious business and not for the faint of heart, for if the stools are not properly cared for, illness and death will surely ensue, not only for whoever is the stool father, but for members of his family as well. It took three years after I met him before he finally offered to take me inside. And each time I have been inside, which only have been a few, I was also dressed in a calico wrap, but led in walking backward. According to the stool father, in the old days if you were called to the stool house because of some transgression and walked in facing forward, you invariably would leave feet first. That is why the inner room has a very low entrance, which requires one to stoop down. When the person was brought out after the stools had passed judgment, the victim's head was knocked against the low overhang, and that is when he or she would be killed.

These were the war stools of his ancestors blackened with blood, possessed of immense power and deep knowledge. I asked him once how he had acquired such detailed (and historically accurate) knowledge of Ewe history and he replied, "The stools, of course." In return for his service the stools have taught him much, protected him through the years, and imparted a fair amount of spiritual power. The stool father was a man who said his piece and did not countenance much. As a result, many in the community didn't particularly care for him, but, nonetheless, they respected him; more important, they feared him.

The uncle, on the other hand, was a staunch Catholic who lived in Lome, the nearby capital of Togo, and, as with many Africans of such a bent, thought traditional religion was nothing but a bunch of superstitious beliefs that were seriously hindering development. For some twenty years he had been a low-level administrative employee of the World Health Organization stationed in what was then called Zaire (the Democratic Republic of Congo). Now retired, he was living on, at least according to him, a sizable pension from WHO, which, given the per capita income in this part of Africa, made him a relatively rich man. He had never spent much time on the other side of the border in Ghana, only coming to Adafienu when family business demanded it, and nothing had ever happened, or was likely to, that would have changed his mind about traditional life. His wealth made him an *amega* (a big man) and, as head of a lineage, someone to reckon with.

By the time the Rastaman and I had arrived on the scene, the air was so poisoned between the two that they were literally having a hard time breathing. The uncle had already suffered one heart attack, and the stool father was in the beginning stages of congestive heart failure. We were merely pawns in what turned out to be one last episode of gamesmanship between two old rivals.

It all started when the uncle sold a piece of property to the Rastaman, the director and lead performer of a folkloric drum and dance troupe based in Lome. They performed a mixture of different African music and dance styles, promoting themselves as the bearers of a "traditional" and "authentic" African culture. They had had some minor success and had toured Germany several times, where the Rastaman had met his German wife.[2] She was the one who put up the funds to buy the property, which initially was to be used as a training site for his troupe. The land was situated directly behind the eastern portion of the land the stool father had given me five years before.[3] He had given me the land because he wanted to see the area developed and thought that having white people on the beach would at least get things started. Unlike Westerners, for whom beachfront property is, for the most part, highly desirable and very expensive, Ewes have no particular desire to be on the seaside. Who wants to be somewhere that requires constant upkeep due to the constant sea breeze (salt in the air corroding everything), where there is a general lack of access to roads and markets, and who would want to live among fishermen, who are considered to be rough and crude people? Most Ewes, in fact, thought we were crazy for building there, to say nothing of the fact that most other Ghanaians thought we were not only crazy, but in constant danger, living among the Ewes with all their *juju*.

It wasn't until we started walling in the part of the property in front of the Rastaman's that I found out that the uncle also had told him and his wife that the land directly in front of theirs wasn't owned by anyone. They were led to believe that they could use it to build facilities to house a cultural center—she had visions of German tourists enjoying seaside views—the uncle knowing full well that the land had been given to me years before. He also knew that this was going to cause me a fair amount of aggravation—an irate German wife, a disgruntled husband, and a land dispute—thus ultimately problems for his nephew, which was exactly what he wanted. The details of how this endgame played itself out, typical of the Ewes, were byzantine and, although fascinating in themselves, a blow-by-blow description of the "he did this; she did that" variety is ultimately beside the point. The point here is the threat, for it was this piece of business that brought the gods.

People say lots of things in the heat of the moment, and often threats are just that, never progressing beyond the verbal. But when the Rastaman tore down part of the wall and Baba and Blackie, one a convicted murderer who had killed a Gabonese diplomat in Togo and the other an armed robber wanted by the Ghanaian police, showed up at our compound, I started to take the threat seriously. I couldn't fathom how things could have gotten to this point over a wall, but they had. The whole convoluted series of events was beginning to spin out of control, taking on a life of its own beyond the intentions of the uncle or his nephew. This was territory way outside the usual bounds of ethnographic research, and, frankly, thinking that my life and my wife's might actually be in danger, I was ready to pack up and head home. But I had responsibilities to more people than just myself, and leaving would be no easy matter. It was at times like this that trying to maintain my in-betweenness, sliding toward one or the other side of the equation, became a little too slippery for comfort.

When Baba and Blackie arrived at our compound looking for me, there was no small irony in the fact that I happened to be at the police station with my wife making a formal complaint against the Rastaman for destruction of property. We had tried to resolve the case through a traditional form of arbitration within the family—the Rastaman was matrilineally related to the uncle—but when, after a meeting of the elders, which included the uncle and the stool father, had heard our two sides and the family ruled that I had a right to build a wall on my property, the Rastaman had refused to accept the results. It was after that meeting that he had torn down part of the wall, swearing that he would never let it be built. The next day I had been summoned to the chief's house, where members of the family had gathered, and told that they could no longer be responsible for the actions of this wayward relative.[4] They had washed their hands of the matter and advised me to go to the police, make a formal complaint, and send the case to court. In the old days this action of the family would have been a serious sanction, but this nephew, the uncle's sister's son, could not have cared less. And that is why I was at the police station and not at the compound when Baba and Blackie arrived.

By the time I got back they had already left, but their presence could still be felt and seen in the eyes of those who had talked to them. They had said they were looking for me because they wanted to hire some white students to play drums for the president of Togo and were willing to pay five million CFAF (the currency used in Francophone Africa and worth about seven thousand dollars at that time)—a rather bizarre story that no one was buying. Several people had recognized them—Blackie had a thick scar that started on his forehead and traveled down past his eye, and Baba was a well-known character in the border town of Aflao—and, given their rather strange excuse for being there, everyone was unnerved.

Whatever their reason, I was taking no chances and immediately returned to the police station. When the inspector heard who had come to our compound, he sent me straight to the district BNI (Bureau of National Investigation) office, the Ghanaian equivalent of the FBI. And once they heard about who was looking for me, they bluntly told me that these two individuals were dangerous and I should not take this lightly, then proceeded to tell me that there was not really much they could do. They had been trying to arrest Blackie for sometime without much luck, and Baba was out on parole. As for the Rastaman, since the case was headed for court and no direct evidence connected the three, their hands were tied. As I left, however, they suggested that my wife and I might want to think about sleeping somewhere else that night.

The Cast

Operating on the "when in Rome" mode, I immediately sent for the local chief's diviner to consult Afa, not only the name of the god, but also that ancient divination system found throughout the Guinea Coast.[5] No traditional-minded Ewe would ever consider confronting any serious situation such as the one I was facing without first checking things out with a *bokɔ*, as Afa diviners are called. Trying to cover all my bases, I also went to see Old Man—actually he was in his early thirties, but that is how he was known in *zongo*, the Islamic quarter situated in Xedzranawo across from the Denu market—and arranged for some added security. If something was headed my way, I was doing my best to be prepared for it on all fronts. Old Man was the local traveling butcher, the kind who comes to your house and will slaughter a ram or goat for you in the traditional Islamic way—the animal is given a small drink of water as a Qur'anic verse is recited, and a quick cut is made in the middle of the throat—something he had done for me more than once.

He was a well-known figure in *zongo*, which also meant he knew most of the *"zongo* boys," those somewhat suspect youths that most Ewes considered to be ruffians, who smoked "wee" and were always ready for a fight. I found Old Man hanging around the market and, after telling him what had happened, asked if he could arrange for a contingent of these youths to act as watchmen during the night. When he heard that Baba and Blackie were looking for me, he didn't hesitate to inform me that I did indeed need extra protection and that he would see what he could do. Shortly after sunset the *zongo* boys showed up and proceeded to organize themselves into details, complete with passwords, to "patrol" the outside of the compound. And although I spent a somewhat restless night, they turned the whole affair into a party. To their disappointment and my relief, nothing happened. Early the next morning they went back to *zongo*, and that is when the *bokɔ* arrived with Afa bag in hand, which contained the *prima materia* of his vocation (but more about the bag later).

Though I knew Old Man only casually, the *bokɔ* was someone I had worked with for years and had consulted many times. As with all the Afa diviners I had ever met, he had a playful, almost trickster spirit about him that was often in contrast to the serious business at hand. But this was not surprising. Afa is all about possibility and paths, and thus the crossroads. And wherever you find the crossroads you will find Legba, the guardian of thresholds but also the trickster nonpareil in this West African religion (Pelton 1980; Herskovits 1958, 1938, vol. 2). Legba of the crossroads, by the way, is not confined to West Africa. The Middle Passage made sure of that. In one famous sighting on the western side of the Black Atlantic, he was seen at a crossroads in the Mississippi Delta at midnight in the guise of a tall dark stranger teaching the legendary bluesman, Robert Johnson, how to "tune" his guitar.

Fig. 6.1 Legba "dressed" at the entrance to a village after a sacrifice (Elise Ridenour)

The relationship between Afa and Legba, destiny and the trickster, fate and the fortunes of chance, is revealed in a large corpus of myth and lore found throughout the Guinea Coast. In 1931 Melville and Frances Herskovits collected one such myth in Dahomey, modern-day Benin.[6] Full of striking imagery and condensed poetics, it is worth one more retelling, if for nothing else but its aesthetic value alone. In the spirit of African storytelling, I have rearranged and interpolated some material from other sources:

Afa and Legba are siblings. They are not exactly brothers, nor are they exactly brother and sister, though they are born of the same parent, Mawu, the supreme deity. Whereas Legba is usually spoken of as male with an insatiable sexual appetite (see p. 3), Afa, as with Mawu, is both male and female.[7] Afa (taken here in her female form) lives on top of a palm tree in the sky and with her sixteen eyes watches over the three realms of Mawu's creation: the earth, the sky, and the sea.[8] When Afa sleeps at night, she closes her eyes, but when she awakes, she is unable to open them by herself. Therefore, every morning Legba climbs the palm tree in the sky and asks Afa which eyes she wants opened. Since Afa does not want anyone to overhear what is said, she puts one palm nut in his hand if she wants two eyes opened, and two palm nuts if she wants one eye. Each eye that is opened looks into one of the sixteen doors of the house of the future that Mawu built when the universe was created. Casting Afa is the key that unlocks these doors that open out into the destinies of the world.

Everything that will ever happen on earth, according to Afa, already has happened in the sky—there *is* nothing new under the sun—and, in that sense, it is a closed and deterministic world. But with that many destinies converging, diverging, and crossing one another, virtually anything is possible, and that is why there is not one door to the future, not one irreversible destiny, but many. Afa is not fatalistic, but shot through with possibility—closing one path always leads to another. The *boko's* art is to navigate these multiple paths, helping to close some and open others. And every opening and every closing is a crossroads where choices are made and destinies taken up or abandoned. That is why every Afavi, a child of Afa, has a Legba installed at his gate when he receives his birth *kpɔli*, the cast he was born with.

We are all born with a *kpɔli*; it is part of who we are as human beings, part of our *se*, our destiny, though not all of us, Ewes included, choose to find out. It is the irony of Afa that the more you know, the less freedom you may end up having in your life (Rosenthal 1998: 186). As one *boko* told me, when you get your *kpɔli*, it often tells you that you will have to give up something you like the most—say, a certain food or drink. Afa may be telling you that you are wasting away your luck and fortune by indulging such a desire and thus shortening your life.

When a *boko* divines, whether it be to find out your life *kpɔli* or to figure out how to clear some path that has been blocked, like Legba, he opens the eyes of Afa. There are two basic ways to do this, both procedures based on three simple rules: (1) take four items, (2) that can take two forms, (3) and organize the results into a lineage—some casts are older than others (Bascom 1969: 10). These simple rules (the last one, however, may not be so simple) generate an exceedingly rich and complex body of material. At the center of these two procedures governed by three rules (a divinatory hemiola, to extend a musical metaphor) and thus at the center of Afa divination is the element of chance. Chance, however, looks like chance only from a lower stratum of being. The aleatory nature of Afa is meant to remove the human equation in establishing the foundation for meaningful action. This is not to say that the agency of the *boko* does not come into play as the divination unfolds. But in throwing the casts, ideally, human volition is factored out. It is Afa who, sitting on top of the palm tree in the sky with a bird's-eye view (sixteen of them), reveals the ways, the ins and outs, of what, from a world's-eye view, seems like randomness. Afa is the alphabet of Mawu, thus the language of the sky. *Bokɔwo* are needed because they are able to read by way of the casts at least some of the vast potential of this language.

There are a myriad of reasons having to do with the vicissitudes of life for which Afa is consulted: someone is sick and what usually works as a remedy works no longer and the person wants to find out why; or a couple is unable to conceive, and if they do, they want to know what ancestral soul (*dzotɔ*) is reincarnated in their new son; or somebody is plagued by troublesome dreams, as the stool father was; or someone is undertaking a new business venture and seeks to ensure success; or success brings envy to that man and he wants to know what trouble might be around the corner and who may be behind it; or relatives seek to find out the cause of death of one of their kin; or someone wants to make sure of a favorable outcome in a land dispute; or wants to know why his crops, or love life, or health is failing; and so on. I had come to Afa in order to find out how to close at least one path that seemed to be getting increasingly dangerous and open another with a more gentle future.

Guns, Ghosts, and Graves

On numerous occasions when I have consulted Afa, the results have been uncannily resonant with the circumstances surrounding the reason why I had sent *adza*, the token payment given to a *bokɔ* to call him to perform *afakaka* (Afa divination). This is not to say, however, that there have not been other times when the connection between my queries and what I was hearing from Afa has seemed tenuous at best. But, by far, in the majority of my encounters with Afa, my situation has been addressed not only accurately, but in very specific terms, and I am not the only ethnographer who has commented on these kinds of "coincidences" (Rosenthal 1998: 169–73).

Afa is deeply situated in a Guinea Coast cultural zone, but so were those other researchers, including myself. After all, isn't that why we do research for extended periods of time? We all were living in a field of action and forces that must have had significant influences on our experiences regardless of our epistemological orientation, our methodological stance, or whether we consciously knew it or not. This is not a matter—for Ewes or ethnographers—of "belief," that catchall term used by anthropologists, sociologists, psychologists, psychiatrists, and numerous others to explain away the uncanny when it is encountered, the placebo effect raised to the level of religion. One does not have to "believe" in Afa—I certainly didn't—for it to work in the way it was intended. Paths are opened and closed continuously in our lives; we are just not usually aware of it. Afa divination is but one way to take off the blinders and earplugs, to borrow a metaphor from Charles Keil (1979: 199), and listen to the possibilities that lie right in front of us. These possibilities, however, are always circumscribed by very particular circumstances in very specific locations. So when the *bokɔ* came that morning to our compound and threw Afa, I really wasn't surprised when my cast came up "GbeNɔli," a *du / kpɔli* all about guns, ghosts, and graves. (When the *gumaga* chain is used [see below] to determine the cast, it is usually referred to as a *du*; when especially consecrated palm nuts are used, the cast is called a *kpɔli* [see n. 10], though these words are often interchangeable.)

Before the initial cast was thrown and GbeNɔli appeared, the *bokɔ*, as he always does, took out his bag of divination objects, the *vodzi*, and poured them on the floor to his right side, the side of strength.[9] As he sifted through this pile of stuff—animal bones, skulls of various birds, kola nuts, cowries, sea shells, old glass trade beads, shards of pottery and porcelain, different kinds of seeds, and other things not so traditional, such as the plastic hand from a doll, a double-A battery, and just about anything else he had found (or, perhaps better put, that Afa had sent his way) that he thought would be of help in reading the mind of Afa—he called out the names of many *voduwo* and *trɔwo*, his ancestors, and the old *bokɔwo* and, by doing so, was calling them to enter those things he was stirring up, to give them power and force, to let them speak the truth.

He then pulled out two *gumaga* chains, open-ended necklaces each strung with eight seeds, which are used to determine the different casts.[10] Each seed on the chain has been split lengthwise, resulting in a seamless convex back side and a concave open front that is naturally divided into two parts by a medial ridge.[11] If the back side of the seed shows its face, which means it is resting, two marks are made; if the concave divided side, which means it is awake, one mark is made. In the calculus of Afa $2 = 1$ and $1 = 2$, and, as we shall see, $4 = 256$. The *bokɔ* holds the *gumaga* chain in the middle, which has slightly more space between the seeds (the others are pretty much equidistant), so that when it is thrown, each side has four seeds that land in various face-up and face-down configurations (rules 1 and 2). Given the fact that there are four seeds on each side of the necklace when thrown, there are statistically sixteen casts (4^2) in which both sides are exactly the same. These are considered the original children of Afa and are the oldest and most powerful casts.[12] Because most of the time both sides of the cast do not land in the statistically rare same configuration, there are a total of 256 possible combinations (16²), each with its own name.[13] Not only are the 256 casts named, but each has numerous verses, myths, parables, stories, and songs associated with it, and each one of these points to specific sacrifices, certain food taboos, behaviors to avoid, such as arguing or worrying too much, places to stay away from, and innumerable other things that can clear the path of one's destiny, or, if need be, change it (though this is possible only to a limited degree). This wealth of knowledge—some have compared a senior *bokɔ*'s training as equivalent to earning a Ph.D. (Ottenberg and Ottenberg 1960)—is a treasure trove of traditional wisdom. And this is only the surface manifestation of an infinitely deep hermeneutical world. Significantly, *bokɔwo* relate to these casts not as signs to be read, texts to be deciphered, or symbols to be contemplated, though they and their clients, in fact, do all of this. Rather they treat the *kpɔliwo* as living entities, each with its own personal history, life story, and particular experiences.[14] Reading a text and "reading" what amounts to another person are two very different things. Hearing a *bokɔ* talk *and* sing to the various casts, seeing him gesture and point as if speaking to another person, is striking, a performative aspect of Afa that can be appreciated only in its recital. Afa is literally alive with meaning.

Holding both of the *gumaga* chains in his hands, the *bokɔ* invoked the "strong cross." Raising his hands to the left, above his head, and to the right, he spoke to each direction:

> *To the left:*
> Ho dzedo ("strong-force-rising / fire / coming")   Where the sun rises

> *Above:*
> Ho dota ("strong-force-rising / course / head")   Where the sun reaches its zenith

> *To the right:*
> Ho yixɔ ("strong-force-rising / go / room")   Where the sun sets

Drawing one plane of the cross through this action now he invoked the second:

To the left:

Yeʋe le ɟume   Thunder God in the sea

To the right:

Agee le Gbeme   God of the Bush

After inscribing this version of the crossroads, he took the *gumaga* chains
and swung them four times, each time grabbing the open ends. On the
fourth throw he touched the middle of the chains to the ground. This is
called "bowing *gumaga* to the ground." Now ready to throw the first cast—
the most important one, for it is the one that rules the day—he placed the
smaller of the two chains in the crook of his arm. The large *gumaga* was
swung another four times, reflecting the eight marks of a cast. On the final
throw he let go, letting the open ends of the chain fall away from him and
land on the ground. The small *gumaga* was put on the floor next to the
thrown chain and the seeds arranged according to the cast. On the right
side he turned all the seeds face up, and on the left, the seeds face down in
the first two positions and face up in the last two, thus GbeŊoli:[15]

11	1
11	1
1	1
1	1

And he sang:

Ex. 6.1. GbeŊoli: Afa song   *(continued)*

GbeŊɔli meka	GbeŊɔli (literally, "Ghost voice") I cast
Nyagblɔla meli nam o	I don't have a spokesperson
Mewɔ naneke o	It does not matter

Ex. 6.1 (*continued*). GbeŊɔli: Afa song

For melodic purposes, when singing this song the three-syllable name "Gbe-Ŋɔ-li" is contracted into two syllables, pronounced "Gbe-Ŋlɔe."

Afa songs are sung to the standard timeline used also for *agbadza* (♩ ♪ ♩ ♩ ♪ ♩), usually sounded by the *bokɔ*, who taps it out using his special Afa stick (*ametɔlɔfi*).[16]

This song plays on the radical *ŋɔli* (ghost). Some Ewes say—though, with just about everything, not all—that ghosts speak with a soft high voice through their noses. In this sense the word is virtually an onomatopoeia due to the nasalized consonant at the beginning. It is said that if you hear a ghost's voice, there is a good chance you will die, or if you hear your name called out in the middle of the night, it is usually a ghost and, if you answer, you will surely die. Here the meaning is clear that although GbeŊɔli's voice (that is the cast) may be small, it is powerful.

Ewe *bokɔwo* consistently associate GbeŊɔli not only with ghosts but also with guns. Of the many stories connected with this cast, the one the *bokɔ* told me that day, one which I had heard before from other *bokɔwo*, was short and to the point: "There were once two guns, one very long that made a loud bang when shot, and one a very short gun, like the one that is used in the thunder god shrine at Nogokpo called *tukpui*, which only makes a small sound when it goes off but is extremely deadly.[17] The short gun shot someone and instantly killed him, but when the long gun spoke and said that he was the one who had done it, everyone believed him because of his loud voice." The *bokɔ* went on to explain that it is like the difference between the gun a hunter uses to kill animals and the one set off at funerals (metal pipes packed with gunpowder). Although the latter makes the bigger sound, only the former has bullets and can kill. The message was obvious: my enemies' threats were just that and I ultimately had nothing to worry about. One cannot rule out, however, the "I was being told what I wanted to hear" syndrome. (It is quite possible the *bokɔ* already had heard about what was happening, since everyone was talking about it.) But what I was hearing was not a story to fit the occasion; it was a story that was organically part of the cast, though it is true that there are many stories with each cast and the *bokɔ* picked this one. Besides, there have been plenty of other times when Afa had told me rather disturbing news, things I definitely did not want to hear, that directly related to my questions, and I knew the *bokɔ* had no idea of why I had summoned him.

Once the cast was established, the next piece of obligatory business was to find out whether what Afa was telling me "already had passed" or was "yet to come," and here is where the age of the various casts comes into play. I was given two items from the *vodzi* pile on the floor, a *hũsaka* seed representing the past and an *adziku* seed for the future, and told to "share them" between my two hands so that the *bokɔ* would not know which hand held what.[18] He then threw the *gumaga* chain twice to determine Afa's answer. If the first cast is older than the second, which it was, he points to his right side, which means Afa has chosen your left hand (the client always sits facing the *bokɔ*) and vice versa.[19] I was holding the *adziku* in my left hand, which meant the thing had yet to come.

Since it was something that was in the future, it was now time to find out which of the six fortunes of the world were on this path. Each of these fortunes was represented by an item from the *vodzi*: long life by a stone, market affairs (meaning having to do with women) by a bead, children by the *adziku* seed, money by a cowrie shell (which was a traditional form of currency), *vodu* by the seed of a silkwood tree, and enemy death by an animal bone. I shared these six items between my two hands, and, through a series of casts, all were eliminated except the animal bone. I would defeat my enemies.[20]

To open this path, however, and given the serious nature of what faced us, we needed to do a *vɔsa*, usually translated as "sacrifice," which, as with many glosses of Ewe words, was far from exact. The radical *vɔ* is most often translated as "evil," and *sa* as "to tie" or "to bind" (Gaba 1997: 90), that is, to tie or bind evil. Both, however, are polyvalent and not so easily pinned down to a one-to-one translation.[21] A *vɔsasa* (the act of doing *vɔsa*) is something much more and sometimes much less than a blood offering. It is meant to both appease whoever or whatever is blocking a path, in part a substitutional calculus and simultaneously a gift to all those deities, spirits, ghosts, and ancestors that come to partake in the offering. For those ghosts and others who are intending evil, the offering is supposed to be accepted in place of the person making the vɔsa. For all the rest it is a gift for them to take and pray for that individual. The nature of the vɔsasa is something that is prescribed by the cast. Some may be relatively simple affairs—a drink or offering of kola, or a piece of cloth—but the one required for GbeNɔli is complicated and relatively expensive. It involves an assemblage of things and acts that adhere into a complex performance. More than a text (as Rosenthal understands it [1998: 242]), vɔsasa is an enactment whose efficacy is in its doing. In this doing it makes a story concrete, collapsing its narrative and thus temporal structure into a collage that is not so much read (something that takes time) as grasped all at once.

You can't perform a vɔsa just anywhere. Location is something very important, something you need to ask Afa about. Once again I was given a pile of objects to share, and once again the gumaga chain was thrown twice to determine which hand Afa had chosen. And through a series of such choices, what remained in my hand at the end was a kola nut. The vɔsasa was to be done at a gorovodu shrine, and that is how my wife and I ended up at Sɔfo Peter's involved in what turned out to be a very involved and sometimes extremely strange affair.

The Gift

The following week we arrived at the shrine of Peter, who, after I told him what Afa had said, had arranged for two senior diviners to officiate over the vɔsasa. Both were fairly old, and both had, as do virtually all bokɔwo, great laughs. When we arrived around 3:00 in the afternoon, they were sitting on mats under a palm-roofed shed in front of one of Peter's houses, cracking jokes—it seems they already had been imbibing—and giving some of the young bosomfowo who were hanging around instructions to bring certain things that were needed for the sacrifice.

After greetings were exchanged, we sat down under the shed and waited as they began making a basket out of freshly cut leaves and twigs in which were placed three clay figures called amɛkoe (literally, "person takes it"), arranged around a miniature clay table, as if people were getting ready to eat, which is exactly what it was meant to be. When a vɔsa is offered, not only does Afa eat, but many voduwo, ghosts, and other spirits come to get their share. On this "table" were placed small, ground-up pieces of all sorts of animals, herbs, and medicines taken from the sɔfo's collection along with freshly cut leaves specific to Afa. This cast also called for a pig's head, which is anathema to the *gorovodu* shrines (see p. 79). But this part of the *vɔsa* relates directly to the *ŋɔliwo*, the ghosts, and, being the problematic souls they are, they must be given their due by being offered this "dirty" animal. This was done by taking a small sliver of a pig's head and adding it to the mix. Next, three small guns carved out of wood were put inside, directly relating to the "short guns" (*tukpui*) mentioned in the GbeŊɔli cast. Then one of the *bokɔwo* got out his Afa divining board and, after pouring termite dust on it, proceeded to mark the sixteen original casts, those whose two sides matched, one at a time. After completing each one and naming it, singing a song for some, speaking deep Ewe proverbs for others, he picked up some of the dust it was drawn in and put it in the basket. He added that seventeenth cast unique to Ewe diviners and finished with TseTula, which closed the door.[22] We were now ready to get down to the serious business at hand.

Two lines were drawn in the sand a few feet in front of the basket, and my wife and I were told to jump over the lines back-and-forth three times, being very careful not to land on them. In this crossing of thresholds, we were moving away from the "house of death" (*kutome*) toward the "house of life" (*agbetome*).[23] We did what was asked, and then sat down on the ground with the basket between the *bokɔwo* and us. A libation was poured, the two *bokɔwo* calling on Afa, the *voduwo*, the ancestors, and all of the ancient diviners to help them in their task, more drinks were had, and a cock was brought inside and its legs were untied. Anything that ties or binds an animal that is to be offered must be removed. According to instructions, I took the bird and touched its beak to the small clay table three times, plucked a few feathers from its head, chest, and tail, and put them into the basket. I hadn't realized this was going to be so participatory, but this was something I had done many times before when offering fowls to the gods. Then I was told to spit in its ass three times, something I had never done before. I asked if I had heard correctly, and was assured that I definitely needed to do this, for spitting would bring what we wanted to come to pass. So spit I did. My wife was spared all this because in Ewe culture the husband's Afa is considered to cover his wife's, a cultural construct my wife was never very comfortable with.

One of the *bokɔwo* then took the chicken from me, pried open its mouth, and, among much squawking, ripped out its tongue, something else I had never seen before and, to say the least, was disturbing to watch.[24] At that moment the *bokɔ*'s jovial persona transformed into a serious countenance that was striking. There was no mistaking that he was "really doing something," as Ewes would say, and that we were really seeing something. The cock didn't have long to suffer, however, for the *bokɔ* immediately picked up a knife and slit its throat, bleeding it into the basket. Things were definitely getting strange and about to get a lot stranger.

The other *bokɔ* now took out a baby chick that was in his bag (I had thought I had heard chirping) and while holding its legs proceeded to wipe it over our bodies while reciting deep Ewe texts in a voice with a timbre reminiscent of Barry White's, though it was perhaps a bit deeper, if that was possible. It was something about cleansing away all the evil that was surrounding us. Then, without warning, he started whacking our backs with the chick until it was dead. My wife was staring at me with a "What the hell have you got me into?" look, and I looked back with an expression that I hoped conveyed "I have no idea." The chick was divided into two parts and put in the basket. While this was going on, the cock had been taken outside and split open. Small bits of farm produce—maize, beans, cassava, groundnuts, onion, and whatever else was around—mixed with red palm oil were put inside, and the bird was closed and placed in the basket. This is called *agbleŋkusogbe* (literally, "farm-eye-thunder god-voice"). The *vɔsa* was for every spirit and ghost; thus the food offered needed to cover all the bases.

To our relief, a break was now in order. All got up to stretch their legs, some went around the side of the shed to relieve themselves, and schnapps and *akpeteshie* were liberally passed around. The *bokɔwo* were now definitely "in the mood," as Ewes would put it, kidding one another and exchanging ribald jokes. Once the *bokɔwo* sat down on their mats and we resumed our position in front of the basket, the *gumaga* necklace was thrown to check in with Afa to see how things were going. The cast came up GbeWoli, another *kpɔli*, about guns and he started singing:

GbeWoli kuɖe vodu (ʃe) xɔme   GbeWoli dies in vodu's room
Hũsiviwo fɔ aza do   Female children of the thunder god take
    the aza (ritual palm branch) and wear it

Ex. 6.2. GbeWoli: Afa song

Although the song does not directly mention guns, the stories surrounding this cast invariably do.[25] Typically, they are in the same mode of a big gun that makes a lot of noise and a small gun that is quieter but more deadly, here usually related to brothers who are hunting. The two bokɔwo agreed that this was a good sign, and another round of drinks was had.

By now it was late afternoon and, after some discussion about how to proceed next, it was finally decided that it was time for the goat. The goat is considered a hot animal and was something else that was prescribed by Afa for the vɔsa when GbeŊɔli appeared. One of the young bosomfowo went to the nearby tree where the goat was tethered and brought it to where we were sitting. Once again, after the rope was removed from its neck, I was told to touch the animal's head to the basket three times, hair was cut from its head, chest, and tail and put in the basket, but this time, thankfully, I didn't have to spit in its ass. After being formally presented to Afa, its throat was slit, as the cock's had been, and bled into the basket. It was taken outside, its left leg was cut off, and its intestines, throat, and heart were removed. All were put in the basket, which by now was overflowing with stuff.

Night had now settled in, and a kerosene lamp was lit so we could see. After another round of drinks, the *gumaga* was thrown, and when Gbe-Ŋɔli appeared once again—a coincidence that was greeted with several "Ahas"—we all knew that everything was in order, so we entered the last phase of the *vɔsasa*. We were told to pick up the basket and start walking without turning around. When we found a place where two roads crossed, we were to leave the basket, turn our backs to it, and go. Under no circumstances should we look back until we arrived at the compound. If the next morning the contents were gone, whether dogs or a person took it, it meant that Afa had accepted the *vɔsa*. If not, well, we would have to consult Afa again to find out why. We did as we were told and a couple of hundred yards from Sɔfo Peter's compound we came to a T in the road. Since there were multiple paths, it was deemed an adequate place, and we left the offering. As instructed, we turned our backs to the *vɔsa*, thus turning our backs on all the evil that was following us, and started to walk away. I was ahead of my wife, and we made it almost back to the shed where the *bokɔwo* were waiting for us when she slipped in the dark and let out a cry. In that moment I knew I had crossed into the mythic realm, for as with Orpheus in the underworld, I instinctively spun around to see if my wife was okay. Someone quickly grabbed me and turned me around, and we proceeded on our way.

Was it all for naught? No one said anything about it. The next morning the basket was gone—a good sign—but when Sɔfo Peter offered a fowl to Kunde to see if everything was in order, and the cock died with its head tucked under its wing—a worrisome sign that shame was coming to our house—Peter decided there was no question about what needed to be done next. No more fooling around; Sakra Bode, the god of the land, would have to be buried at our compound to protect us. He said it would take him a few days to make the fetish, but not to worry since he had written down Baba's, Blackie's, and the Rastaman's names on a piece of paper and put it in Kunde's house, his *kpome*. They were now "registered" with the shrine.

While we were off consulting Afa, the Rastaman was not sitting on his hands. Tearing down walls and sending out very scary looking guys were not the only things he was up to. In an attempt to get the notorious Ghanaian bureaucracy involved—something that would slow down if not stop any project—he went to the District Town and Planning offices, complaining that I didn't have a permit to build a wall. He was informed that you don't need a permit to build a wall and summarily dismissed. Being a "Rasta" is not really an advantage when dealing with the Ghanaian civil service. He came back the next day, this time with his wife, who, being a German national, had more credibility in the eyes of Ghanaian bureaucrats, and they both protested that the wall had encroached on their property. This time two officials came out to the site, looked at the wall, located the boundary markers, took a few measurements, and returned to their office to check their files. Finding everything in order, and, to my surprise, not asking for a "gift" from me, they dropped the case. But the Rastaman was definitely not through. The next thing I knew, a committee of concerned fishermen showed up at our compound to find out if I really was building a wall that would extend into the sea, as the Rastaman had claimed. They informed me that they couldn't let that happen, for it would seriously disrupt their net fishing. I told them that I had no intention of doing such a thing, that the sea would carry away such a wall anyway, and informed them that I would never build or do anything that would interfere with their livelihood. Reassured by what I had said, they left, and I never heard anymore about my supposed "sea wall."

Not content to try only such mundane means as gossip and bureaucratic meddling, the Rastaman also seemed to be active on more esoteric fronts. Ewes have a reputation among themselves and other Ghanaians for knowing and using what is generically called *juju* along the Guinea Coast.[26] As I stated before, I have had more than one Ghanaian warn me to be careful in the Volta Region on precisely this account (cf. Geurts 2002: 124–26). One day during all of this I was walking down my usual path from the compound to the roadside when I came across something odd. On the right side of the path was a chameleon. That was unusual in itself, for they are rarely seen, but this one was desiccated and inverted: its head and stomach were pointed skyward and its legs had been bent back. No chameleon ever naturally died in that way. I had been headed to Sofo Peter's shrine, and when I got there, I told him about it. It sounded suspicious, so he advised that I collect it—"Pick it up with something else and make sure you don't touch it"—and bring it to the shrine. But when I came back in the afternoon it was gone. It was also around this time that I became much more careful about what I ate and drank. I had heard and knew of more than one person whose suspicious death was rumored to be the result of an undetectable poison. Was I getting paranoid? Perhaps. But I wasn't in the mood to take any chances. And that is where I found myself, watching where I was walking and what I was eating and drinking, when Peter came to bury Sakra Bode.

The Burial

This wasn't the first time that something was going to be buried in our compound. Over the years various *sofowo*, *bokɔwo*, and a few *midawowo* (thunder god priests) had buried a variety of things there for general protection, good fortune, and assorted other reasons that related to immediate concerns. Usually these burials were conducted in front of the gates and doorways, the place where Legba rules. The latest such burial took place in the interval between the GbeŊɔli reading when Afa was consulted and the *vɔsasa* at Peter's shrine.

When GbeŊɔli revealed itself that day the *gumaga* chain was thrown, the *bokɔ* told me that there was another side to the cast besides guns and killing, and it had to do with holes and what goes in them, specifically graves. Sometimes, he informed me, the ground above a grave in your compound may open up. (Traditionally Ewes would bury their dead within the confines of the compound, sometimes even underneath the house, as happened with Anibra.) If this happens, then it means that the dead are calling someone to come join them. In order to avoid a death in the family you need to find out what the dead want and dig a hole, put that thing inside, and cover it. Of course the way to find out who is calling and what they want is through Afa.

A few days after the initial divination, the *bokɔ* returned around dusk and said he had come to finish this part of the *kpɔli*, the cast. He had brought a bag containing a special stick (*fe*), several different kinds of leaves, some powder, and the head of a python. Pieces of all these things were ground up and rubbed on the stick, which was then divided into five parts. We waited for night to come and under the cover of darkness went to the four corners of the compound. At each place the *bokɔ* dug a hole with his hands, put in a piece of the stick, sprinkled more medicine on top, and then, to my surprise, took off his pants and used his buttocks to push the sand into the hole. Sometimes the way you close a hole is as important as what you put in it. When you bury something with your buttocks, it is as you were when you were born. The only one who can defeat such a medicine, the *bokɔ* explained, is someone who would enter the compound naked, and then I would know for sure who my enemy was. After doing this at the four corners, he did the same burial in the middle of the compound, thus enacting the crossroads, for the four cardinal directions intersect in a middle that is simultaneously a horizontal and vertical axis that connects the upper and lower realms, another invocation of the "strong cross." And this was pretty close to where we finally decided to bury Sakra Bode.[27]

Several weeks after the Afa burial, and a few days after the *vɔsa*, Peter arrived one night at our compound with Sakra Bode in hand. He was with two of his senior *bosomfowo*. One was his brother, the second in command at the shrine who always does the prayers for Bangle; the other, the man who on special occasions "outdoors" Ketetsi. When he does this, he wears a white calico toga with a white calico wrap around his head while he holds the Bangle fetish upright in his two hands. With extremely slow and measured steps, one foot in front of the other, as if under a great weight, he circumambulates the courtyard in front of the shrine. I have seen him do this several times, and every time his right eye freezes and bulges out of its socket, giving him a very strange and disconcerting visage. It wasn't that he was possessed by Bangle, as a *trɔsi* would be; rather, the power of Ketetsi was so great that the force pulsing through his body as a result of holding the fetish was overwhelming. Although it was Peter's hand that actually fashioned Sakra, it was the *bosomfo* who was carrying the bag that held the god.

Sakra, we decided, should be buried near some newly planted coconut trees, not exactly in the center of the compound but close to it. As we all knelt on our haunches, libations were poured by the light of a flashlight, and the two *bosomfowo* dug a hole in the sand about two and a half feet deep with their hands. The one who carried Bangle reached into the bag and pulled out a small clay pot covered in white, blue, and red cloth (the colors of the gods) and handed it to Peter. The top had a lid with a small hole in the center, but it was not large enough to see what was inside. What was inside was Sakra Bode, god of the land, and, as I would later learn, a little piece of each of the other gods.

Sɔfo Peter handed me the pot, and I was told to place it in the hole, making sure it sat well. I had heard this expression before when, during libations to the ancestors, the calabash bowl with maize-meal water (*dzatsi*; literally, "welcoming water") was put on the ground and turned from side to side, and that is what I did with the pot. Peter and the *bosomfowo* laughed, surprised that I knew about this. Schnapps was liberally poured on the god straight from the bottle, reminiscent of a cow sacrifice (see p. 89), and four piles of gunpowder were "shot" around the hole. A cat—well, actually a kitten—was pulled out of the bag and was given to me to hold. I was told to whisper in its ear what I wanted in life and handed it back to the *sɔfo* who gave it to one of the *bosomfowo*. I knew what was coming next, but I still cringed every time it happened. But when you bury Sakra Bode you have to give a cat or you will have "done nothing at all." So the cat was sacrificed, its head cut off, its lungs put in its mouth, and then put on top of Sakra. A cock that Peter had brought was untied and I touched its beak to Sakra four times. Peter took the bird from me, cut feathers from its head and tail while praying, pulled back its wings and head, exposing its neck, and made one quick slash across its throat. The blood poured out over Sakra for a minute or so, and then he cut deep into the throat and the blood gushed. This only lasted a few seconds before the fowl was thrown. It flopped around the courtyard, seemed to die on its stomach, but, with one last gasp, stood straight in the air and plopped on its back—a blessing and a relief. The cat's head was removed and buried in front of the main gate, kola and kaolin were thrown inside the hole, and, with one last pouring of schnapps, the hole was filled in with sand—no bare ass this time. Ten years after I had first started dealing with these northern gods, Sakra Bode—and along with him a part of all the gods—was now installed in the center of the compound, to protect my family from all those who would do us harm.

Closing the Door

Several years have passed now since the wall was torn down and our lives were threatened. The stool father finally died from congestive heart failure—he was my *mɛgbetɔ*, my "back," and will be sorely missed. They say that when an old man dies, one who is spiritually powerful, it will rain at his funeral. When the stool father was buried there was a torrential downpour all day. I always figured it was just one last parting shot at his uncle, who, being the family head, had to officiate over much of the proceedings. With no one to fight with, the *tɔɖia*, the uncle, retired back to Lome and is rarely seen these days on this side of the border, even for family business. The last I heard, Baba had also "retired" and was running a small drinking bar near the border in Aflao, and rumor has it that Blackie was finally captured by the Ghanaian police but for some inexplicable reason let go. As for the Rastaman, I haven't seen him since, except occasionally in court as the Ghanaian legal system plods its way along.

What to make of all of this, frankly, I am not quite sure. It all seemed to have a destiny, a trajectory of its own, in which I really didn't have much say. Once again faced with a strangeness that often offended my sensibilities—pulling out the tongue of a live chicken, beating a chick to death on my back, cutting off the head of a cat—I found myself turning my back, sometimes literally, on those sensibilities, accepting what was happening within a field of action of which I could have only a faint understanding, though this was something I had been studying for years. As the Ewe proverb says,

Tso vado kple dzɔ kpleke	The cut [grafted] plant and the one
womesɔ o.	born with roots are not the same.

But this is not to say that most Ewes involved in such matters somehow had a clear understanding of what was going on either, a ready-made, ready-to-hand explanation of these events.

Traditional Ewe religious practice is full of ambiguity; thus few people agree on many things, including whether Mawu, the supreme deity, is male, female, or both. Priests and diviners know what to do, but it doesn't follow that they know exactly the meaning of those acts. Much of this is supposed to be in the dark, literally and figuratively, for it is neither in the understanding nor, contrary to the majority of "received" opinion, in the beliefs of those who partake in such things. Efficacy here is not predicated on faith or belief, but in the doing, and you don't need to know why in order to act. In fact, sometimes you don't even need to be there.

Coda

Opening the Door

I was sitting with the other adehawo, *singing brekete songs and beating the akpé, when out of the corner of my eye I saw a bright light coming from inside the shrine. I turned toward the light, and standing in the doorway of the shrine was a woman with long, flowing hair dressed all in white; it was Tseriya. She looked at me and began to dance, twirling as she came toward me. I felt a tremendous joy and stood up to greet her, and that was the last thing I remembered until I found myself sitting in back of the shrine, exhausted. It has been two years now since my mother first came to me and I became her wife. I am told that when she comes she does many things: healing the sick, giving advice, warning of danger. I wouldn't know because I am not there. It is not me who does such things, but Tseriya.*

—Testimony of a trɔsi

When two atoms of hydrogen are combined with an atom of oxygen, you get water. It is the same with the gods. When you put the right ingredients together you get a gorovodu.
—KWASI ANIBRA

As I am writing this book, Sɔfo Peter came yesterday unexpectedly and told me that, in the middle of the night, Tseriya had possessed one of her wives. She was singing loudly outside his house, and, before he could get up to open the door to see what was going on, she broke it down and entered his room. She told him she had come to warn me that someone had thrown something in my compound, but Sakra had sacked it. Thwarted in his efforts, the person was going to come back with evil on his mind and try to do harm. To protect us, Sɔfo Peter must bury two wooden guns and offer a chicken in front of each doorway to our compound. He should not delay, but do this immediately, which was why he was there. A warning delivered under such dramatic circumstances, directly from the mouth of a god, was not to be taken lightly, and the next day we arranged to bury the guns and split the chickens.

Around 10:00 in the morning Peter showed up with three chickens, plus the guns and some gunpowder. He had three chickens instead of two, because we decided to also make the yearly sacrifice to Sakra and might as well do them both at the same time. It had been the year before when the first annual offering had been made. Shortly after returning to Adafienu that summer I had gone to visit him at his shrine. After I made obligatory prayers to the gods, asking for the standard health and wealth, he informed me that we needed to make a sacrifice to Sakra, something simple like a chicken. I thought he was talking about the Sakra Bode in his shrine and asked him why, thinking that one of the *trɔsiwo* or Sakra himself had made this request of me through cowrie divination. "It has been a year since we buried him in your compound," he replied, "and we need to let him know you are back."

A few days later Peter arrived with a well-fed *Gallus domesticus* in hand, without a doubt the most sacrificed animal in Africa. Following greetings, he stood up, walked straight to a place near the middle of the compound, and put his foot down. "Here's the spot," he said confidently, and instructed his brother who was with him to start digging. About two feet down, there was Sakra just as we had left him, the clay pot covered in red, white, and blue cloth. We offered kola and schnapps, I touched the chicken's head to the top of the clay pot four times, and the bird was bled over the fetish. The chicken died on its right side, which was acceptable, since that was Sakra's side, although a death on the back would have been better. If it had died on the left, Kunde's side, it would have meant that Sakra had refused and we would have had to consult Afa. It should be obvious by now that the Ewe reading of the way a chicken dies is indeed a thick text. We buried Sakra once more, and there he remained, protecting the compound, at least that is what I thought.

When I came back the following year, there was no need for reminders; it was I who told Peter that we should tell Sakra I had returned. And that is when we decided to combine the protection Tseriya had prescribed with the offering to Sakra Bode. On the appointed day Peter arrived, accompanied by the same *bosomfowo* from the first time we buried Sakra. After a libation was poured in front of the side gate, the chicken was killed, but instead of being thrown to see which way it landed, it was split down the middle, pried apart, and placed face up in the hole. If a bad spirit came, it should take the chicken instead of someone inside. To both sides of the chicken the wooden guns were placed, one pointing to the right, the other to the left. Five piles of gunpowder were poured inside and set off, invoking the crossroads. The whole offering was then buried, and the same process was repeated at the front gate.

Finished with this ritual prescription from Tseriya, Peter walked over to a spot in the middle of the compound and, as before, put down his foot. But this time he looked puzzled. He said that he had not felt anything underneath. The two *bosomfowo* who were assisting started digging, but there was nothing there. They kept digging and found the old kola and some of the kaolin from the previous year but still no Sakra Bode. I was mystified, but Peter said that Sakra had probably moved somewhere else in the compound, or had buried himself deep into the ground: "Gods do those sorts of things." I, however, couldn't get my mind around what had happened to Sakra. I had seen it there the year before and knew it must be somewhere close. I reasoned that Peter had either misjudged the spot, or, given the nature of shifting sands, it was somewhere nearby. I told him that I was sure it was here and we should try to find it. He didn't seem that concerned but agreed, and someone went to get a hoe. A half an hour later we had a good portion of the middle of the compound dug up, but Sakra was nowhere to be found. Peter offered that Sakra could have decided to go very deep or, for some reason unbeknownst to us, had decided to leave altogether. He suggested we consult Afa to find out, but, regardless of what we learned, he would make a new Sakra. This time, however, we should put some cement over it (probably for my benefit and peace of mind) to make sure we knew where he was.

And this eventually came to pass. A bokɔ was consulted, and when the

Ahɔ lem loo	Scorpion caught me
SaLɔso, ahɔ lem loo	SaLɔso, Scorpion caught me
Bokɔnɔ, bedzee! Awunɔ, bedzee!	Diviner, it should come on! Diviner, it should come on!
Enua le kɔme adatɔ	The thing is in the termite mound, strong one
Ekɔkutɔ ha adatɔ	Those who are digging in the termite mound are also strong
Ahɔ lem loo	Scorpion caught me

Ex. C.1. SaLɔso: Afa song

cast for SaLoso revealed itself, he started singing (see ex. C.1). In this song, SaLoso represents the snake god, Da, and the scorpion a human being. Da, unlike a *gorovodu*, cannot be made by hand but is always found by digging in a termite mound. This is a difficult task, for he may keep shifting his position, constantly moving inside the mound. He doesn't want just anyone catching him, because the person who takes care of him has to be spiritually strong. Was it mere coincidence that we had summoned Afa to find the buried Sakra and this cast had appeared? Perhaps. No doubt about it, however, Sakra was still there; we just couldn't find him. All well and good, but, according to Peter, we still needed to bury a new one and put cement over it. It seemed simple enough, so I agreed. The cement thing, however, took on a life of its own, and, by the time it was finished, I got not only another god of the land but also a small shrine to go along with it, not something I had exactly planned on. When Peter had mentioned the cement covering for Sakra, I had gone to the market the next day and bought some cowries to put in the cement so it would be more like the Sakra Bodes I had seen in the shrines. It was just an afterthought, something that happened to cross my mind.

Peter and his brother showed up a couple of days later with a new Sakra and, as before, proceeded to bury the clay pot covered in the colors of the gods—this time, however, not in the center of the compound but off to the side of the main house in a more private area away from public eyes. The burial went pretty much as it had the first time, except for the intention to make the site more permanent. As he was starting to lay the cement over Sakra I gave the cowries I had bought to Peter, who exclaimed "Aha," and the next thing I knew a mound was being constructed complete with a hole in the top to give Sakra his drink and food directly. The cowries were embedded in concentric circles around the hole, but eight were kept back for divination, to see what Sakra had to say when I prayed. The ground in front was plastered, including an opening where libations for the ancestors could be poured. Peter consulted with his brother as they looked at what they had done to see if they had forgotten anything—they had. There was no rock to knock on Sakra's door. A suitable one was quickly found, and, with some of Kunde's medicine underneath, it was embedded in the plaster next to the mound. Before they left, Peter informed me that a small shelter needed to be built over the mound so that rain would not get into the hole. I didn't have just Sakra Bode; I now had, more or less, a Sakra Bode shrine.

The next day Peter, this time with the *bosomfo* who carries Ketetsi, came back to finish the process. We knocked on Sakra's door, which was now covered by a small shed, and called his name four times. Realizing there was no *kpome* to receive the kola and kaolin we were offering, we quickly made three sandcrete blocks that were lying around into a makeshift one in back of the mound. Peter threw the cowries, and they came up even: the prayers had been accepted. A cock was thrown and died on its stomach with its wings outstretched and its head bent back. Although a chicken dying on its stomach is usually not a good sign, when its wings were outstretched like this it meant that Sakra was covering me; the house was protected by the gods. Finally, Peter asked me to fetch a stool so I would have something to sit on when I prayed. I brought out a small carved one I had bought in the Ashanti Region years before. He placed his hands on my left shoulder while the *bosomfo* did the same on the other. They said a prayer while tapping my back seven times, and then both sat me down on the stool. As they did this, Peter declared that I was now a *sofo* and could pray directly to Sakra. Of course, this didn't mean I was a priest; it takes much more than this to become the head of a shrine—I wasn't even a member, had never "eaten the *vodu*." But it did give me the sanction to sit on a stool and pray. And maybe that is why we couldn't find Sakra. He wanted something more than merely being buried in the middle, in-between the ethnographic crossroads of being-there-and-away.

It was shortly after this, on a Denu market day, that I was walking through the maze of inner stalls when I heard someone call out "Sofo! Sofo! Woezo [Welcome]." I turned around expecting to see Kpesusi, or Peter, perhaps Kwamiga, but nobody was there. The fishmonger who had called out the first time repeated her greeting, and that is when I realized she was welcoming me.

Tradition exists only in constantly becoming other than it is.
—HANS-GEORG GADAMER, "Reply to My Critics"

Postlude

To write of divine horsemen is to write of leaving. Whether buried in the sand or the turn of the dance, northern gods are always on the move, every arrival a departure, every being-there a being-away. To think that such an existence ever ceases to be in flux is an illusion nurtured by the desire for narrative assurance. This constant leave-taking imparts to Brekete a feel for that which is not there, an absence that echoes across these chapters. Neither a lack to be replaced through relentless excavation nor a debt to be repaid in lengthy exegesis, this absence has a surplus of meaning that cannot be captured, only pointed to in its leaving. Those who inhabit these pages—gods and their wives, priests and diviners, strangers and neighbors (who sometimes turn out not to be very neighborly)—are not just memories fashioned into the written word, the grain of different voices remembered from a particular point of view. On the contrary, they *are* there in the telling of what was left behind, the remains of ritual carried forward in this book.

These remains are found in the flow of libation and sacrifice, united in the gush of the poured gift; felt in the jubilation of a sunlit afternoon, when you can touch and be touched by the gods; heard in the prayers to *gorovoduwo* who sit on the earth, and now every Friday to a different type of northern god, one of the Book; seen in the practice of divination, where the casts of Afa reveal the language of the sky and the throw of the cowries gives voice to the material silence of the fetishes; encountered in the burial of a god who blesses and protects, and that of priests, some of whom left this world sooner than expected, though according to their own words they died precisely on time. But most of all, although few who have studied these shrines have considered it as such, these remains can be found, seen, heard, and felt most intensely in the play of the drums, the singing and clapping of the *adehawo*, the rhythm and movement of the dance, in sum, the musical experience of Brekete, a poured gift of a special kind.

Here musical structure itself takes on the dimensions of an ontology of energy, the *force vitale* of a saturated and animated engagement with the world. Here the cold fusion of cross-rhythms gives more than it receives. It is nothing less than the heart and soul of a Black Orpheus, a musical journey of retrieval that is fundamental to African ritual life.[1] In this ontology, the rationality of certainty is transformed into the certainty of relationality. No rhythm stands alone; one part always invites another. To fill in the ellipses of Senghor's ontological turn quoted at the end of chapter 1, "I feel the Other Person, I dance the Other Person, therefore I am" (cited in Bâ 1973: 115). In this dance, sound and object collapse. No distance separates call from response, color from sound, human from god, threes from twos. Musical experience is a clearing at the center of the crossroads where paths intersect and intertwine; it is a chiasm, the flesh where deities and devotees grow older together, making music together (Schutz 1951).

There are moments in Brekete that at least seem perfect, when everything is in its right place, when gods are there and *trosiwo* are away, and the rest of us are caught in-between the sublime countenance of the god's turn, an infinite balance no mortal can attain—only those who are not there can move in such ways. When this turn happens, all else turns with it and the world becomes *trance*-figured. The dance of divine horsemen is not merely one more event among many, a happening that takes up space and time. Rather, space and time are denied, and in this denial mysteriously recovered in a musical mode of being. Within this musical field, things are neither far nor near, here nor there, but always-already profoundly in-between, heard in a continual round of retrieval, a true re-petition, a call that is already a response. For the Brekete shrines of West Africa, this calling response is the sound of northern gods riding in a southern land.

Notes

Southern Lands

1. Quoting "hall-talk" among French anthropologists and sociologists working with Ewe speakers in Togo, Judy Rosenthal (1998) reports the prevailing opinion: "Here no two persons will tell you the same thing about the same cult. . . . The south is a nightmare for an ethnographer" (45–46).

2. "Guinea Coast" refers here and elsewhere in this book specifically to the countries that lie along the Gulf of Guinea.

3. In Ewe religious practice, virtually all thunder god shrines have within their precincts a special enclosure dedicated to Da. Greene (1996: 95) reports that Yeve, the name of the thunder god "religious order," came from the middle Slave Coast in the 1700s and consisted of three separate deities: "Hebieso or So, Agbui or Avleketi, and Voduda or Da." (See also Herskovits 1938, vol. 2: 193–94.)

4. Three-Town is not its official name, what you would find on the government books, or what outsiders call the place, but a compromise decided upon by the town elders. When the government finally built a secondary school for the community, instead of arguing about the school

title, what town of the three it would be named after, it became the Three-Town Senior Secondary School. The look of the towns is typical of those dotted along the west coast of Africa: on either side of the main road are a series of small shops, each mostly specializing in one kind of commodity—building supplies, dry goods, cloth, CDs, and so on—and interspersed between the shops, here and there, are drinking bars serving shots of gin, beer, and minerals (sodas) to accompany the local cuisine served at chop bars from large pots of the stew of the day.

5. According to Crapanzano, Hermes was a "phallic god and a god of fertility" (1992: 44), which he equates with the "phallic-aggressive" act of interpretation, of penetrating the meaning of things and conveying such understanding to others, thus the inherent violence of all translation, which always must leave something behind in its additive attempt to bring all that is there forward. (See also Goldman 1942 on the origin of the Greek "herm," a stone boundary marker that evolved into a phallic form, from which Hermes got his name.)

6. More precisely, the cover is a photograph of a mixed media artwork "Remains of Ritual" (Ridenour 2007).

Northern Gods

1. "Shrine" refers both to the physical place where the gods are housed and to the group of people who belong to such ritual spaces. The term "medicine," according to Allman and Parker (2005: 174), seems to have first been applied to these northern gods by J. B. Danquah (a lawyer and one of the "Big Six" Ghanaian nationalists) in order to medicalize, thus legitimize, these "fetishes" in the eyes of colonial officials who were planning to ban them. However, Goody (1961: 145) independently uses this idiom, presumably by applying the LoDagaa term *tii* (medicine) to these shrines. He argues that the ritual commerce in medicine shrines, at least for the Ashanti, was going on much earlier than previously reported (Goody 1957a: 358).

2. I am using the term "gods" here, and throughout this book, because this is the translation the Ewes themselves use when speaking of these deities in English.

3. Recently, Judy Rosenthal (1998) has written of the widespread presence of Brekete in southern Togo in her study of this shrine. Her use of Lacanian notions of the Real to approach the phenomenon of spirit possession brings a different perspective to understanding this complex way of being. As to the origin of these gods, however, her conclusion that they were the spirits of northern slaves (100–3) is not part of the discourse of the members or priests I worked with, including the paramount priest of all of the Brekete shrines. Although Rosenthal weaves the idea of the gods as spirits of slaves in the main body of her text, she does acknowledge in a footnote that "not all agree that they are the spirits of slaves," suggesting that this is a "secret," which not all shrine members know (251 n. 3; see also 104). Allman and Parker's (2005) recent important work, however, would seem to confirm a lack of slave narrative in northern shrines that migrated south. The ritual complex of Tongnaab, the main focus of their book, for example, has nothing to do with slave spirits, nor do the many other shrines that are mentioned. See also Ward (1956), Goody (1957a), Debrunner (1959), Field (1960), McCleod (1975), and Werbner (1979) for the absence of slave spirits in these traveling fetishes. Ward, in fact, states that the Brekete god Kunde (spelled "Kune" in her account) was a "local earth spirit" (53). This is not to say that the "hot" spirits of slaves do not constitute a whole arena of action (Greene 1996), just that it is not happening within the confines of Brekete. Rosenthal does make a point that slave spirits are more explicitly connected with another "Vodu order," Mama Tchamba, with which she worked (104).

4. Most of this literature has concentrated either on these gods in their homeland or how they were received among the Akan. In comparison, there has been little work done on these northern gods in Ewe communities (see, however, Rosenthal 1998; Fiawoo 1968; and Hill 1981).

5. For passing reference to the fact that these gods danced, see Allman and Parker (2005: 52), Debrunner (1959: 116), Fortes (1936: 598), and Freeman (1898: 148, quoted in Goody 1957a: 359), to name but a few examples from ethnographic data on these shrines in their place of origin in northern Ghana. On the south see, for example, Ward (1956: 56), Fiawoo (1968: 80), Field (1960: 55–62), and Kramer (1993: 46–47). This lack of attention to dance and musical phenomena also holds true for Rosenthal's book (1998), which deals specifically with Brekete. We read about something she calls a "*brekete* rhythm" (6), but nothing of what it sounds like or how it is produced. Likewise, Rosenthal makes much of the fact that these northern gods possess people who dance but offers only brief descriptions of how this dance moves. I am not saying that every researcher who deals with these shrines needs to be an ethnomusicologist, or that the work they have done has not been valuable, but that still does not alleviate the fact that much of what is central to ritual praxis for these northern shrines remains silent. The one major work on music in Brekete shrines is Richard Hill's master's thesis (1981), which, though rather thin on the ethnography, offers the most detailed musical analysis of Brekete to date. For Nigeria, McCall's *Dancing Histories: Heuristic Ethnography with the Ohafia Igbo* (2000) takes ritual dance seriously, providing a nuanced account of his experience.

6. There is, of course, Jean Rouch's famous, or infamous, depending on your point of view, film *Les Maîtres Fous* (1954), shot on the outskirts of Accra, the current capital of Ghana. The film takes us inside a yearly ritual of a different set of northern gods, the Hauka, who came from Niger instead of northern Ghana (see Stoller's [1995] study of the Hauka in their homeland). These gods of the city, gods of technology, gods of power, as Rouch calls them, were the embodiment of the power of the colonial other—others othering others in a very postmodern move, according to much of the subsequent commentary on this film (Stoller 1992; Taussig 1993). Given Rouch's *cinéma vérité* style, the ritual happenings, including the sacrificing and eating of a dog, the aspect of the film that has caused the most controversy, are given an immediacy unparalleled in ethnographic film at that time. What is telling for the point being made here, however, is the glossed-over fact that at its premiere showing at the Musée de l'Homme for the International Conference on Ethnographic Cinema, it was a silent film, with Rouch providing the commentary from the projection booth (Rouch 2003; Stoller 1992). The film had been shot before synchronous sound recording, and, in the rush to show the film at the conference, there had not been enough time to add the sound track. Rouch, of course, eventually did, in which we hear snatches of the one-stringed fiddle, the *gayia*, and the gourd drums, but the music, for the most part, is ambient background for Rouch's narrative voice telling the story of the Hauka, a perfect metaphor for the fate of musical experience in these studies.

7. Particularly in regards to northern gods, the anthropological discourse around mimesis, rethought by Taussig (1993), Kramer (1993), and Stoller (1995), situates these migratory fetishes—wearing the red fez, embodying colonial memories, practicing sympathetic magic in a new mode—in an alternate and more nuanced understanding. While this metonymic turn has brought much to the study of spirit possession in Africa, it also has subtly devalued the ontological claims of the lived experience of trance. According to this discourse, the possessed may think others direct them, but they are enacting their own agency, their own history, for various purposes and reasons.

8. Edith Turner has attempted to address this issue in her work (1992, 2006).

9. "Négritude," a term coined by Aimé Césaire and Léon Damas, was a literary, cultural, philosophical, and political movement that they started along with Senghor while they were students in Paris (Jules-Rosette 1992: 39; Mudimbe 1988: 83). Césaire from Martinique, Damas from French Guiana, and Senghor from Senegal shared the experience of French colonization, and the desire to legitimize, thus recover from the Western gaze, the black heritage of Africa. By reacting to the "white myth," however, négritude has been criticized as still being caught in its racist web (Taylor 1989). (For other criticisms of its philosophy see Wiredu 1980 and Hountondji 1983.) The Black Atlantic is a phrase that comes from Robert Farris Thompson's *Flash of the Spirit* (1983), its geographic reach appropriate for the present discussion (see also Gilroy 1993; and Matory 2005).

10. Somewhere along the line I heard Christopher Waterman use this phrase.

Chapter 1

1. A shorter version of chapter 1 appears in *Aesthetics in Performance: Formations of Symbolic Construction and Experience*, edited by Angela Hobart and Bruce Kapferer (New York: Berghahn Books, 2005). Excerpts from this shorter version may also be found in "Northern Gods" and chapter 5.

2. While this metaphor is widespread throughout the Guinea Coast, and its analogies hold true for possession among Ewes, it is not as forefronted in the indigenous discourse about trance as, for example, it is among the Yoruba and Fon peoples, to say nothing of the fact that it is the dominant trope in Bori possession found in the Sahel region among Hausa speakers, and in Zar cults found in the Sudan, Ethiopia, and elsewhere. The term "divine horsemen" is taken from Deren's (1953) work on Haitian Vodou.

3. Bangle's name is not pronounced as in the English "bangle," a piece of jewelry. The stress is put on the first syllable (*ba*), followed by a nasalized consonant cluster (*ng*) said along with the final *le* but as one syllable (*ngle*).

4. *Trɔ* is a word that has no fewer than thirteen entries in Westermann's incomparable Ewe dictionary (Westermann [1928] 1973: 244–45), depending on tonemic variation and nasalization. Among its many meanings are "to turn," "to change," "to return," and "deity." Turning into a deity along with the turning aspect of the dance is a suggestive etymological link, though in the first usage the vowel is nasalized, which is phonemic in the Ewe language. Nasalization for *trɔ* is not marked in the rest of the text since the word always refers to the gods. The radical *si* indicates betrothal, usually in the sense of being possessed by a god. Banglesi, for example, would be a wife of Bangle; *trɔsi*, the wife of a god in general. In this context both men and women can become wives.

5. When the term *brekete* is used to indicate the drum or the music instead of the name of the shrine, it is in lowercase and italicized.

6. Matory (1994) makes a similar point about the moral superiority of women and possession among the Yoruba: "The possession religions of Oyo North cast women as exemplars and leaders of a moral order credibly rivaling the national state" (496). This is in contradistinction, for example, to the widespread phenomenon of prostitutes being the main adherents in Bori cults found among Hausa-speaking peoples of the Sahel.

7. This style of chicken divination is also found in northern Ghana, the original home of these kola-nut gods (see Fortes 1936: 600; Debrunner 1959: 119; Allman and Parker 2005: 147).

8. This does not take into account the Jungian notion of synchronicity, which, however, is not generally part of scientific or lay understandings in the West. This is not to

deny that there are instances where people do subscribe to something approximating meaningful coincidences though this is not systematic as in divinatory practices in Africa.

9. Sanya Kompo is a secretary in the sense that s/he keeps account of all that you do whether good or bad. No one seemed to know why s/he is also called god of the stone. There are varying opinions of whether Sanya is male or female (see chap. 2), though I have always thought of Sanya as female, perhaps because it is very rare to encounter a male *trɔsi* possessed by this god. Debrunner (1959: 107) states that this fetish came from "Kupo at Senyon near Bole (hence Senya-Kupo)," while Field (1960: 90) locates the shrines of "Senyon Kupo" as coming from "Senyon near Wa." There was even a trading company called Senyakupo, which formed in 1928 in Kumasi (Allman and Parker 2005: 176).

10. According to some *sɔfowo*, Lahare is the Eweized version of Alhaji, an honorific title designating a man who has made the pilgrimage to Mecca.

11. During this period, the Northern Territories Protectorate of the Gold Coast (the official title of the north under British rule), with its general lack of exploitable resources and relatively sparse population, was marginal to colonial interests, which had been concentrated on the coast and central forest regions (Watherson 1908). This does not mean the British left northerners to themselves; rather, they instituted indirect rule and appointed paramount chiefs, distorting traditional social and political structures. See Allman and Parker's (2005) recent important work on this subject. Specifically in regards to how this affected the northwestern part of the Northern Territories, where Kunde is alleged to have come from, see Lentz (2006).

12. This belief in the occult powers of northern Muslims could be found throughout Ghana. *Mallams* (Muslim scholars), for example, had long been ensconced in the Asantehene's court, offering protection through talismans, advice by way of divination, and other forms of spiritual help (Wilks 1980; Bravmann 1983; Hiskett 1984; Parker 2004).

13. On strangers in Ghana see Peil (1979). For a more general discussion of the sociology of the stranger see Simmel (1950) and Schutz (1964).

14. The story of the migration from Nigeria, especially their extended stay in Togo at Notsie under the "cruel" king Agɔkɔli, is something every Ewe knows by heart. Geurts (2002: 114–16) theorizes that this story goes so deep in the Ewe psyche that, when recounted (at least for the Anlo Ewe with whom she worked), it involves a physiological reaction.

15. Hausa-speaking peoples are concentrated in northern Nigeria, but there are also significant numbers found in southern Niger and to a lesser extent in northern Ghana. Many Hausas are traders and have long frequented southern lands, conducting all kinds of business (Peil 1979: 126–27).

16. The overlay of Islam that has been superimposed on Brekete, as thin as it is, does not seem to have been a part of the reception of northern gods among the Akan, though Debrunner (1959: 132) does comment on an emerging process of Islamization. In general, these "inland fetishes" were understood to come from shrines tied to local acephalous societies in the Ashanti hinterland, their power derived from outside the boundaries of "civilization" (Rattray 1932; Goody 1957a; Allman and Parker 2005). Islam for the Ashantis was definitely not part of this discourse. See chapter 2 for how the face of Islam has deepened and become more prominent in Brekete.

17. The term "Dagarti" is considered to be a holdover from colonial times and carries certain pejorative connotations. The preferred term is either "Dagara" or "Dagaba," though these designations also are problematic (Lentz 2006: xi). I am retaining the name

Dagarti because this is how most Ewes refer to these people, which for them does not carry any kind of negative intent.

18. In Dagarti country, there were villages that were predominantly Islamic and others that resisted both Islam and Christianity, holding on to traditional religion. But the dominant face of Christianity among the Dagarti did set them off from other northern peoples. See Goody (1975: 101–2), and especially Lentz (2006: 153–74), for a fuller discussion of the complex history of Catholicism in the Upper West Region.

19. It is very likely that the queen mother might have heard of these gods from Ewe fishermen who had temporary encampments along the Black Volta, which runs through the center of Dagarti country (Goody 1957b: 76).

20. See Ward's (1956) account of an Ashanti man acquiring "Kune" (Kunde) in 1946 from the north. Also, Parker (2004: 408) writes that in the early twentieth century two fetishes—Sakrabundi and Aberewa—were brought to Sunyani and then to Kumasi from the Dagarti as part of an antiwitchcraft movement. In the Brekete pantheon Ablewa (the Ewe-derived spelling of Aberewa, which means "old woman" in the Twi language) is the mother and Sakra Bode is the god of the land. It is entirely possible that Kodzokuma acquired these two fetishes while living in Kumasi and incorporated them into what became the Lahare Kunde shrine, though shrine lore insists that he personally received these gods from the Dagarti. Regardless, it seems that it was the innovation of Kodzokuma to incorporate what had been many different fetish shrines into a single pantheon of gods complete with familial ties.

21. When the Ewes finally arrived in the Volta Region from their long migration, they had split into three main groups: the northern Ewe, who settled places such as Kpando; the southern Ewe, dominated by the Anlo; and a more peripheral group, the Tano, located on the banks of the Volta River.

22. The Dagarti had shrines for earth deities, ancestors, and nature spirits and shrines referred to as "medicines," with many of these crossing territorial and ethnic boundaries (Goody 1957a: 359). Exactly which type of shrine / fetish came south is unclear, though most likely it was the latter. Allman and Parker (2005), however, cite the extensive influence of at least one earth shrine (Tongnaab) that was brought to the forest regions. When they were brought south, first to Akan territory, they were transformed into witch-finding shrines and then transformed once again when they were introduced to the eastern coast. Here these northern gods lost their explicit association with witch finding, which has never been as much of a concern among the coastal Ewes (see Fiawoo 1968: 73), and were recontextualized within the parameters of long-standing Vodu practices, while retaining their strong moralistic bent, something that was not as typical of the Vodu gods. Werbner (1979) discusses a similar process for the Boghar shrine, which also originated in northern Ghana.

23. I have adopted the term "spirit-god" to translate *vodu* from Gideon Foli Alorwoyie (personal communication).

24. The Brekete gods may also have been related to, or influenced by, the widespread Bori possession cults found throughout the Sahel. Greenberg (1941) takes Bori as an Islamized version of the pre-Islamic *iskoki* spirits of the Hausa-speaking Maguzawa, non-Muslim Hausas, who were originally from the area around Kano State in Nigeria. Hausa Muslims, on the other hand, particularly the *mallams* (Islamic scholars), took the *iskoki* to be *jinn* spirits of the Qur'an and reinterpreted them as either spirits who had been converted to Islam, the white *jinn*, or those who had not, the pagan black *jinn*, all of them assimilated into a rather elaborate Bori pantheon. These spirit-gods, as in the Brekete pantheon, are arranged in family relationships, take sacrificial blood as sustenance, pos-

sess their initiates on a regular basis, speak of this possession in terms of brides and divine horsemen, are costumed in spirit-specific garb, take Friday and Sunday as holy days (see chap. 2), are summoned to "the sound of appropriate drum rhythms, and converse directly with spectators through the mouths of those possessed" (Greenberg 1941: 57). While there are strong similarities that relate Brekete to Bori, there are also significant differences: Bori has considerably more deities in its pantheon (Brekete has nine, depending on who is doing the counting), and Bori in principle is open ended but with at least several hundred named spirits (Erlmann 1982: 49, cites over four hundred), who are more precisely articulated and elaborated within a strict hierarchy. The traits of Brekete gods are much more generalized, in keeping with southern practices, and are not arranged in such a hierarchical manner. Bori live in the well-defined sacred city of Jangare (Besmer 1983); there is nothing comparable in Brekete. The whole discourse around *jinn* is also totally absent, and the question of whether the Brekete gods have converted to Islam is an open one depending on whom you talk to. Significantly, though Greenberg mentions drum-specific rhythms, most of the literature cites the importance of spirit-specific melodies supplied by the *garaya* (two-stringed plucked lute) and the *goge* (single-stringed spike fiddle), instead of drumming (Besmer 1983: 51; Ames and King 1973: 258; Erlmann 1982: 51). The style of northern drum that was brought south and adopted for Brekete ceremonies is similar to the *gun-gon* snared double-headed drum of the Dagbamba, which, interestingly, is generally not used for possession. In Chernoff's (1979) extended discussion of playing Dagbamba music he never mentions spirit possession in relation to this drum. Locke (1990: 49) states that *brekete* is the term non-Dagbamba typically use in reference to the *gun-gon*. An Akan proverb cited by Appiah (1993: 813) sums up the point being made here: "A matter which troubles the Akan people, the people of Gonja take to play the brékété drum." He goes on to say that "the brékété drum is one [the Gonja] play for entertainment at dances, and represents fun" (813). What was important was not its former function, but that *brekete* was a northern drum suitable to be played for northern gods. (See Masquelier 2001 for a more recent book dealing with Bori in Niger.)

25. At about the same time Brekete arrived among the Ewe, Tigare took root in the Cape Coast region among the Fante (Field 1960: 90). Mainly an antiwitchcraft movement, it spread like wildfire across the Guinea Coast, arriving under the name of Atinga in Nigeria, where it once again moved north and was, ironically, appropriated by a newly emergent Muslim bourgeoisie (Matory 1994: 503–4; see also Apter 1993). During this same period Alafia (derived from the Hausa word for health and strength) also started to crop up in the eastern coastal communities of the Volta Region, though many say that this shrine was just an earlier version of Brekete. There are a few Alafia shrines still around (one has painted on its outside wall a picture of a bearded man in northern smock, holding a knife and leading a dog on a chain, all reminiscent of Kunde), and I did see one Tigare shrine that was for the most part moribund. It was obvious that the fetishes had not been given sacrifices or libations for some time (they were totally dried out) and the drums were in a state of disrepair to the point of not being playable. Tigare shrines, however, seem to still be active in the Ashanti Region (Ter Ellingson, personal communication).

26. See Locke (1990: 26–27) for a description of the *gun-gon* drum from which the *brekete* drum was adapted. Chernoff (1979: 44) describes the same drum, which he calls *gongon*.

27. Chernoff comes to a similar conclusion: "Africans use music and the other arts to articulate and objectify their philosophical and moral systems, systems which they do not abstract but which they build into the music-making situation itself, systems which we can understand if we make an effort" (1979: 37). Those, however, who have a hard

time with ethnophilosophy would never even consider the possibility (Hountondji 1983; Wiredu 1980; also see Masolo 1994; Apter 1992; and Irele 1981 for a general discussion). Kwame Gyekye (1987) strongly defends the possibilities of an African philosophy, though he does so largely through a specific Akan perspective.

28. Ghana exports electricity to Togo and Benin, to the dismay of many Ghanaians, who experience load shedding and periodic outages.

29. All the buildings, typical of villages, are constructed out of mud, usually with ce- ment floors, and called *anyixɔ* (literally, "mud room").

30. *Bosomfo* is most likely a Twi term adopted from *obosomfo*, meaning the priest of an *obosom* shrine as distinct from the *suman* type of shrine, though the differences do not seem to be sharp. The former are "high gods" (Rattray 1927), the latter "personal shrines and charms" (Goody 1957a: 358).

31. Ade ritual is now usually directed to ancestral hunters, because wild game is scarce.

32. Rosenthal (1998) stresses the "lawful" and lawgiving nature of Kunde. This empha- sis on morality and upholding the laws of the shrine offers a counterexample to Lewis's (1999: 80–96) analysis of "main and marginal cults." In a patrilineal society such as the Ewe, where jural power for women is circumscribed, the predominance of women pos- sessed by foreign deities in Brekete would seem to fit at least some of his parameters for a peripheral cult, which he states are not directly concerned with the "maintenance of gen- eral morality" (81). Brekete *trɔwo*, unlike traditional *voduwo*, are explicitly concerned with such issues, which, in fact, sets them apart (see chap. 1, n. 22, and chap. 2, p. 50).

33. This style of singing, called *hamekɔkɔ* (literally, "detailing in a song"), which in- cludes some use of harmony, is found in other music-making situations, such as funerals and wake keepings at other shrines, for example, the thunder god shrine, Yeʋe.

34. *Senterwa* is a cognate of the English "sentry."

35. A native speaker of Twi told me that Điamlo was an Ashanti warrior whose name is derived from the Twi word *điamlo*, meaning cooked food. He further explained that, according to Ashanti tradition, this king did not eat cooked food for forty days before he went into battle and, therefore, could not be defeated. Although he did not recognize the word *atsidzé*, or what language it was, he assumed this was some kind of praise song. Sɔfo Peter thought that *atsidzé* might be a Fante word meaning "Can you challenge me." Hill (1981: 224) translates *atidzé* from the same song as an Ewe word meaning "guilty con- science." Westermann ([1928] 1973) does not list the word.

36. I am following Heidegger's ontological argument here as laid out in *The Fundamen- tal Concepts of Metaphysics* (1995).

37. Aren't horses, though, at least aware of the difference between being ridden and galloping free? There is no doubt that the horse senses a difference, a weight on its back, but that doesn't mean that he detects it, knows it *as* something, is actually aware that something else is controlling his direction and movement. Animality is all about captiva- tion and compulsion, taken by behavior, absorbed into environments, not worlds. To know something *as* something on the other hand is to have a world, a leap no horse to my knowledge has yet taken, regardless of the amount of anthropomorphizing we may do on their behalf.

38. This does not mean that a horse has no world at all. Animals, according to Heidegger (1995), are poor in world (*weltarm*), and that paucity has meaning only as a middle term between the lack of a world (*weltlos*) for something like a stone, and the rich and intricate fabric of the world-forming (*weltbildend*) hermeneutical "as," of being-in-the-world. But neither can a horse when it is ridden be reduced to a bundle of

conditioned reflex arcs firing off inside the nervous system of *Equus caballus*. Rather—to truncate an intricate analysis of Heidegger's about the difference between organisms which have capacities and equipment that are ready-to-use—riding a horse is a matter of moving into its field of instinctive drives "not in the so-called 'interior' of the animal, but in the ring of the interrelated drivenness of instinctual drives as they open themselves up" (Heidegger 1995: 255). These "disinhibiting rings" of behavior, characteristic of animality, overlap with rings of other horses and other animals, resulting in a rather narrow, though complex, range of capacities released under the appropriate conditions: running, mating, grazing, fighting, and, of course, being ridden, which appropriates a horse's basic sociality of being part of a herd and the hierarchy that comes with it. This is in stark contrast to the "rings of contextuality" that emanate from human comportment, those webs of significance, to invoke Weber, characterized by their unfinished nature. Here captivation and compulsion give way to possibility and preference.

39. "Ekstatic" is taken from Heidegger's ([1927] 1996) language of Temporality that traces its Greek etymology to *ek-stasis*, "out of place," which fits very well with the phenomenon under discussion.

40. Merleau-Ponty's (1968) ontological terminology of the flesh points to the intertwining—what he calls the chiasm—of seeing and having the inherent ability to see oneself as visible, of touching one's left hand with the right, which leads to the conclusion that object and subject are a binary illusion that in fact does not exist. This implies a "wild logos," a primary awareness of the world being aware of itself. And while Merleau-Ponty concentrates on the visible, the same could profitably be said of the heard, for we also hear our own voice and, although it may sound like it is coming from inside our heads, from the vibrations made from our vocal chords, which of course it is, it is not coming from inside our brains. All language, as Heidegger reminds us, is out there. For Merleau-Ponty subject and object are made of the same stuff—flesh. It is not a thing but the in-between.

41. The dark formula refers to fragment 62 of Heraclitus: "Immortals are mortal, mortals are immortal; living the other's death, being dead in the other's life" (Sweet 1995: 27). This particularly ambiguous fragment of Heraclitus, seems, in the present context, applicable to the phenomenon of spirit possession. The one possessed "dies" in order that the god may manifest him or herself in the world of the living. It is through this "death" of mortals that immortals "live."

Chapter 2

1. The transliteration of *salah* is often rendered as *salat*. I am following usage as understood by members of Brekete.

2. The term *gorovodu* is meant to specifically reference the gods in their material manifestation as objects.

3. Eric Charry (2000) has commented on these elements of Islamic prayer as being the most common in sub-Saharan Africa.

4. The complete *shahada* is as follows:

Ashhadu anal ilaha illallah (2×)	I bear witness that there is no deity but Allah
Ashhadu anna Muhammadar rasulullah (2×)	I bear witness that Muhammed is the Messenger of Allah

This version is taken from one of the many "how-to" prayer booklets printed in Lagos, Nigeria, and sold throughout West Africa. The following is the more common transliteration of the *shahada* (Rippin 2006):

ashhadu an lā ilāha illa llāh
wa-ashhadu anna Muhammadan rasūlu llāh

5. This is not to say that Christianity has not been an ongoing presence for the past several hundred years, or that it hadn't increased its presence before the 1990s.

6. Spectators, in my usage, are people who are drawn to an event that is not specifically performed with the intention of establishing an actor-observer relationship as is the case with an audience.

7. According to the Qur'an, man was created from clay and *jinn* from fire. As with humans, the *jinn* are personalized beings that have the ability to believe or not believe, thus a certain amount of free will that will be called to account on judgment day (The Holy Qur'an n.d. 371–72 n. 929). Surat 15: 26–27:

26. We created man from sounding clay,
    From mud molded into shape;
27. And the Jinn race, We had
    Created before, from the fire
    Of a scorching wind.

Also Surat 55: 14–15:

14. He created man
    From sounding clay
    Like unto pottery,
15. And He created Jinns
    From fire free of smoke:

8. Parrinder, writing in 1960, states that while "Islam dominates almost the whole of the interior and Sudanese areas of West Africa, and it has made progress in some of the coastal areas, notably in Western Nigeria, Sierra Leone, Guinea and Senegal . . . [It] has had little effect upon Eastern Nigeria, the south of Dahomey and Ghana, and the southern Ivory Coast" (41). It remains much the same today, at least in Ghana, where Muslims make up only 15 percent of the population (Ghana 2000 census [Ghana Statistical Service 2005]).

9. *Bisi*, also spelled *bese*, is the Akan word for kola nut, and Kwasi is the day name for males born on Sunday.

10. Speaking of northern shrines among the Ashanti, Kramer remarks that "the one thing which was really new about the shrines of the foreign deities were the costumes, which were hitherto unknown from the traditional mediums in trance" (1993: 45). He includes two black and white photographs of Kunde possession, complete with one of the *trɔsi* wearing a red fez (46–47).

11. The *adhan* always has had a connection to Africa. The first person whom Muhammad chose to call the faithful to prayer, over the objections of some of his followers, was Bilal, an African slave.

12. In two very interesting passages in Lévy-Bruhl's *How Natives Think* ([1926] 1985: 111–12), he cites numerous instances of "native" peoples singing in languages in which they have no competency. For Lévy-Bruhl, these examples speak to the "prelogical" prodigious memory of primitive peoples. While not supporting his problematic thesis, here, it supports my point that attributing agency to the meaning of lyrics sometimes leads analyses astray.

13. Ululation, although not entirely absent among Ewe women, is not nearly as present as, for example, among the Tumbuka I worked with in Malawi. Among the Ewe, this may be a nod to northern practice, where it is much more prominent.

14. The suffix *za* indicates festival music. Ablewaza, therefore, means festival music of Ablewa.

Chapter 3

1. See Herskovits (1938, vol. 2: 307–8) for a description of similar delays in giving sacrifices among the Fon.

2. Schnapps is by far the most expensive drink bought for the gods. There is a lively business in counterfeit schnapps (mostly out of Nigeria along with a whole host of other fake goods) complete with authentic-looking seals. The following is taken from the label of a J.H. Henkes Schnapps carton: "J. H. Henkes, Starbrand, Prize-Medal, Aromatic Schiedam Schnapps. The finest Schnapps it is possible to produce and the most refreshing drink in hot climates. *Please note label and brand and beware of spurious imitations*" (italics in original).

3. The same kind of wifely intercession can be seen between the thunder god Xebieso and his wife Avleketi.

4. Ablewa's perceived problematic nature may have something to do with her possible associations with an antiwitchcraft movement and its attendant poison ordeal before she became part of the Brekete pantheon. See Parker (2004) for an account of the Aberewa (Twi spelling) antiwitchcraft movement among the Ashanti. According to Debrunner (1959), who lists twenty laws for adherents of the Aberewa shrine, "[She] was ruthless in stamping out all opposition to her dictates" (115), and, quoting a source from 1919, "she had been sent down to earth to protect men and to prolong their lives, but finding so many evildoers, she was greatly incensed and destroyed indiscriminately rich and poor, young and old alike. It was even said that Aberewa dispatched to eternity more people than those poisoned and killed by all sorcerers and witches whose power she came to abolish" (121).

5. I have seen this knife only one time. I was in an antiquary shop in Lome, Togo, when on the top shelf containing a collection of old fetishes I spotted a Bangle. It was dried out, and about half the body was gone. Sticking out of the inside was a knife, just as Sofo Peter had told me.

6. The senior god in a pantheon is often demarcated by special treatment and practices. The left hand, according to Islamic practices, should be used for toilet hygiene and never for eating. In general, the left hand is seen as the hand of Satan.

7. See Akyeampong (1996) for a history of alcohol policy in Ghana.

8. Whether this is the universal violent act, as Girard (1987) would claim, or the rebound of violence that Bloch (1992) assumes, is open to question. Can we really assume, as so many have, that all sacrifice is inherently violent? The Ewes certainly don't think so. For the majority of Ewes, violence is either something human beings do to each other or retribution from the gods. As far as animals are concerned, it is virtually nonexistent, occurring only on those rare occasions when the field is reversed and an animal attacks a human.

9. Speaking about offering sacrifices to the ancestors, Senghor (1974: 41) makes a similar point: "For as powerful as they may be, the Dead do not possess *life*, and they are not able to procure for themselves those 'earthly sustenances' which give so intense a sweetness to living. In return for this care the gods bestow their blessings" (italics in original).

10. From a story in the *Daily Graphic* newspaper (March 23, 2005) about dog meat in the Northern Region: "Added to the pito drink, is the almighty dog meat delicacy. Dog meat, in fact, is very expensive as I have learnt and indeed the price of a full-dog is higher than that of a goat or sheep on the market. While a goat khebab or sheep khebab sells at between 1,000 and 2,000 [cedis], a piece of dog meat sells at 5,000, and those who like it are prepared to buy as they enjoy their pito."

11. On rare occasions an adult dog and cat may be sacrificed, but this requires *bosom-fowo* who are especially trained to handle these animals. Although I never saw one of these sacrifices, I have heard several accounts of sacrificial priests being severely bitten and scratched during one of these offerings.

12. In my fifteen years of working with Kunde this rule was never broken. Fiawoo (1968: 74) also reports that "animals sacrificed to Nana Kunde are forbidden to members." This is in stark contrast to Rosenthal's (1998: 51) account of a dog being offered during a cow sacrifice: "Every morsel of the dog was eaten." She goes on in a footnote (251 n. 6) to state that a story was circulating that someone had the dog "cooked in a sauce, and served to priests and trosiwo, saying it was beef. 'Everyone loved it,' the story went. Gorovodu worshipers in Dogbeda still break into laughter when this tale is repeated." For the Kunde members I have worked with, this breach of one of the most serious taboos would not be met with laughter, but shock.

13. On the high status of dogs in American society, Marshall Sahlins (1976) comments, "There is even an enormous industry for raising horses as food for dogs. But then, America is the land of the sacred dog" (171).

14. The idea of "pet" is starting to creep into some sectors of Ghanaian society.

15. Blier (1995: 172), quoting Guédou (1985: 227–28), makes the same point for the Fon: "[The human] is the master of all that lives, of all that breathes. . . . All that exists in the universe should contribute to the life of this superior being . . . [who] kills creatures to safeguard life." Also see Tempels's (1959: 65) understanding of an African ontology: "Inferior forces, on the other hand (animal, plant, mineral) exist only, and by the will of God, to increase the vital force of men while they are on earth." Senghor (1974: 190) echoes this same hierarchical ontology when he states that "from God, to the least grain of sand and by way of Man, the universe is seamless. . . . Man in his person is the center of this universe."

16. Along the Guinea Coast, doves do not always carry this symbolic load. Doves, in fact, are sometimes considered harbingers of war, associated with "death-accompanying battles" (Blier 1995: 224). If you have ever seen wild doves in action, constantly challenging each other over territory, then you can understand where this notion comes from.

17. At first take, it would seem that Heidegger would be spinning in his grave to read that his ontological analysis of "das Ding" was being appropriated to such things as fetishes, especially African ones. However, in several places Heidegger discusses the potential positive benefits of studying what he calls "primitive Dasein" ([1927] 1996: 47, 112–13; 2000: 15). According to Heidegger, "The life of primitive peoples can have positive significance as a method because 'primitive phenomena' are often less concealed and less complicated by extensive self-interpretation on the part of the Dasein in question. Primitive Dasein often speaks to us more directly in terms of a primordial absorption in 'phenomena' (taken in a pre-phenomenological sense). A way of conceiving things which seems, perhaps, rather clumsy and crude from our standpoint, can be positively helpful in bringing out the ontological structures of phenomena in a genuine way" ([1927] 1996: 76). This kind of Lévy-Bruhlian approach to primitive absorption, "clumsy and crude" from the Western perspective (read especially German) of "advanced Dasein" (Heidegger

[1927] 1996: 415), of course, is saturated with ethnocentric prejudices, but the foregoing discussion does point to the fact that fetish as "thing" might not have been totally foreign to his thinking.

18. As do all vessels, a glass or a bottle has a base and sides that are responsible for its self-standing and make it independent and self-supporting. But the thingly nature of the vessel is not contained in the shape and impermeability of its material, nor in its intended purpose, that is, its use for holding what is poured into it. As Heidegger (1975: 169) makes clear in his discussion of a jug holding wine, "When we fill the jug with wine, do we pour the wine into the sides and bottom? At most, we pour the wine between the sides and over the bottom. Sides and bottom are, to be sure, what is impermeable in the vessel. But what is impermeable is not yet what does the holding. When we fill the jug, the pouring that fills it flows into the empty jug. The emptiness, the void, is what does the vessel's holding. The empty space, this nothing of the jug, is what the jug is as the holding vessel. . . . The vessel's thingness does not lie at all in the material of which it consists, but in the void that holds." Science doesn't see a void here, only the exchanging of one substance (air) for another (a liquid). But this tells us nothing of the jug's void or the holding of a jug qua jug. "Science always encounters only what *its* kind of representation has admitted beforehand as an object possible for science" (170). Measured ob-jects (*Gegenstand*) that stand over against us may have started out as things but under the gaze of science are things no longer.

How then, Heidegger questions, does a jug's void hold that which is poured into it? The void of the jug holds in a twofold manner, as a taking in and keeping. Taking and keeping belong together, are of one piece, themselves held together in the giving nature of that which is poured out. This "gathering of the twofold holding into the outpouring" is what Heidegger calls the "poured gift" (172). It is in the outpouring of the poured gift that jugs presence as jugs and, if it is a consecrated outpouring for the gods, libations as libations: "In giving the consecrated libation, the pouring jug occurs as the giving gift. The consecrated libation is what our word for a strong outpouring flow, 'gush,' really designates: gift and sacrifice. 'Gush' . . . is the Greek *cheein*, the Indoeuropean *ghu*. It means to offer in sacrifice. To pour a gush, when it is achieved in its essence, thought through with sufficient generosity, and genuinely uttered, is to donate, to offer in sacrifice, and hence to give" (173). Sacrifice and libation are tied together in the outpouring. If Heidegger could have overcome his myopic view of Africa as the home to "primitive Dasein"—he cites the "Hottentots" of what was then German Southwest Africa (Nambia) (2000: 15)—he might have spoken of African shrines as well as Greek temples.

Chapter 4

1. What is presented here is a southern Ewe perspective, of how the *sofowo* and *adehawo* with whom I worked understood Anibra's death.

2. Given that *agbadza* is a war drum, there is also a sense here of taunting an enemy in war; i.e., when I kill you, you will stay dead forever.

3. Presumably, there are now also plenty of taxi drivers and policemen, and a fair share of bankers and politicians as well, though these professions are rarely mentioned. Tsiefe is understood as timeless, thus thought of and felt as a traditional way of life. This understanding of a mirrored world of the dead is widespread in West Africa (Herskovits 1938, vol. 2:240)

4. This burying of hair and nails is tantamount to burying the *luvɔ*, a kind of shadow soul. *Yɔfofo* takes place anywhere from four to seven or eight days after burial, depending on which clan you belong to. There are short-term clans and long-term clans.

5. The lead drummer in a Brekete shrine, one who is also responsible for taking care of the drums, including giving them sacrifices, is called *awuku*, the entire drumming group *awukuwo*.

6. Titibigu was Kodzokuma's nickname, meaning "he gives freely."

7. See Herskovits (1938, vol. 2: 240), who cites the same practice for the Fon, and, of course, in Greek mythology there is Charon, who, for a price, ferried the newly dead across the river Styx.

8. McCall (2000: 130, 146) cites a similar idea of bringing wares into the world as part of the negotiation of one's destiny among the Ohafia Igbo people of Nigeria. This seems to be a widespread notion in this part of West Africa.

9. Westermann ([1928] 1973: 6) defines "bome" as "on the farm," and in a second, separate entry, as "the underworld." The place where souls wait to be born is also referred to as *amɛdzɔfe* (literally, "person-birth-place") (Fiagbedzi 1977: 98).

10. Westermann ([1928] 1973: 87) describes *gbetsi* as "the promise to return within a fixed time given by a person (an *aklama*) who is going to leave the underworld in order to enter a new-born child's body." The radical *gbe* means voice, sound, or language, and the radical *tsi*, among its many meanings, signifies both old and water. Thus *gbetsi* could mean "old words," or "water words." *Aklama*, a kind of guardian spirit, is sometimes explained as the "soldier" that the *bomenɔ* attaches to the *gbetsi* to make sure what is said is carried out.

11. Rosenthal (1998: 264) refers to this kernel as the *dzɔgbese,* which she defines as "the beginning-beginning of a person before conception, a kernel of desire that wishes itself into this life." She differentiates the *dzɔgbese* (in her book she does not use the international phonetic symbol ɔ) from the desire of the *dzɔtɔ* (ancestral soul). Westermann ([1928] 1973: 29) does not list this word but does cite "dzɔgbe" as "the week-day on which the *aklama* has entered one's body." He also gives a second definition as "fate, destiny," which in Rosenthal's term probably refers to the last syllable, *se,* which as Se is the god of destiny.

12. The exception to this practice was when an important chief died. Sometimes the burial would be put off for weeks or, on rare occasions, even months. The body would be prepared with special herbs and soaked in *akpeteshie* and a local form of kerosene. This is not to say, however, that the body did not suffer the ravages of time.

13. Traditionally, it was after the burial (*amɛɖiɖi*; literally, "person lowering") that the family would get together to decide when to hold the grand funeral (*tsɔga*), the final obsequies. This could take place from one month to one year later, depending on how long it would take to accumulate the necessary funds and when an appropriate date could be found to accommodate everyone that needed to be there and wanted to come. With the ability to postpone burial due to the advent of refrigerated mortuaries, more family and friends were able to attend these mortuary rites, often coming from different parts of the country or abroad, where they worked and lived. Thus burials became bigger and bigger events and started to take on some of the characteristics of grand funerals. They also became more and more expensive. When coupled with the costs of a grand funeral months later, the expenses of funerals could send familes into debt for years over the death of a prominent member. To try to curb what it considered an unnecessary waste of scarce economic resources, the government, in the name of development, began a campaign in the 1990s—particularly aimed at Akan funerals in the Ashanti Region, which were extravagant in the extreme—to persuade families to forgo grand funerals in favor of combining them with burials. It seems that families, at least in the Volta Region where I did my fieldwork, were only too happy to find an excuse to get out from under this financial burden, and, though this was not the only reason—for example, there was also pres-

sure from churches to adopt Western-style burial-funerals—over the past five to six years grand funerals, while not completely disappearing from the cultural landscape, have been significantly reduced. When I first started coming to this part of Ghana, hardly a month would pass without a grand funeral taking place, glorious musical affairs with hundreds, sometimes thousands of people. But this practice, going back hundreds of years, is now much more rare. In its place are "grand burials" (amɛɖiɖiga), to coin a new phrase.

14. Virtually the same music which in one case can engender multiple instances of possession trance, in another does nothing of the kind, one more empirical confirmation of Rouget's (1985: 167–68) obvious point, made by Rousseau (1966: 60) two centuries earlier, that there is no one-to-one causal relationship between particular rhythms, pulses, tempos, melodies, or sounds and bodies in trance. However, this is not to say that there is no physiological relationship whatsoever between music and trance—Rouget's hardened position—just that it is not genetic. The physiological relationship between music and trance may be much subtler than attempts at such gross causal determinations can explain.

15. Agbadza, or atrikpui, as it was then called, was part of an earlier unified music-culture of the Ewes (Fiagbedzi 1977: 57–58; Jones 1959: 162–63), dating from the last part of the seventeenth century. The northern Ewes, for whatever reason, left this music behind, developing different traditions, which have been in place for generations (Agawu 1995). It was the southern Ewes who kept agbadza alive and developed it from predominantly a war drum into funeral music.

16. What makes this dance beautiful, according to Ewes, is how the back moves, particularly how the shoulder blades come together. This movement is not initiated by the arms, as novices (read yevu) usually try to perform this dance, but the arms move as a result of bringing the shoulder blades together. This is a subtle difference but crucial to the correct feeling and look, for it leaves the arms free and loose.

17. German Christian missions, both Catholic and Presbyterian, were active in the northern Volta Region; towns often split between the two denominations (Gavua 2000b: 20).

18. In 2001 roughly seven thousand cedis equaled one U.S. dollar.

19. The phrase ŋku nɛ is not actually sounded, but implied. The kagaŋ is played with two long thin sticks hit flat against the head, giving a dry, sharp sound. The transcription (ex. note 4.19) is meant to highlight the fact that the right-hand stroke interestingly outlines a steady equidistant articulation. The left hand's first stroke (the syllable yi) is almost a sixteenth grace note; its exact placement is open to individual interpretation.

Ex. note 4.19. Kagaŋ drum pattern for agbadza

20. The Ewe language, as are most African languages (Greenberg 1948), is tonemic; therefore, speech can be transformed into the tonal and rhythmic patterns of drumming, or, for that matter, into any medium that has the ability to articulate such differences (bells and rattles also can talk). For the sogo drum this is accomplished through the manipulation of open and stopped strokes played with the hands on different parts of the drumhead (see Pantaleoni 1972b for a description and Jones 1959 [vol. 1, plates XII–XVII]

for photographs of the various hand strokes and their placement). For the *kidi*, open and stopped strokes are played with sticks, but without movement of these strokes on different parts of the drumhead. *Kagaŋ* is also played with sticks but doesn't use stopped strokes.

21. I am speaking here mainly about talking drums within the context of dance drumming. When such drums as the *atumpani* speak the drinking names of the ancestors at funerals, or announce the arrival of important personages such as chiefs outside dancing contexts, the purely linguistic function of the drumming gains some ascendancy.

22. What I am calling "beat" is what Arom calls "pulse," and pulse is what he terms the "smallest operational value" (1989: 92). My usage of "pulse" is resonant with Hood's concept of density referent, the "fastest pulse discounting momentary doubling or tripling" (1971: 114).

23. For *agbadza* played outside the framework of Brekete, the *gankogui* double-iron bell is used. In the context of Brekete, however, the *atoké* boat-shaped bell is usually used.

24. One way to understand the timeline is that it groups itself naturally into two unequal parts marked at each end by double strokes. As a pattern, two events (one stroke followed by a double stroke) are brought into close proximity to three events (two strokes followed by a double stroke). Though not in the strict ratio of 2:3, the timeline echoes that principle, creating a kind of phenomenal hemiola (see chap. 5 for a discussion of the term "hemiola").

25. See Chernoff (1979: 112–13), however, for an insightful discussion of the power of repetition in African music.

26. This may be an example of what Lévy-Bruhl ([1926] 1985: 182) calls concrete numeration: "If a well-defined and fairly restricted group of persons or things interests the primitive ever so little, he will retain it with all its characteristics. In the representation he has of it the exact number of these persons or things is implied: it is, as it were, a quality in which this group differs from one which contained one more, or several more, and also from a group containing any lesser number. Consequently, at the moment this group is again presented to his sight, the primitive knows whether it is complete, or whether it is greater or less than before." Instead of dismissing Lévy-Bruhl's thinking and "primitive" terminology out of hand as a misguided evolutionary discourse (which in many respects it is), a more nuanced reading may reveal important insights (see Littleton's [1985] introduction to *How Natives Think*). Here we find a possible resonance with rhythmic praxis. In other words, instead of "persons or things," we might posit the same kind of phenomenon for Ewe percussion ensemble music. Ewes seem to grasp the rhythmic structure of music such as *agbadza* in one fell swoop, being able to instantly hear any deviation from the concrete numeration of a given set.

27. This also could be interpreted as employing the principle of offbeat timing or shifted "counterbeats" (Locke 1982: 237).

28. Thompson (1983: xiii) cites such African musical features as "the *dominance of a percussive performance style* (attack and vital aliveness in sound and motion); [and] *a propensity for multiple meter* (competing meters sounding all at once)" as prominent elements of this cross-Atlantic music culture (italics in original). The energy of this music culture is what Thompson refers to in the context of the "*visual* and *philosophic* streams of creativity and imagination" as the "flash of the spirit."

29. The "regulative dance beat" may not be isomorphic with the assumed metrical structure of the timeline of the bell pattern, but in cross-metric relation to it (see chap. 5, p. 152).

30. Willie Anku (1997: 212) makes a similar point: "The most significant aspect of 'multirhythm' perception in drumming is that the various composite patterns are heard in integration and not as isolated units."

31. *Force vitale* comes from Father Placide Tempels's book *Bantu Philosophy* (1959), a concise distillation of his thought after having lived in what was then the Belgian Congo for some twelve years as a missionary (Fabian 1971). His understanding of an African ontology has had an influential, though controversial, reception. A translation of the original Dutch (1945) into French (*La philosophie Bantoue* [1949]) was the first book published by the legendary *Présence Africaine*, the literary home of négritude. Although it has been roundly criticized on many fronts (see Mudimbe 1988 for a full discussion of both criticism and support for Tempels's position and Apter 1992 for a response to Mudimbe), its fundamental conclusion, that the ground of a Bantu ontology is "the concept of 'force' . . . bound to the concept 'being'" (51), has echoed across a wide array of texts: Senghor uses the term extensively in his writings, and Herskovits speaks of its conclusion approvingly [cited in Tempels 1959: 38 n. 1], as do, surprisingly, Evans-Pritchard [1965: 113] and, not so surprisingly, Jahn [1961]). Here, I want to recover this ontology of vital force from its moorings in an essentialist discourse of "Bantuness" and understand it within the horizons of musical experience in African ritual life. According to Tempels, Africans live within an understanding that "each being has been endowed by God with a certain force capable of strengthening the vital energy of the strongest being of all creation: man" (46). This ontology is a dynamic rather than a static conception of being—"force is being, being is force" (51). The concept of the *force vitale* would seem to be an excellent fit for the energy-producing quality of much African music. As a side note, Tempels obviously took music seriously, having documented over two thousand songs, though, to my knowledge, these have not been published.

32. His funeral was less than a month after September 11, 2001, and overseas air travel was still difficult. This, combined with my responsibilities at the university, precluded such a trip.

Chapter 5

1. In Kpando there was plenty of wood available, and the *brekete* drums initially were made in the same style as the wood *gungon* drums of the north.

2. Mami Wata gods are found throughout the Guinea Coast (Drewal 1988; Jell-Bahlsen 1989). Greene (2002: xvii) reports that these kinds of gods were introduced into Anlo territory in the 1930s.

3. See Chernoff (1979: 11–15) for a similar story of receiving a specially prepared drumstick.

4. Agɔsu is the name given to a male born breech first, as I was. This kind of birth, taken in the West as a medical problem (babies can suffocate), is considered auspicious in Ewe culture, for if the baby survives, he is born with his feet ready to hit the ground running. In Brekete, many *sɔfowo* know me by this name.

5. Part of this proverbial saying may be in the Fon language.

6. Not only is this bell pattern found in many different kinds of Ewe music, but it is also heard throughout West Africa and into parts of central and southern Africa (Jones 1959; King 1960), suggesting that it carries considerable historical depth. It survived the Middle Passage, remaining intact in much of the ritual music of Candomblé, Santería, and Vodou, reemerging transformed into such popular rhythmic forms as the *clave* pattern. The timing of *abey*, just as the timing of *agbadza*, embodies rhythmic principles that

Fig. note 5.8 Rubin face / goblet

gave forth a distinctive Black Atlantic aesthetic (Thompson 1983: xiii), namely, the rhythm of the crossroads.

7. By using the term "body," I am not referring to one half of a duality, the other of which is mind, but, rather, to Merleau-Ponty's (1962) phenomenological concept of a body-subject as a primordial "montage du monde." Here I am pointing to a particular form of this assembly, the musical body.

8. This creates a shadowed duet that Pantaleoni (1972a: 60) calls the principle of the silhouette: "Just as a silhouette exists as the line between a background and a foreground, Anlo timing exists as the interaction of the play of the bell with the play of each of the other parts." The Rubin face / goblet (fig. note 5.8) adds the dimension of shifting perspectives to the idea of the silhouette.

9. See Friedson (1996, chap. 5) for a similar account of acoustical illusions in Tumbuka drumming.

10. Part of what happens in this shifting may be a result of confusing where the double strokes of the bell are oriented. In other words, the double strokes exchange places, resulting in the addition of one stroke where the auditor expects a double stroke. Locke (1982: 223–24) also comments on this shifting quality of the bell in his seminal article on Ewe timing techniques.

11. Locke agrees that in southern Ewe dance drumming "a pattern may be heard differently depending on the metric vantage point of the listener" (1982: 223). However, he backs away from the strong position of polymeter I am arguing for here, namely, that there are always at least two meters copresent at all times. For Locke, "no matter how prominently a 'countermeter' is mentally or acoustically accented the primary duple / quadruple stream of beats is never negated or replaced" (224). While I agree that the duple / quadruple beat is never negated, I would argue that neither is the "countermeter."

12. The term hemiola comes from the Greek *hemiolia*, meaning a half (*hemi*) and a whole (*holos*) ($\frac{1}{2} + \frac{2}{2} = \frac{3}{2}$). Originally referring to the interval of a justly tuned perfect fifth (a musical interval produced by a string that is by a half longer than another string [Forster 2000, chap. 3, sec. 18], thus in a ratio of 3:2, which is also the intervallic relationship between the first and second partials of the overtone series), during the fifteenth century it shifted its reference to rhythmic phenomena (Rushton 2001: 361–62).

13. Of the many composers who have utilized this rhythmic technique, Brahms might be perceived as most closely tied to its use.

14. Charles Rosen (1998) argues that the integrity of the authentic cadence is at the core of functional tonality. If the V–I harmonic progression is taken as expressing the underlying principle of the P5, which is based on a ratio of 3:2 (the second partial of the overtone series [see Hindemith's (1942) discussion on the relationship between the overtone series and consonant-dissonant chordal movement]), then, perhaps, we are dealing with some kind of fundamental musical insight that in one system is realized through an intervallic relationship, and in the other through rhythm. This, of course, does not mean that all music cultures would have come to this insight or to utilize its potential.

15. One scholar who has paid serious attention to hand clapping in African music is A. M. Jones (1964).

16. The clapping of the *adehawo* (shrine members) is often augmented by the use of *akpé* concussion sticks (flat, palm-shaped pieces of wood with handles). This does not alter the point being made here that both hands, whether they are holding *akpé* sticks or not, are actively engaged in making the sound.

17. When I have taught this pattern to Western-trained musicians and nonmusicians alike, it has been my experience that the tendency is to clap in 6 as an initial orientation. Why should this be so? If one looks at the notation, strokes 7, 1, and 2 mark out the first three beats of the 6-beat meter, with the next four strokes in an offbeat relationship. On the surface this phenomenal pattern, in fact, suggests this 6-beat (2 pulses per beat) meter much more strongly than it does the 4-beat (3 pulses per beat) meter, something totally ignored in analyses that argue a basic 4-beat meter as primary.

18. Since we can't lead other people's lives, this possibility, of course, has to remain speculation. But I think there are some hints to support this thesis. I have always been struck by the way Ewe master drummers who are teaching Western-trained musicians count beat structures when they are asked to. This is hard to put into words, as with all things such as this, but it is not the same way of counting as we do it. When Western musicians count meter, it tends to be punctuated, a marking of the beginning, or front part of the "beat." Ewe drummers whom I have heard (Gideon Alorwoyie and Godwin Agbeli to name two) tend to elide the count, connecting the beat count in a legato style instead of punctuating it. I found myself doing something similar when playing with polymetrical clapping. If I feel / clap the meter in 6, for example, letting that beat dominate, but count the 4 beat, I end up counting in a similar legato style.

19. Kolinski (1973: 501–2) argues that "a performer or listener is not capable of a truly polymetric perception." However, he goes on to conclude that while "polymetric perception is inconceivable," polymetric ensemble playing is not only possible but "provides for a most intriguing and stimulating experience."

20. Geurts (2002: 283) translates *seselelãme* as "hearing or feeling in the body, flesh, or skin: a cultural category for sensation, emotion, disposition, and vocation."

21. Locke (1982: 222), in his example 3a and 3b, shows this part for *"kagaŋ 1."* In other styles such as *ageshi* and *atsiagbekɔ, kagaŋ* plays its two-note riff four times to one cycle of the bell, which in standard percussion notation would be called an offbeat eighth-note pattern, which would align with a 4-beat metrical scheme (*"kagaŋ 2"* in Locke's example). There is, however, another way to understand this pattern other than one based on this beat structure. It can also be understood in relation to a 6-beat configuration, which presents an interesting relationship between the *kagaŋ* part and the beat structure. Here each articulation of the two-stroke figure of the *kagaŋ* aligns itself in a shifting pattern that hooks, or locks, into the six beats (ex. note 5.21). The first stroke of the *kagaŋ* comes

Ex. note 5.21. *Kagaŋ* drum pattern for *agbekɔ*

after the first beat, as Locke shows it (i.e., starting after what I have labeled the last stroke of the bell), with the second stroke of the *kagaŋ* aligning itself with the second beat. The next repetition of the *kagaŋ* part shifts its orientation, with the first stroke coming *on* the third beat. This whole sequence covers six pulses and is repeated exactly for the second half of the bell pattern. What this points to is the fact that we cannot assume out of hand, as is usually done, that when the *kagaŋ* plays its pattern four times in one cycle of the bell's timing, it is articulating a continuous offbeat eighth-note figure.

22. The timeline, when given a meter by scholars, is usually ⅛. The timing of the foot pattern, however, divides each of the four beats in half, indicating, if anything, a ¼ meter for the dance steps.

Chapter 6

1. Sakra Bode has had a relatively long history in the written records of Ghana. We first read of this northern god in R. A. Freeman's 1898 account of his travels in Ghana nine years before. As recounted by Goody (1957a: 359): "on reaching Odumasi in the north his party was greeted by a fetish dance. The deity worshipped was the great inland fetish, Sakrobundi, or Sakrobudi." (See also chap. 1, n. 20, for another account of this fetish.)

2. The connection between African folkloric groups and Germans is fascinatingly explored in Debra Klein's (2007) *Yorùbá Bàtá Goes Global: Artists, Culture Brokers, and Fans.*

3. Actually, it was a fifty-year lease, because foreigners cannot legally own land in Ghana.

4. As many anthropologists already have pointed out, matrilineal relations still play an important part in patrilineal societies such as that of the Ewes.

5. The Fon call it Fa (Herskovits 1938, vol. 2); the Yoruba, Ifa (Bascom 1969).

6. The Herskovitses didn't record this with an audio recorder, not even a wire one, but, as the narrator spoke, using a portable typewriter, they typed an English translation of a Dahomean who was translating the original Fon into French. The rich body of material they recorded in this way is quite an achievement and continues to be a rich source of material. This particular version is largely taken from Herskovits's *Dahomean Narratives* (1958) and also recounted in the second volume of his *Dahomey: An Ancient West African Kingdom* (1938), but it is not an exact quotation.

7. The full name of the supreme deity among the Fon is Mawu-Lisa. Mawu is the female form and related to the moon, while Lisa is the male component and related to the sun (Herskovits 1938, vol. 2: 101). Geurts (2002: 172) also cites Ewe informants as saying that "*Mawu* is the female principle and *Lisa* is the male principle" and goes on to elaborate on this concept, filling out the name with Segbo, which gives her the full name Mawu-Segbo-Lisa. She translates this as "that one that exceeds or surpasses destiny and

total power and that exists inextricably entangled and intertwined" (173). Geurts is taking the idea of destiny from the first part of the middle name Segbo, giving her Se, the god of destiny. The people with whom I worked called the middle name Sogbo, which is also the name of special beads worn for the thunder god shrine, Yeve. The name probably also relates to So, from the last part of Xebieso's name, and may refer to the thunder god's manifestation in lightning, which he hurls to the ground to strike those who have committed some wrongdoing. Although there does seem to be a fair amount of evidence that at one time this dual aspect of the supreme deity (male-female) was a widely held view among the Ewe, today, most (though once again not all) state that Mawu is the only name and that He is most definitely male. Abotchie in his *Social Control in Traditional Southern Eweland of Ghana* (1997: 65) refers to Mawu as the male supreme deity, and Gaba (1969: 65) puts it succinctly: "Mawu has sex: he is male. As the creator and sustainer of the universe, he is father." This may be a result of the influence of Christian missions, something Geurts alludes to. For a historical treatment of Mawu and how the German Bremen Mission (Nordeutsche Missionsgesellschaft) may have influenced Ewe conceptions see Meyer (1999) and Greene (2002).

8. In the majority of myths, however, Afa is depicted as male.

9. The Ewes consider the right side male and stronger, the left side female and weaker. The Ewe word for the right hand is ɖusi (the hand that eats), and for the left, miasi (the feces hand).

10. The other way of casting Afa, palm-nut divination, is considered the older and more reliable, though it is used more infrequently than the *gumaga* chains because it takes considerably more time to determine the cast. In this method the *bokɔ* holds specially consecrated palm nuts (*hukuwo*) in his left hand. The number can vary according to how many a hand can handle, but it is usually between ten and sixteen. With the other hand he attempts to grab all of them at once with an upward grasping motion. If one palm nut remains in the open hand then, echoing the way Afa lets Legba know how many eyes to open, two marks are made in termite dust (sometimes a combination of kaolin powder and maize flour is used) that has been poured on a special Afa board. If two nuts are left, then one mark is made (rule 2), and if none or more than two remain, then no mark is made and it is done again. This procedure is repeated until eight double or single marks are recorded in two rows of four (rule 1), which gives the *kpɔli* (cast). This is called "beating Afa" (*afafofo*), as in beating a drum (*vufofo*), and is usually reserved for more formal occasions, such as a yearly session to "welcome back one's head" or a major sacrifice offered to Afa, or when someone becomes an Afavi and receives his own set of *hukuwo* (palm nuts).

11. It is the *avini* seeds taken from the "king of the trees" that reveal the cast; the beads, which are strung in between the seeds, have no significance in this regard. The beads, however, beyond providing an aesthetic dimension, serve the function, as Bascom (1969: 29–30) points out, of making the necklace flexible (beginners use seeds tied on leather straps, which is much more rigid therefore liable for certain configurations to come up consistently), allowing for the random nature of the process to come through unhindered. Beads help to free the necklace into possibility.

12. The casts are arranged according to age (rule 3), and each cast is further paired with its "opposite," or what also may be called its turning (*totrɔ*), or what it changes into (something to my knowledge no other researcher has commented on, including Bascom). Let me offer a few examples to make this clear. The oldest and by far most powerful *kpɔli* is when all the seeds of the *gumaga* land face up. Coincidence is meaningful in Afa, and the chances for this cast are rare. Given the 2 = 1 formula, the cast consists of two rows of

1	1	11	11	11	11	1	1	1	1	11	11
1	1	11	11	1	1	11	11	1	1	11	11
1	1	11	11	1	1	11	11	11	11	1	1
1	1	11	11	11	11	1	1	11	11	1	1
Gbe-medzi		Yeku-medzi		Woli-medzi		Di-medzi		Loso-medzi		Aŋɔli-medzi	

Fig. note 6.12 Paired sets of Afa casts

one mark and is called Dzongbe or Gbe-medzi. The radical *gbe* is what is important here, because it gives the cast its name. Gbe-medzi turns into its opposite, the next-oldest cast, Yeku-medzi, when all the seeds land back side up, producing two rows of two marks. This is followed by the pair Woli-medzi and Di-medzi (fig. note 6.12). As can readily be seen, the pairs are in a mirrored relation: in Woli-medzi the inner marks are changed into their opposites, producing Di-medzi. One more example should make this clear. Loso-medzi, the fourth cast, transforms itself into Aŋɔli-medzi, the fifth. Whereas in the former, one mark occupies the two top positions and two marks the bottom two positions, in the latter, this is reversed, with two marks on top and one mark below. This pairing of *kpɔliwo* is followed for all of the sixteen original casts and may be a memory aide for the *bokɔ* when first learning the casts. This process is nothing more than pure mathematical sequencing of sixteen possibilities into paired sets. Is this mathematical sensibility of a pattern containing the seeds of its opposite evident in other aspects of Ewe culture? Musical praxis—how the different parts of a percussion ensemble interact, one part complementing the other, often in some kind of mirrored relationship, how master drummers construct their variations, and how these variations seem to organically transform themselves—is highly suggestive.

13. The sixteen original casts have only one name, since *medzi* is not identificatory, but a term borrowed from the Yoruba where Afa is believed to have originated. *Medzi* is the Yoruba word for the number two and probably relates to the fact that both sides of the cast are the same in these original sixteen *kpɔliwo*. The other 240 are named by reading the cast from right to left. In other words, if the right side shows Yeku-medzi and the left side Woli-medzi, then the cast is called YekuWoli and assumes its rightful place by age in the lineage of the 256 *kpɔliwo*. In the combinatorial casts, age usually is determined by the right side of the cast, which gives the first part of the *kpɔli's* name.

14. This is an important distinction often glossed over or not mentioned in the literature on this divinatory system. It is not that certain *kpɔliwo* fall under the aegis of certain *voduwo* and deities, as Herskovits reports (1938, vol. 2: 211–12), rendering the casts as merely signs of the various gods, but that the *kpɔliwo* themselves are a kind of spirit entity.

15. There are variations on all of these procedures, according to the predilections and training of individual *bokɔwo*. For example, instead of using two chains, some *bokɔwo* use three. The first chain that is thrown is left on the ground; the other two used to determine questions.

16. One of the signatures of the song is the melodic movement of a perfect fourth in the first measure beginning immediately after the sixth eighth-note pulse (c″–g′–c″–g′), producing an almost yodeling effect. The melodic line and text are interwoven with the timeline in very precise ways, with the vocable "yee" coming exactly on the eighth pulse coinciding with a bell stroke. The two previous notes are evenly spaced, beginning immediately after the fourth stroke of the bell's timeline (pulse six), thus the use of an artificial grouping of five sixteenth notes to approximate this rhythmic movement. This same rhythmic configuration also can be found in the song GbeWoli (see ex. 6.2).

17. Nogokpo (sometimes spelled Nogo-Kpo) is considered one of the most powerful Yeυe shrines (thunder god shrines) in this part of the Guinea Coast and is greatly feared (Abotchie 1997: 81). The motto at this shrine is "The truth shall set you free," that is, if you have been brought to Nogokpo for a "case" and do not tell the truth, Xebieso will strike you dead with a thunderbolt. Any person in the general area who has been killed by lightning is usually taken to the shrine, along with all of their possessions, and put in the sacred grove. I was allowed once to walk through this grove, as long as I did not speak and didn't really look to either side of the path. In my peripheral vision, I saw human skulls, motorcycles, electric fans, and various other sundry items, a very strange experience, to say the least.

18. The word *hūsaka* contains the radical *hū*, which refers to a Vodu priest (*hūnɔ*). *Adziku* literally means "to bear, to die," and when the word is duplicated, *dzikudziku* refers to a woman whose children die shortly after they are born (Westermann [1928] 1973: 24). The *adziku* seed also is used to represent the good fortune of having a child, and it would make sense to relate this seed to something that was coming.

19. If both casts come up with the same *du* on the right side, then, regardless of the left side of the casts, the right side is considered older and the second throw is taken as merely confirming the first throw; thus the left hand of the client is chosen. However, if one of the original sixteen casts appears, it trumps any combinatorial *du*. In other words, if GbeWoli were the first cast and Woli-medzi the second, then Woli-medzi would be considered the older of the two casts even though "Gbe-medzi" (the oldest cast) showed on the right side of the first cast.

20. If it had been something already past, then the five misfortunes of the world would have been queried: sickness (*edɔ*) represented by the black seed of the *logo* tree (silkwood), death (*eku*) by an animal bone, problems (*enya*) by a cowrie, *vodu*-trouble by a *hūsaka* seed, or all-will-spoil (*ahe*; literally, "poverty") by a broken piece of porcelain.

21. Westermann ([1928] 1973) gives no fewer than twelve entries for *vɔ* (270) and ten for *sa* (206), if you include differences in prefix, nasalization, and tone. For *vɔsasa*, however, he merely gives the following: "1. sacrifice, offering. 2. purification, expelling an evil spirit" (271), and the verbal form *sa vɔ*. He also gives the next entry after *vɔsasa* as *avɔsasa* (tying a cloth), which would seem to indicate that he sees these two words as having distinct and separate meanings. Rosenthal, however, translates "vossa" as "literally, the tying of the cloth" (1998: 234). This spelling of *vɔsasa* or *vɔsa*, where the *s* is doubled, is unique to her.

22. When asked to give the sixteen original casts, Ewe *bokɔwo*, however, add one wrinkle to the mathematically tight process of paired sets (see this chapter n. 12) that other diviners, such as the *babalawo* Ifa diviners of the Yoruba, do not do—they invariably end with a seventeenth *kpɔli*, TseTula, which is one of the combination casts. TseTula is said to be the last and youngest of all the casts and thus closes the door of Afa, and closing the door, as we have seen, is something very important to Ewe sensibilities.

23. Westermann translates *tome* as "a place surrounded by people" ([1928] 1973: 237). Richard Burton refers to "Ku-to-men, or Deadland, [as] the place which receives the 'midon,' or ghostly part of man proceeding from him after death" (cited in Herskovits 1938, vol. 2: 239 n. 1).

24. Herskovits (1938, vol. 2: 115, 120) reports that during the consecration of a set of drums the priest killed a chicken and tore out its tongue, and the same was done during the head shaving of initiates in the Mawu-Lisa cult.

25. GbeWoli in this song stands for someone like a *midawo* (thunder god priest) who dies and whose female members have to wear special ritual things, such as dried palm

branches, before he is buried. This cast also is associated with water trouble, and, if this is your birth *kpɔli*, you need to be careful around rivers, the sea, and other bodies of water, lest you drown. You also cannot hang your bathing sponge on a line to dry, because the dripping water represents tears and means someone in your family will die.

26. In Ishii's (2005) discussion of northern shrines in the Eastern Region of Ghana, she cites the reputation the Ewes have as "potential users of frightening magic" (283). The transformation of these shrines from antiwitchcraft to "anti-magic" ones was mostly directed at countering what was perceived to be Ewe farm laborers' use of the short gun called *tukpui*. (See the previous comments in this chapter on this type of spiritual weapon [p. 168].)

27. It makes sense to bury the god of the land. The ground is his abode, after all. As god of the land, Sakra Bode parallels other gods such as Anyigbatɔ (literally, "owner of the land") and Sakpata, found throughout the Guinea Coast and often referred to mistakenly, in the literature, as the god of smallpox. Instead of being the god of a disease, Sakpata only let this terrible scourge loose upon those who offended him (see Herskovits's [1938, vol. 2] description of this god among the Fon). Rosenthal cites Anyigbatɔ as "another form of Sakpata" (1998: 61). Anyigbatɔ, however, is a giant who is said to roam the night. You can always hear him coming because of the numerous shells of land snails hanging from his body, which clang and rattle as he walks, and you can always tell an Anyigbatɔ fetish because it invariably has these snail shells attached to it. Sakra Bode, however, doesn't carry this load of disease and night wanderings. Rather, he is, in a sense, Bangle's back, the stool upon which Bangle and his entourage sit (see fig. 1.2).

Postlude

1. Sartre's famous phrase, "Orphée noir," comes from the title to his preface to *Anthologie de la nouvelle poésie nègre et malgache de langue française*, edited by Léopold Senghor (1948).

Glossary

This glossary is intended for English speakers; therefore, it is arranged alphabetically to approximate English usage. For example, the letters $d/ḍ/dz$, g/gb, k/kp, $n/ŋ$, and $v/ʋ$ are not treated as separate categories, as they are in some Ewe dictionaries; x does not follow h, as in Westermann ([1928] 1973); and nominal prefixes such as a are not divested from their roots and are alphabetized accordingly.

abey: predominant musical style in Brekete ritual life

Ade: god of hunting and hunters

adehawo (literally, "the hunting group"): members of a Brekete shrine

adewu: special hunter's shirt with attached talismans worn during animal sacrifices

adza: token payment to summon an Afa diviner

Afa: god of divination; a form of Ewe geomancy; called Ife by the Yoruba

afakaka: performing Afa divination

afemeku (literally, "house death"): to die of natural causes at an old age *agbadza*: the classic style of Ewe drumming; originally played for war, now performed at funerals

aklama: a kind of guardian spirit

akpe: thank you

akpé: wooden concussion clapping sticks

akpefofo (literally, "thanks-beating"): clapping

akpeteshie: locally distilled gin made from palm wine or sugar cane

alilɔ: kaolin (white clay) used in Brekete shrines as an offering

ama (pl. *amawo*): herbs / plants; medicine; used to make fetishes

amatsi: special herb water used in shrines

amɛɖiɖi (literally, "person lowering"): burial

amɛdzɔdzɔ (literally, "person-born-born"): reincarnation

amɛdzro: stranger

amegashi: a diviner, most often female, who deals with hot spirits and Mami Wata gods

apentema (Akan): footed drum borrowed from the Akan and adapted for use in Brekete music; plays a free-floating complement to the lead drumming

ase: unmetered ritually charged songs; the term, probably borrowed from the Yoruba language, points to ritual energy, power, life force

atike (literally, "tree-root"): traditional medicine

atikeɖeviwo (literally, "children of the medicine"); alternately, *atikeɖuviwo* ("children who eat the medicine"): another name for members of the Brekete shrine

atikevodu: a medicine shrine

atoké: boat-shaped iron bell; plays the timeline in Brekete music

awuku: lead drummer in a Brekete shrine; responsible for taking care of the drums, including giving them sacrifices

awukuwo: *brekete* drumming group

bokɔ: an Afa diviner

bome: place where souls wait to be born

bomenɔ: the caretaker of unborn souls

bosomfo (pl. *bosomfowo*): especially initiated sacrificial priests

Brekete: a "kola-nut" shrine from northern Ghana

brekete (lowercase): northern-style snared double-headed drum; played with a curved bent-wood stick

buta (Hausa): striped plastic kettle used by Muslims for ablutions; used in Brekete shrines as a container for *amatsi*, the herb water of the gods

cedi (Akan): cowrie shell; name of the Ghanaian currency

Da: the snake god

ɖoɖo: hourglass-shaped tension drum

du (see also *kpɔli*): an Afa cast; usually called *du* when the *gumaga* chain is used to determine the cast

dzekple: maize flour boiled with salt; traditional food served in ritual contexts

dzogbe (literally, "desert"): a place enclosed in palm branch fencing, only accessible to initiated members; in Brekete, reserved for Bangle who deals with "hot" vodus, and spirits of people who died violent deaths

dzɔtɔ: ancestral soul; what is reincarnated

fetatrɔtrɔ (literally, "the year head turning"): triennial cow sacrifice

gankogui: iron-forged double bell

gbetsi: final words spoken before birth declaring what one will do in this life, including the promise to return (i. e., die) at a specific time in a specific way

gorovodu (pl. *gorovoduwo*): another name for a kola-nut god; particularly, the spirit-gods in their material form; fetish

gumaga: open-ended necklace / chain strung with eight seeds, used to determine the different casts of Afa divination

gun-gon (*gungon*): snared double-headed drum of the Dagbamba; also called *brekete*

hũnɔ: priest of a Vodu shrine

juju: substances intended to cause harm

kagaŋ: small high-pitched support drum in Ewe percussion ensembles; played with a thin flexible stick flat against the head, it produces a distinctive steep-fronted attack, dry, with virtually no sustain

Ketetsi (Akan): praise name for Bangle; a strong man

kidi: main response drum in Ewe percussion ensembles; in *abey*, used as a support drum

kodzogbe: this world

kpome (literally, "in the oven"): the home of a spirit-god; a half-walled cubicle where the fetish is kept and sacrifices and libations offered

kpomega: administrative head of a Brekete shrine, distinct from the priest and owner of the shrine

kpɔli (see also *du*): an Afa cast; one of 256 specific pattern / arrangement of eight items, each having the possibility of taking two different forms; named, with particular stories, songs, taboos, and prescriptions for ritual action; usually called *kpɔli* when consecrated palm nuts are used to determine the cast

Lahare Kunde: official name of the Brekete shrine; "Lahare" is explained by some priests as the Eweized version of "Alhaji" (an honorific title designating a man who has made the pilgrimage to Mecca)

lātagbagba (literally, "breaking of the animal head"): ritual performed on the last day of a major sacrifice, when the animal's head is cooked and various parts given to the gods

lātsoha (pl. *lātsohawo*) (literally, "animal-cutting-song"): god-specific songs sung after animal sacrifices

lātsovu (literally, "animal-cutting-drum"): drumming played for the *lātsohawo*, sacrificial songs

Legba: god of the crossroads and thresholds, of the door, the gate; linguist of the gods

luvɔ: a kind of shadow soul

mallam: Muslim scholar; an honorific title given to a learned and respected Islamic man

Mami Wata: water spirit-god associated with wealth; also an important divinatory deity used by *amegashi* diviners

Mawu: the supreme deity

midawo: male priest of a thunder god shrine

ŋɔli: ghost

ŋudɔdɔ: wake keeping

ŋutila: flesh; the body of a human or animal

pito: fermented millet drink (favorite of northern Ghanaians) *salah*: transliteration of the Arabic word for prayer as used by members of Brekete shrines

sɔfo: priest of a kola-nut god shrine

Se: god of destiny

senterwa (pl. *senterwawo*): a cognate of the English "sentry"; especially appointed women who attend to the needs of those possessed by the gods

sogo: the master drum used for *agbadza*; played with hands

tɔɖia: uncle (father's younger brother)

tɔgbui: grandfather; chief; address of respect

trɔ (pl. *trɔwo*): deity, usually referring to a kola-nut god from the north: distinguished from vodu spirit-gods of the Guinea Coast

trɔsi (pl. *trɔsiwo*): the "wife" of a kola-nut god; someone possessed

tsiami: linguist; the chief's spokesman (one should not speak to a chief directly but through the linguist)

Tsiefe: deadland; a mirrored world of this life where ancestors go after they die

tsifofodi: libation

tsila: talisman; usually leather amulets worn for protection

tukpui: "short gun" used as a kind of *juju*

vodu: spirit-god of the Guinea Coast

vodzi: various objects used and collected by Afa diviners to help them in divination

vɔsa: a sacrifice usually prescribed through Afa divination

vɔsasa: the act of doing a *vɔsa*

vú: drum

vù: blood

vùmeku (literally, "died in the blood"): to die prematurely as a result of some kind of accident or other misfortune

Xebieso: thunder god

yevu: white person

Yeve: thunder god shrine

yɔfofo (literally, "beating the grave"): the final burial ritual when part of the fingernails, toenails, and hair are interred

zongo: Islamic, or "stranger," quarter

Bibliography

Abaka, Edmund. 2005. *Kola Is God's Gift: Agricultural Production, Export Initiatives and the Kola Industry of Asante and the Gold Coast c. 1820–1950*. Athens: Ohio University Press.

Abotchie, Chris. 1997. *Social Control in Traditional Southern Eweland of Ghana: Relevance for Modern Crime Prevention*. Accra: Ghana Universities Press.

Agawu, V. Kofi. 2006. "Structural Analysis or Cultural Analysis? Competing Perspectives on the 'Standard Pattern' of West African Rhythm." *Journal of the American Musicological Society* 59 (1): 1–46.

———. 2003. *Representing African Music: Postcolonial Notes, Queries, Positions*. New York: Routledge.

———. 1995. *African Rhythm: A Northern Ewe Perspective*. Cambridge: Cambridge University Press.

Agbodeka, Francis, ed. 1997. *A Handbook of Eweland*. Vol. 1, *The Ewes of Southeastern Ghana*. Accra: Woeli Publishing Services.

Akyeampong, Emmanuel Kwaku. 2001. *Between the Sea and the Lagoon: An Eco-social History of the Anlo of Southeastern Ghana*. Athens: Ohio University Press.

————. 1996. *Drink, Power, and Cultural Change: A Social History of Alcohol in Ghana, c. 1880 to Recent Times*. Portsmouth, NH: Heinemann.

Allman, Jean, and John Parker. 2005. *Tongnaab: The History of a West African God*. Bloomington: Indiana University Press.

Alorwoyie, Gideon Foli. 2003. Personal communication with author.

Alorwoyie, Gideon Foli, and David Locke. n.d. *Agbadza Music by Gideon Foli Alorwoyie*. Edited, transcribed and introduced by David Locke.

Ameevor, Phillips Kwabla Megabuio. 1994. *Aŋlɔawo fe Hogbetsotso kple Kɔnu Aɖewo*. Tema: Tema Press.

Amenumey, D. E. K. 1989. *The Ewe Unification Movement: A Political History*. Accra: Ghana Universities Press.

Ames, David W., and Anthony V. King. 1973. "Igbo and Hausa Musicians: A Comparative Examination." *Ethnomusicology* 17 (2): 250–78.

————. 1971. *Glossary of Hausa Music and Its Social Contexts*. Evanston, IL: Northwestern University Press.

Amira, John, and Steven Cornelius. 1992. *The Music of Santeria: Traditional Rhythms of the Batá Drums*. Tempe, AZ: White Cliffs Media Company.

Anku, Willie. 1997. "Principles of Rhythmic Integration in African Drumming." *Black Music Research Journal* 17 (2): 211–38.

Anyidoho, Kofi. 1997. "Ewe Verbal Art." In *A Handbook of Eweland*, vol. 1, *The Ewes of Southeastern Ghana*, edited by Francis Agbodeka, pp. 123–52. Accra: Woeli Publishing Services.

Appiah, Kwame Anthony. 1993. "Thick Translation." *Callaloo* 16 (4): 808–19.

Apter, Andrew. 1993. "Atinga Revisited: Yoruba Witchcraft and the Cocoa Economy, 1950–1951." In *Modernity and Its Malcontents: Ritual and Power in Postcolonial Africa*, edited by Jean Comaroff and John Comaroff, pp. 11–128. Chicago: University of Chicago Press.

————. 1992. "'Que Faire?' Reconsidering Inventions of Africa." *Critical Inquiry* 19 (1): 87–104.

Armstrong, Robert G. 1954. "Talking Drums in the Benue–Cross River Region of Nigeria." *Phylon* 15 (4): 355–63.

Arom, Simha. 2006. "An Ethnomusicologist Reexamines the Organization of Musical Time." Keynote address, Ninth International Conference on Music Perception and Cognition. Bologna: Alma Mater Studiorum, University of Bologna.

————. 1991. *African Polyphony and Polyrhythm: Musical Structure and Methodology*. Translated by Martin Thom, Barbara Tuckett, and Raymond Boyd. Cambridge: Cambridge University Press.

————. 1989. "Time Structure in the Music of Central Africa: Periodicity, Meter, Rhythm, and Polyrhythmics. *Leonardo* 22 (1): 91–99.

Bâ, Sylvia Washington. 1973. *The Concept of Negritude in the Poetry of Léopold Sédar Senghor*. Princeton, NJ: Princeton University Press.

Baka: People of the Forest. 1988. VHS. National Geographic Society and WQED Pittsburgh.

Barber, Karin. 1981. "How Man Makes God in West Africa: Yoruba Attitudes Toward the Orisia." *Africa* 51 (3): 724–45.

Bascom, William. 1969. *Ifa Divination: Communication between Gods and Men in West Africa*. Bloomington: Indiana University Press.

Bastide, Roger. 1978. *The African Religions of Brazil: Toward a Sociology of the Interpenetration of Civilizations*. Translated by Helen Sebba. Baltimore: John Hopkins University Press.

Bebey, Francis. 1975. *African Music: A People's Art*. Translated by Josephine Bennett. New York: L. Hill.

Becker, Judith. 2004. *Deep Listeners: Music, Emotion and Trancing*. Bloomington: Indiana University Press.

Bell, Catherine. 1992. *Ritual Theory, Ritual Practice*. New York: Oxford University Press.

Besmer, Fremont E. 1983. *Horses, Musicians, and Gods: The Hausa Cult of Possession-Trance*. South Hadley, MA: Bergin and Garvey Publishers.

Blacking, John. 1973. *How Musical Is Man?* Seattle: University of Washington Press.

Blier, Suzanne Preston. 1995. *African Vodun: Art, Psychology, and Power*. Chicago: University of Chicago Press.

Bloch, Maurice. 1992. *Prey into Hunter: The Politics of Religious Experience*. Cambridge: Cambridge University Press.

Boddy, Janice. 1994. "Spirit Possession Revisted: Beyond Instrumentality." *Annual Reviews of Anthropology* 23:407–34.

———. 1989. *Wombs and Alien Spirits: Women, Men, and the Zār Cult in Northern Sudan*. Madison: University of Wisconsin Press.

Bourdieu, Pierre. 1977. *Outline of a Theory of Practice*. Translated by Richard Nice. Cambridge: Cambridge University Press.

Bourguignon, Erika. 2004. "Suffering and Healing, Subordination and Power: Women and Possession Trance." *Ethos* 32 (4): 557–74.

———. 1968. "World Distribution and Patterns of Possession States." In *Trance and Possession States*, edited by Raymond Prince. Montreal: R. M. Burke Memorial Society.

Brandel, Rose. 1959. "The African Hemiola Style." *Ethnomusicology* 3 (3): 106–16.

Bravmann, René A. 1983. *African Islam*. Washington, DC: Smithsonian Institution Press.

Brown, Karen McCarthy. 1991. *Mama Lola: A Vodou Priestess in Brooklyn*: Updated and expanded edition. Berkeley: University of California Press.

Carrington, John F. 1949. *Talking Drums of Africa*. London: Carey Kingsgate Press.

Charry, Eric. 2000. "Music and Islam in Sub-Saharan Africa." In *The History of Islam in Africa*, edited by Nehemia Levtzion and Randall L. Pouwels, pp. 545–72. Athens: Ohio University Press.

Chernoff, John M. 1979. *African Rhythm and African Sensibility: Aesthetics and Social Action in African Musical Idioms*. Chicago: University of Chicago Press.

Clifford, James. 1988. *The Predicament of Culture: Twentieth-Century Ethnography, Literature, and Art*. Cambridge, MA: Harvard University Press.

———. 1983. "On Ethnographic Authority." *Representations* 2:118–46.

Crapanzano, Vincent. 1992. *Hermes' Dilemma and Hamlet's Desire: On the Epistemology of Interpretation*. Cambridge, MA: Harvard University Press.

Csikszentmihalyi, Mihaly. 1990. *Flow: The Psychology of Optimal Experience*. New York: Harper and Row.

Damasio, Antonio. 1999. *The Feeling of What Happens: Body and Emotion in the Making of Consciousness*. New York: Harcourt Brace and Company.

Debrunner, Rev. H. 1959. *Witchcraft in Ghana: A Study on the Belief in Destructive Witches and Its Effect on the Akan Tribes*. Kumasi: Presbyterian Book Depot.

Deren, Maya. 1953. *Divine Horsemen: Voodoo Gods of Haiti*. New York: Chelsea House Publishers.

Donovan, James W. 2000. "A Brazilian Challenge to Lewis's Explanation of Cult Mediumship." *Journal of Contemporary Religion* 15 (3): 361–77.

Drewal, Henry. 1988. "Performing the Other: Mami Wata Worship in Africa." *Drama Review* 32 (2): 160–85.

Duthie, A. S. 1996. *Introducing Ewe Linguistic Patterns: A Textbook of Phonology, Grammar, and Semantics*. Accra: Ghana Universities Press.

Eliade, Mircea. 1964. *Shamanism: Archaic Techniques of Ecstasy*. Translated by Willard R. Trask. Princeton, NJ: Princeton University Press.

Ellen, Roy. 1988. "Fetishism." *Man*, n.s., 23 (22): 213–35.

Ellis, A. B. [1890] 1965. *The Ewe-Speaking Peoples of the Slave Coast of West Africa: Their Religion, Manners, Customs, Laws, Languages, Etc*. Chicago: Benin Press.

Epega, Afolabi A., and Phillip John Neimark. 1995. *The Sacred Ifa Oracle*. San Francisco: Harper San Francisco.

Erlmann, Veit. 1982. "Trance and Music in the Hausa Boorii Spirit Possession Cult in Niger." *Ethnomusicology* 26 (1): 49–58.

Evans-Pritchard, E. E. 1965. *Theories of Primitive Religion*. Oxford: Oxford University Press.

———. 1962. *"Social Anthropology" and Other Essays*. New York: Free Press.

———. 1937. *Witchcraft, Oracles and Magic among the Azande*. Oxford: Clarendon Press.

Fabian, Johannes. 1971. *Jamaa: A Charismatic Movement in Katanga*. Evanston, IL: Northwestern University Press.

Fiagbedzi, Nisso. 1977. "The Music of the Anlo: Its Historical Background, Cultural Matrix, and Style." Ph.D. dissertation, University of California, Los Angeles.

Fiawoo, Dziigbodi Kodzo. 1968. "From Cult to 'Church': A Study of Some Aspects of Religious Change in Ghana." *Ghana Journal of Sociology* 4 (2): 72–87.

Field, Margaret J. 1960. *Search for Security: An Ethno-Psychiatric Study of Rural Ghana*. Evanston, IL: Northwestern University Press.

———. 1940. "Some New Shrines of the Gold Coast and Their Significance." *Africa: Journal of the International African Institute* 13 (2): 138–49.

Fleurant, Gerdès. 2007. "Haitian Vodou and Its Music." In *Music in Latin America and the Caribbean: An Encyclopedic History*, vol. 2, *Performing the Caribbean Experience*, edited by Malena Kuss, pp. 237–50. Austin: University of Texas Press.

Forster, Cristiano M. L. 2000. *Musical Mathematics: A Practice in the Mathematics of Tuning Instruments and Analyzing Scales*. San Francisco: Chrysalis Foundation Press. Online at www.chrysalis-foundation.org.

Fortes, Meyer. 1936. "Ritual Festivals and Social Cohesion in the Hinterland of the Gold Coast." *American Anthropologist* 38 (4): 590–604.

Freeman, Richard Austin. 1898. *Travels and Life in Ashanti and Jaman*. Westminster: Archibald Constable and Company.

Friedson, Steven M. 2009. www.remainsofritual.com.

———. 2005. "Where Divine Horsemen Ride: Trance Dancing in West Africa." In *Aesthetics in Performance: Formations of Symbolic Construction and Experience*, edited by Angela Hobart and Bruce Kapferer, pp. 109–28. New York: Berghahn Books.

———. 1996. *Dancing Prophets: Musical Experience in Tumbuka Healing*. Chicago: University of Chicago Press.

Gaba, Christian R. 1997. "The Religious Life of the People." In *A Handbook of Eweland*, vol. 1, *The Ewes of Southeastern Ghana*, edited by Francis Agbodeka, pp. 85–104. Accra: Woeli Publishing Services.

———. 1969. "The Idea of a Supreme Being among the Anlo People of Ghana." *Journal of Religion in Africa* 2 (1): 64–79.

Gadamer, Hans-Georg. 1990. "Reply to My Critics." In *The Hermeneutic Tradition: From Ast to Ricoeur*, edited by Gayle L. Ormiston and Alan D. Schrift, pp. 273–97. Albany: State University of New York Press.

———. 1976. *Philosophical Hermeneutics*. Berkeley: University of California Press.

Gavua, Kodzo, ed. 2000a. *A Handbook of Eweland*. Vol. 2, *The Northern Ewes in Ghana*. Accra: Woeli Publishing Services.

———. 2000b. "A Brief History." In *A Handbook of Eweland*, vol. 2, *The Northern Ewes in Ghana*, edited by Kodzo Gavua. Accra: Woeli Publishing Services.

Geertz, Clifford. 1988. *Works and Lives: The Anthropologist as Author*. Stanford, CA: Stanford University Press.

———. 1983. *Local Knowledge: Further Essays in Interpretive Anthropology*. New York: Basic Books.

———. 1973. *The Interpretation of Cultures*. New York: Basic Books.

Geurts, Kathryn Linn. 2002. *Culture and the Senses: Bodily Ways of Knowing in an African Community*. Berkeley: University of California Press.

Ghana Statistical Service. 2005. *2000 Population and Housing Census of Ghana*. Accra: Ghana Statistical Service.

Gilroy, Paul. 1993. *The Black Atlantic*. Cambridge, MA: Harvard University Press.

Girard, René. 1987. *Things Hidden since the Foundation of the World*. Translated by Stephen Bann and Michael Metteer. Stanford, CA: Stanford University Press.

Goffman, Erving. 1974. *Frame Analysis: An Essay on the Organization of Experience*. Cambridge, MA: Harvard University Press.

———. 1961. *Encounters: Two Studies in the Sociology of Interaction*. Indianapolis: Bobbs-Merrill Company.

Goldman, Hetty. 1942. "The Origin of the Greek Herm." *American Journal of Archaeology* 46 (1): 58–68.

Goody, Jack. 1975. "Religion, Social Change and the Sociology of Conversion." In *Changing Social Structure in Ghana: Essays in the Comparative Sociology of a New State and an Old Tradition*, edited by Jack Goody, pp. 91–106. London: International African Institute.

———. 1961. "Religion and Ritual: The Definitional Problem." *British Journal of Sociology* 12 (2): 142–64.

———. 1957a. "Anomie in Ashanti?" *Africa: Journal of the International African Institute* 27 (4): 356–63.

———. 1957b. "Fields of Social Control among the LoDagba." *Journal of the Royal Anthropological Institute of Great Britain and Ireland* 87 (1): 75–104.

Greenberg, Joseph H. 1948. "The Classification of African Languages." *American Anthropologist*, n.s., 50 (1): 24–30.

———. 1941. "Some Aspects of Negro-Mohammedan Culture-Contact among the Hausa." *American Anthropologist*, n.s., 43 (1): 51–61.

Greene, Sandra. 2002. *Sacred Sites and the Colonial Encounter: A History of Meaning and Memory in Ghana*. Bloomington: Indiana University Press.

———. 1996. *Gender, Ethnicity, and Social Change on the Upper Slave Coast: A History of the Anlo-Ewe*. Portsmouth, NH: Heinemann.

Guédou, Georges A. G. 1985. *Xo et gbé langage et culture, chez les Fon (Bénin)*. Paris: Société d'Etudes Linguistiques et Anthropologiques de France.

Gyekye, Kwame. 1987. *An Essay on African Philosophical Thought: The Akan Conceptual Scheme*. Cambridge: Cambridge University Press.

Heidegger, Martin. 2001. *Zollikon Seminars: Protocols—Conversations—Letters*. Translated by Franz Mayr and Richard Askay. Edited by Medford Boss. Evanston, IL: Northwestern University Press.

———. 2000. *An Introduction to Metaphysics*. Translated by Gregory Pried and Richard Holt. New Haven, CT: Yale University Press.

———. 1995. *The Fundamental Concepts of Metaphysics: World, Finitude, Solitude*. Translated by William McNeill and Nicholas Walker. Bloomington: Indiana University Press.

———. 1977. "The Age of the World Picture." In *"The Question Concerning Technology" and Other Essays*, translated by William Lovitt, pp. 115–54. New York: Harper Colophon Books.

———. 1975. *Poetry, Language, Thought*. New York: Harper and Row.

———. [1927] 1996. *Being and Time*. Translated by Joan Stambaugh. Albany: State University of New York Press.

Heidegger, Martin, and Eugen Fink. 1979. *Heraclitus Seminar*. Translated by Charles H. Seibert. Tuscaloosa: University of Alabama Press.

Herskovits, Melville J. 1958. *Dahomean Narratives: A Cross-Cultural Analysis*. Evanston, IL: Northwestern University Press.

———. 1938. *Dahomey: An Ancient West African Kingdom*. 2 vols. New York: J. J. Augustin Publishers.

Hill, Richard T. 1981. "Possession-Trance and the Music of the Blekete Cult of Southeastern Ghana." Master's thesis, University of Ghana.

Hindemith, Paul. 1942. *Craft of Musical Composition*. Bk. 1, *Theoretical Part*. Translated by Arthur Mendel. New York: Associated Music Publishers.

Hiskett, Mervyn. 1984. *The Development of Islam in West Africa*. London: Longman.

Hobart, Angela, and Bruce Kapferer, eds. 2005. *Aesthetics in Performance: Formations of Symbolic Construction and Experience*. New York: Berghahn Books.

The Holy Qur-ān: English Translation of the Meanings and Commentary. Revised and edited by the Presidency of Islamic Researches, IFTA, Call and Guidance. The Custodian of The Two Holy Mosques King Fahd Complex for The Printing of The Holy Qur'ān.

Hood, Mantle. 1971. *The Ethnomusicologist*. New York: McGraw-Hill.

Horton, Robin. 1971. "African Conversion." *Africa* 41 (2): 85–108.

Houk, James T. 1995. *Spirits, Blood, and Drums: The Orisha Religion in Trinidad*. Philadelphia: Temple University Press.

Hountondji, Paulin. 1983. *African Philosophy: Myth and Reality*. Bloomington: Indiana University Press.

Irele, Abiola. 1981. *The African Experience in Literature and Ideology*. London: Heinemann.

Ishii, Miho. 2005. "The Transformation of Suman Shrines in Southern Ghana." *Journal of Religion in Africa* 35 (3): 266–95.

Jahn, Janheinz. 1961. *Muntu: The New African Culture*. New York: Grove Press.

Janzen, John M. 1992. *Ngoma: Discourses of Healing in Central and Southern Africa*. Berkeley: University of California Press.

Jeanpierre, W. A. 1969. "Sartre's Theory of 'Antiracist Racism' in His Study of Negritude." In *Black and White in American Culture: An Anthology from the* Massachusetts Review, edited by Jules Chametzky and Sidney Kaplan, pp. 451–54. Amherst: University of Massachusetts Press.

Jell-Bahlsen, Sabine. 1989. *Mammy Water: In Search of the Water Spirits in Nigeria*. Berkeley: University of California Extension Center for Media and Independent Learning.

Jones, A. M. 1964. "African Metrical Lyrics." *African Music* 3 (3): 6–14.

———. 1959. *Studies in African Music*. 2 vols. London: Oxford University Press.

Jules-Rosette, Bennetta. 1998. *Black Paris: The African Writers' Landscape*. Urbana: University of Illinois Press.

———. 1992. "Conjugating Cultural Realities: Présence Africaine." In *The Surreptitious Speech: Présence Africaine and the Politics of Otherness, 1947–1987*, edited by V. Y. Mudimbe, pp. 14–44. Chicago: University of Chicago Press.

Kauffman, Robert. 1980. "African Rhythm: A Reassessment." *Ethnomusicology* 24 (3): 393–415.

Keil, Charles. 1979. *Tiv Song: The Sociology of Art in a Classless Society*. Chicago: University of Chicago Press.

King, Anthony. 1960. "Employments of the 'Standard Pattern' in Yoruba Music." *African Music* 2 (3): 51–54.

Klein, Debra. 2007. *Yorùbá Bàtá Goes Global: Artists, Culture Brokers, and Fans*. Chicago: University of Chicago Press.

Kolinski, M. 1973. "A Cross-Cultural Approach to Metro-Rhythmic Patterns." *Ethnomusicology* 17 (3): 494–506.

Kramer, Fritz. 1993. *The Red Fez: Art and Spirit Possession in Africa*. Translated by Malcom Green. London: Verso.

Kwant, Remy C. 1963. *The Phenomenological Philosophy of Merleau-Ponty*. Pittsburgh: Duquesne University Press.

Law, Robin. 1980. *The Horse in West African History: The Role of the Horse in the Societies of Pre-colonial West Africa*. Oxford: Oxford University Press.

Lefever, Harry G. 2000. "Leaving the United States: The Black Nationalist Themes of Orisha-Vodu." *Journal of Black Studies* 31 (2): 174–95.

Lentz, Carol. 2006. *Ethnicity and the Making of History in Northern Ghana*. Edinburgh: Edinburgh University Press.

———. 1994. "A Dagara Rebellion against Dagomba Rule? Contested Stories of Origin in North-Western Ghana." *Journal of African History* 35:457–92.

Léon, Argeliers. 2007. "Music in the Life of Africans and Their Descendants in the New World." In *Music in Latin America and the Caribbean: An Encyclopedic History*, vol. 2, *Performing the Caribbean Experience*, edited by Malena Kuss, pp. 17–27. Austin: University of Texas Press.

Lévy-Bruhl, Lucien. [1926] 1985. *How Natives Think*. Translated by Lilian A. Clare. Princeton, NJ: Princeton University Press.

Lewis, I. M. 1999. *Arguments with Ethnography: Comparative Approaches to History, Politics and Religion*. London: Athlone Press.

———. 1986. *Religion in Context: Cults and Charisma*. Cambridge: Cambridge University Press.

———. 1971. *Ecstatic Religion: An Anthropological Study of Spirit Possession and Shamanism*. Baltimore: Penguin Books.

Lex, Barbara W. 1979. "The Neurobiology of Ritual Trance." In *The Spectrum of Ritual: A Biogenetic Structural Analysis*, edited by E. d'Aquili et al., pp. 117–51. New York: Columbia University Press.

Littleton, C. Scott. 1985. "Lucien Lévy-Bruhl and the Concept of Cognitive Relativity." In *How Natives Think*, by Lucien Lévy-Bruhl, translated by Lilian A. Clare, pp. v–lviii. Princeton, NJ: Princeton University Press.

Locke, David. 1990. *Drum Damba: Talking Drum Lessons*. Crown Point, IN: White Cliffs Media Company.

———. 1982. "Principles of Offbeat Timing and Cross-Rhythm in Southern Eve Dance Drumming." *Ethnomusicology* 26 (2): 217–46.

———. 1978. *The Music of Atsiagbeko*. 2 vols. Ann Arbor, MI: UMI Dissertation Services.

Marshall, John. [1955] 1995. "Ostrich Mating Dance-Game." VHS. Excerpt from *Bitter Melons*, John Marshall filmmaker. Watertown, MA: DER. In *The JVC / Smithsonian Folkways Video Anthology of Music and Dance of Africa*, vol. 3, *Kenya, Malawi, Botswana, South Africa*. Barre, VT: Multicultural Media.

Masolo, D. A. 1994. *African Philosophy in Search of Identity*. Bloomington: Indiana University Press.

Masquelier, Adeline. 2001. *Prayer Has Spoiled Everything: Possession, Power, and Identity in an Islamic Town of Niger*. Durham, NC: Duke University Press.

Matory, J. Lorand. 2005. *Black Atlantic Religion: Tradition, Transnationalism, and Matriarchy in the Afro-Brazilian Candomblé*. Princeton, NJ: Princeton University Press.

———. 1994. "Rival Empires: Islam and the Religions of Spirit Possession among the Oyo-Yoruba." *American Ethnologist* 21 (3): 495–515.

Maurer, R. L., V. K. Kumar, L. Woodside, and R. J. Pekala. 1997. "Phenomenological Experience in Response to Monotonous Drumming and Hypnotizability." *American Journal of Clinical Hypnosis* 40 (2): 130–45.

McCall, John. 2000. *Dancing Histories: Heuristic Ethnography with the Ohafia Igbo*. Ann Arbor: University of Michigan Press.

McLeod, Malcolm. 1975. "On the Spread of Anti-witchcraft Cults in Modern Asante." In *Changing Social Structure in Ghana: Essays in the Comparative Sociology of a New State and an Old Tradition*, edited by Jack Goody, pp. 107–17. London: International African Institute.

Merleau-Ponty, Maurice. 1968. *The Visible and the Invisible*. Translated by Alphonso Lingis. Evanston, IL: Northwestern University Press.

———. 1962. *Phenomenology of Perception*. Translated by Colin Smith. London: Routledge and Kegan Paul.

Métraux, Alfred. 1972. *Voodoo in Haiti*. New York: Schocken Books.

Meyer, Birgit. 1999. *Translating the Devil: Religion and Modernity among the Ewe in Ghana*. Trenton, NJ: Africa World Press.

Moerman, Daniel E. 1979. "Anthropology of Symbolic Healing." *Current Anthropology* 20 (1): 59–77.

Mudimbe, V. Y., ed. 1992. *The Surreptitious Speech: Présence Africaine and the Politics of Otherness, 1947–1987*. Chicago: University of Chicago Press.

———. 1988. *The Invention of Africa: Gnosis, Philosophy, and the Order of Knowledge*. Bloomington: Indiana University Press.

Neher, Andrew. 1962. "A Physiological Explanation of Unusual Behavior in Ceremonies Involving Drums." *Human Biology* 4:151–60.

———. 1961. "Auditory Driving Observed with Scalp Electrodes in Normal Subject." *Electroencephalography and Clinical Neurophysiology* 13:449–51.

Nelson, Kristina. 1985. *The Art of Reciting the Qur'an*. Austin: University of Texas Press.

Nketia, J. H. Kwabena. 1974. *The Music of Africa*. New York: W. W. Norton and Company.

———. 1957. "Possession Dances in African Societies." *Journal of the International Folk Music Council* 9:4–9.

Nukunya, G. K. 1969. "Afa Divination in Anlo." *Research Review* 5 (2): 9–26.

Ong, Walter. 1977. "African Talking Drums and Oral Noetics." *New Literary History* 8 (3): 411–29.

Oohashi T., N. Kawai, M. Honda, S. Nakamura, M. Morimoto, E. Nishina, and T. Maekawa. 2002. "Electroencephalographic Measurement of Possession Trance in the Field." *Clinical Neurophysiology* 113 (3): 435–45.

Ottenberg, Simon, and Phoebe Ottenberg. 1960. "Introduction." In *Cultures and Societies of Africa*, edited by Simon and Phoebe Ottenberg, pp. 3–84. New York: Random House.

Pantaleoni, Hewitt. 1972a. "Three Principles of Timing in Anlo Dance Drumming." *African Music* 5 (2): 50–63.

———. 1972b. "Toward Understanding the Play of Sogo in Atsĩa." *Ethnomusicology* 16 (1): 1–37.

Parker, John. 2004. "Witchcraft, Anti-witchcraft, and Trans-regional Ritual Innovation in Early Colonial Ghana: Sakrabundi and Abrewa, 1889–1910." *Journal of African History* 45:393–420.

Parrinder, E. G. 1960. "The Religious Situation in West Africa." *African Affairs* 59 (234): 38–42.

Peek, Philip M. 1994. "The Sounds of Silence: Cross-World Communication and the Auditory Arts in African Societies." *American Ethnologist* 21 (3): 474–94.

Peil, Margaret. 1979. "Host Reactions: Aliens in Ghana." In *Strangers in African Societies*, edited by William A. Shack and Elliott P. Skinner, pp. 123–40. Berkeley: University of California Press.

Pelton, Robert D. 1980. *The Trickster in West Africa: A Study of Mythic Irony and Sacred Delight*. Berkeley: University of California Press.

Pietz, William. 1987. "The Problem of the Fetish," pt. 2, "The Origin of the Fetish." *Res* 13:23–45.

Rattray, R. S. 1932. *The Tribes of the Ashanti Hinterland*. 2 vols. Oxford: Oxford University Press.

———. [1927] 1969. *Religion and Art in Ashanti*. Oxford: Clarendon Press.

———. 1923a. "The Drum Language of West Africa." Pt. 2. *Journal of the Royal African Society* 22 (88): 302–16.

———. 1923b. "The Drum Language of West Africa." Pt. 1. *Journal of the Royal African Society* 22 (87): 226–36.

Ricoeur, Paul. 1981. "Narrative Time." In *On Narrative*, edited by W. J. T. Mitchell, pp. 165–86. Chicago: University of Chicago Press.

Ridenour, Elise. 2007. *Remains of Ritual I*. Mixed media. Collection of artist. Denton, TX.

———. 2006. *The Welcoming*. Photography. Collection of artist. Denton, TX.

Rippin, Andrew. 2006. "Witness to Faith." In *Encyclopaedia of the Qur'an*, vol. 5, edited by Jane Dammen McAuliffe, pp. 488–91. Leiden: Brill.

Roberts, Allen F., and Mary Nooter Roberts. 2002. "A Saint in the City: Sufi Arts of Urban Senegal." *African Arts* 35 (4): 52–73.

Robinson, David. 2004. *Muslim Societies in African History*. New York: Cambridge University Press.

Rosen. Charles. 1998. *The Classical Style: Haydn, Mozart, Beethoven*. Expanded version. New York: W. W. Norton and Company.

Rosenthal, Judy. 1998. *Possession, Ecstasy, and Law in Ewe Voodoo*. Charlottesville: University of Virginia Press.

Rouch, Jean. 2003. *Ciné-ethnography*. Edited and translated by Steven Feld. Minneapolis: University of Minnesota Press.

Rouget, Gilbert. 1985. *Music and Trance: A Theory of the Relations between Music and Possession*. Translated by Brunhilde Biebuyck. Chicago: University of Chicago Press.

Rousseau, Jean-Jacques. "Essay on the Origin of Languages Which Treats of Melody and Musical Imitation." In *On the Origin of Language*, translated by John H. Moran and Alexander Gode, pp. 5–74. New York: Fredrick Ungar.

Rushton, Julian. 2001. "Hemiola." In *The New Grove Dictionary of Music and Musicians*, 2d ed., vol. 11, edited by Stanley Sadie. London: Macmillan Publishers.

Sahlins, Marshall. 1976. *Culture and Practical Reason*. Chicago: University of Chicago Press.

Salah: The Muslim Prayer. n.d. Lagos, Nigeria: Al-Balagh Publishers.

Sartre, Jean-Paul. 1969. "Black Orpheus." In *Black and White in American Culture: An Anthology from the* Massachusetts Review, edited by Jules Chametzky and Sidney Kaplan, pp. 415–50. Amherst: University of Massachusetts Press.

Schutz, Alfred. 1964. "The Stranger." In *Collected Papers*, vol. 2, *Studies in Social Theory*, edited by A. Broderson, pp. 91–105. Boston: M. Nijhoff.

———. 1962. *Collected Papers*, vol. 1, *The Problem of Social Reality*. Edited by Maurice Natanson. Boston: M. Nijhoff.

———. 1951. "Making Music Together: A Study in Social Relationship." *Social Research* 18 (1): 76–97.

Seeger, Charles. 1961. "Semantic, Logical and Political Considerations Bearing upon Research in Ethnomusicology." *Ethnomusicology* 5 (2): 77–80.

Senghor, Léopold Sédar. 1974. *Freedom 1: Negritude and Humanism*. Translated by Wendall A. Jeanpierre. Ann Arbor: UMI Dissertation Services.

———, ed. 1948. *Anthologie de la nouvelle poésie noire et malgache de langue française*. Paris: Presses Universitaires de France.

Shack, William A., and Elliot P. Skinner, eds. 1979. *Strangers in African Societies*. Berkeley: University of California Press.

Simmel, Georg. 1950. "The Stranger." In *The Sociology of Georg Simmel*, translated by Kurt Wolff, pp. 402–8. New York: Free Press.

Stoller, Paul. 1995. *Embodying Colonial Memories: Spirit Possession, Power and the Hauka in West Africa*. New York: Routledge.

———. 1992. *The Cinematic Griot: The Ethnography of Jean Rouch*. Chicago: University of Chicago Press.

Taussig, Michael. 1993. *Mimesis and Alterity: A Particular History of the Senses*. New York: Routledge.

Taylor, Patrick. 1989. *The Narrative of Liberation: Perspectives on Afro-Caribbean Literature, Popular Culture, and Politics*. Ithaca, NY: Cornell University Press.

Tempels, Placide. 1959. *Bantu Philosophy*. English translation by Colin King. Paris: Présence Africaine.

Temperley, David. 2000. "Meter and Grouping in African Music: A View from Music Theory." *Ethnomusicology* 44 (1): 65–96.

Thompson, Robert Farris. 1983. *Flash of the Spirit: African and Afro-American Art and Philosophy*. New York: Random House.

Turner, Edith. 2006. *Among the Healers: Stories of Spiritual and Ritual Healing around the World*. Westport, CT: Praeger.

———. 1992. *Experiencing Ritual: A New Interpretation of African Healing*. Philadelphia: University of Pennsylvania Press.

Turner, Victor W. 1986. "Dewey, Dilthey, and Drama: An Essay in the Anthropology of Experience." In *The Anthropology of Experience*, edited by Victor W. Turner and Edward M. Bruner, pp. 33–44. Urbana: University of Illinois Press.

———. 1968. *The Drums of Affliction: A Study of Religious Processes among the Ndembu of Zambia*. Oxford University Press. Reprint, Ithaca, NY: Cornell University Press, 1981.

Vaillant, Janet G. 1990. *Black, French, and African: A Life of Leopold Sedar Senghor*. Cambridge, MA: Harvard University Press.

Vega, Marta Moreno. 1995. "The Yoruba Orisha Tradition Comes to New York City." *African American Review* 29 (2): 201–6.

Walker, Shelia S. 1972. *Ceremonial Spirit Possession in Africa and Afro-America*. Leiden: E. J. Brill.

Ward, Barbara E. 1956. "Some Observations on Religious Cults in Ashanti." *Africa: Journal of the International African Institute* 26 (1): 47–61.

Watherson, A. E. G. 1908. "The Northern Territories of the Gold Coast." *Journal of the Royal African Society* 7 (28): 344–73.

Webb, James L. A., Jr. 1993. "The Horse and Slave Trade between the Western Sahara and Senegambia." *Journal of African History* 34 (2): 221–46.

Werbner, Richard P. 1979. "'Totemism' in History: The Ritual Passage of West African Strangers." *Man*, n.s., 14 (4): 663–83.

Westermann, Diedrich. [1930] 1973. *Gbesela Yeye or English-Ewe Dictionary*. Berlin: Dietrich Reimer.

———. [1928] 1973. *Evefiala or Ewe-English Dictionary*. Berlin: Dietrich Reimer.

Wilcken, Lois. 1992. *The Drums of Vodou*. Tempe, AZ: White Cliffs Media Company.

Wilks, Ivor. 1980. "The Position of Muslims in Metropolitan Ashanti in the Early Nineteenth Century." In *Islam in Tropical Africa*, 2d ed., edited by I. M. Lewis, pp. 144–65. Bloomington, IN: International African Institute in association with Indiana University Press.

Wiredu, Kwasi. 1980. *Philosophy and an African Culture*. Cambridge: Cambridge University Press.

Zabana, Kongo. 1997. *African Drum Music: Slow Agbekor*. Accra: Afram Publications.

Index

The index is alphabetized approximating English usage (see "Glossary").